THE OLD TESTAMENT

LONDON AGENTS
SIMPKIN MARSHALL LTD.

The Old Testament

A REINTERPRETATION

By

STANLEY A. COOK, Litt.D.

Regius Professor of Hebrew in the University of Cambridge ;
Fellow of the British Academy ; Joint-Editor of the
"Cambridge Ancient History"

CAMBRIDGE
W. HEFFER & SONS LTD

LONDON
SOCIETY FOR PROMOTING CHRISTIAN KNOWLEDGE
NORTHUMBERLAND AVENUE, W.C.2

NEW YORK
THE MACMILLAN COMPANY

First Published 1936.

PRINTED AND BOUND IN GREAT BRITAIN
AT THE WORKS OF
W. HEFFER AND SONS LTD.
CAMBRIDGE, ENGLAND.

Preface

MODERN knowledge and modern needs call for a reinterpretation of the Bible, for although it is said to be one of the "best sellers" of the day it is questionable whether it is as intelligently understood as it is widely bought. The Bible grew up in the course of what were, relatively speaking, only a few centuries and under the influence of certain profound historical vicissitudes. It won a unique place as the foundation of Western religion and theology, and influenced the course of Western thought more than any other book. Such has been the part it has played in the past that we cannot be indifferent to its future. Yet it holds an insignificant position in estimates of the future, although it was its evident real and immediate meaning for human destiny that made it shape the culture of the West.

Meanwhile, since the Renaissance and the Reformation, and more particularly during the last two or three generations, immense advances have been made in our knowledge of man, his beliefs and his environment. Most emphatic of all has been the progress of Biblical studies. On the one side is the use of the Bible in non-Biblical research (e.g. ancient history), and, on the other, is the modern critical study of its contents in order to understand the development of history and religion within its pages. All the manifold enquiries are, it is true, somewhat scattered, incomplete and, owing to the nature of the problems that arise, often inconclusive. But much has been achieved—more, in fact, than has been assimilated, for it is no easy task to place the Bible upon the new background of our increasing knowledge of history and religion. As many Bibles as readers one might sometimes imagine!

To many people the Bible, and especially the Old Testament, will seem to be of mainly antiquarian interest, and of personal value only to the devout—certainly of no particular significance for up-to-date thought. On the other hand, those who appreciate the religious value of the Bible will be convinced that the God whose hand they see in its pages is the God of all history, and that a deeper comprehension of the Divine Power in the past will give a clearer outlook upon the future. Here the Bible is of cardinal importance, because it ranges over some unique epochs in past history, and the better we can understand these the surer is our knowledge of human destiny or—shall we say?—of the genuinely held convictions that have hitherto proved so powerful.

For a constructive view of the Bible and its religion as a whole, a judicious estimate of that much misunderstood book, the Old Testament, is indispensable; and to that book which has suffered so much from friends and foes alike, the present volume is confined. It is an attempt to give the reader a brief and very general introduction to it. It begins with the English Bible and goes back behind this translation, behind the Hebrew original, as transmitted to us, and behind the classification into "canonical" and "apocryphal" writings (Ch. I–II). It is then shown that the Hebrew text and contents were once in a somewhat unfixed state, and that on a variety of grounds the necessity of "criticism" made itself felt from an early date (Ch. III). Thus, what we may call the "Approach to the Old Testament" takes us behind the "canonical" text, contents, history and religion; it justifies the course of modern research, and we reach the present position in its criticism.

The systematic study of the contents of the Old Testament is now at the stage where much more attention must be paid to the "Land and the Scene": geographical research, excavation, and the evidence of ancient contemporary monuments. These give us a picture of the land, and of the external circumstances in which the history and religion of Israel took shape, and of the greater world of history and religion amid which to place them. The pages devoted to what is now an immense field are inevitably slight, but they may serve to provide a preliminary introduction to its many sub-divisions (Chs. IV–V).

The remaining chapters deal with the religion of the Old Testament, with special reference to its more permanent values and the main historical developments to the rise of Christianity. The "higher" religion of Israel cannot be severed from the contemporary religious conditions, and only from a comparison with other religions can one appreciate its most distinctive ideas. After some account of the general Israelite mentality (Ch. VI), emphasis is laid upon the extremely realistic conceptions of the practical relations between Yahweh, Israel and her land, since these constitute the Old Testament's contribution to the development of the more "philosophical" problems of the relations between God, Man and the Universe (Ch. VII). Not less, but even more realistic were the convictions of the Unseen, God, and the gods, spirits, and the dead (Ch. VIII).

These convictions were concentrated upon Yahweh; and to the prophets is due the teaching of "ethical monotheism," a One and Only God of Righteousness, ruling the Universe. It was a noble and permanent ideal, though it was invariably difficult to maintain it by the side of popular religion, polytheistic speculation and the practical problems of life (Ch. IX). In the work of the prophets we see something of the conditions of life and thought which they strove to purify; and their activities culminate in the age of the "Second Isaiah," the water-shed between two great stages of history and religion (Ch. X). The prophets gave new life to an older Israel, and the subsequent developments prove how profoundly vital was Israel's "Rediscovery of God" in and about the sixth century B.C.

The rich and varied movements of the post-exilic centuries —the Torah (or Law), the Psalter and "Wisdom"—the effect of Persian and Greek impacts, and increasing disintegration carry us insensibly into the New Testament period (Ch. XI). Finally (Ch. XII), another "prophetic" movement sprang up; the Torah as intermediary between God and Israel was replaced by a Person, and there was a parting of the ways. So, the drama of Israel ends with the birth of a new Israel, and Christianity grew up out of a national tragedy. It is in the light of these happenings that a "Reinterpretation" appears to be called for, and some concluding pages refer briefly to the lines it would take, viz. (*a*) the historical development of Israel, (*b*) the nature of the religious developments in and behind the Old and New Testaments, and (*c*), in particular, the significance of the "Israel" idea. In the Old Testament some fundamental religious ideas, not unique in themselves, were uniquely shaped by Israel. But this "Israel" was not a single, unbroken ethnical unity; and a new "Israel" carried them on further, in the history of Christianity. There is a sense, therefore, in which the fundamental ideas of God and Man are independent of the various forms they have taken in history, and there is no reason to believe that the development has reached its limit.

As this volume aims at conciseness the Biblical references are numerous. It is hoped that they will not be passed over by the serious reader, who may be recommended the use of the Revised Version with its indispensable marginal readings (see p. 13). The bibliographical and other additional notes, the chronological summary and the arrangement of the Index will, it is also hoped, facilitate reference.

Much that stood in need of rather technical "critical" discussion has been reserved for another occasion; and since these pages are concerned only with the Old Testament, matters that would arise in a reinterpretation of the religion of the Bible as a whole find no place.

In a critical study of the Old Testament from the standpoint of world history and religion, the free use of the forms "Jehovah"[1] and "God" is to be deprecated; it is surely desirable to endeavour to replace the not unfamiliar notion that God Himself has changed in the course of ages by the fact that it is men's conceptions that have undergone change.

For the map of Palestine I am indebted to Messrs. John Bartholomew and Son and the Syndics of the Cambridge University Press, and for permission to use that of the Persian Empire I have to thank the Delegates of the Clarendon Press, Oxford.

[1] For the form Yahweh, see p. 41 and note 2.

It remains for me to express my deep indebtedness to my friend the Rev. F. S. Marsh, now Lady Margaret's Professor of Divinity, who read the book in typescript at an early stage, and not only made many criticisms and suggestions, most of which I have gratefully accepted, but also increased my obligation to him by verifying the Biblical references. He is not, however, responsible for my opinions or mistakes. My indebtedness to other scholars will be seen from the bibliographical notes ; and to my wife, as ever, I owe much for a self-sacrifice and devotion which have smoothed my path and eased my labours.

Cambridge,   STANLEY A. COOK.
March, 1936.

The following abbreviations may be noted here: A.V. (Authorised Version); R.V. (Revised Version); E.V. (English Version); mg. (margin); Ez. (Ezekiel); BS (Ben Sira or Ecclesiasticus); M.T. (Massoretic Text, see p. 17); LXX (the Septuagint). Other abbreviations (e.g. J, E, etc.) are explained in the Index.

Contents

xi

B

CHAPTER I

The English Bible

THE Bible is a work of Oriental origin which became the Sacred Book of the Western World, and exercised an incalculable influence upon its civilization. Only in modern times have we come to know something of the circumstances amid which it grew up, and the study of what is the most remarkable book in the world is very different now from what it was in the past. To-day we approach it and view it in the light of our knowledge of the Universe and of ourselves. We know more than our ancestors knew of the immensity of this Universe in space and in time, of the dawn and evolution of life, and of the earliest history of Man. We know how recent—relatively speaking—is the appearance of Man, and how extremely "modern" is that relatively brief period over which his history can be traced. Of the Ancient Near East we learn more and more every year, and, inevitably, we approach the Bible in a way undreamed of by our forefathers.

We can look back upon the few centuries of the growth of western civilization and follow the transition from earlier to later attitudes to the Bible. Though never inaccessible, the Bible was not generally read until, after the invention of printing in the middle of the fifteenth century, it became an open book. At that time, discoveries in the heavens and on earth—astronomy and exploration—were beginning to broaden men's outlook, and yet another world was being opened up by the recovery of the classical literature of Greece and Rome. Revolt against extravagant allegory and against an arid scholasticism and an awakening religious and social consciousness were the marks of the Renaissance and the Reformation. Men turned to the Bible to read it for themselves; it was the book of their mother-tongue. There grew up a new religious spirit which treated the Bible, not as a mysterious book in a strange language, but as an intelligible record of God's dealings with Man in actual

history. It had a new and living interest; and, in the words
of the historian J. R. Green, "England became the people
of a book, and that book was the Bible." So the sixteenth
century inaugurated the "new learning," the "modern"
world, the world in which we live. The change was not
made without a struggle, and Biblical students have continually to remember the memorable utterance of Erasmus:
"by identifying the new learning with heresy, you make
orthodoxy synonymous with ignorance."

The Renaissance and the Reformation made no absolute
break with the past. The Reformers introduced new lines
of thought by their historical treatment of Scripture, but
they went no farther than the state of current learning
allowed. They replaced an old dogmatism by a new one;
and their successors, who treated the account of a Divine
Revelation as the very revelation itself, made the Bible a
book of written Law and not of Inspiration, and were apt
to find the fresh knowledge as distasteful as did the
"Unreformed" Church from which they had parted.[1]

Among the many causes, often working independently,
which have brought Biblical study to its present stage,
has been the use of the Bible in other than purely religious
or theological interests. In 1583 Joseph Scaliger treated
the history of Israel, i.e. Old Testament history, as an
integral part of ancient history; and John Selden's researches
in Semitic mythology (1617) and John Spencer's work on
Israelite ritual (1685) began to demonstrate, what has since
become increasingly manifest, that the Bible cannot be
isolated from its original environment, the stage upon which
its drama was played. In fact, the Bible has proved an
invaluable source to students of secular history, anthropology,
archaeology, folk-lore, sociology and psychology. It is
helpful, therefore, to have in one's mind—or, if possible,

---

[1] When the great Scotsman, William Robertson Smith, who
combined a knowledge of the old Oriental world with an interest in
anthropological research and a deeply religious spirit, defended Old
Testament criticism (1881), he was anxious to show that, radical
though his methods of criticism might seem to be, they were in
entire harmony with the religious principles and the intellectual
methods of the giants of the Reformation.

before one's eyes—a map of the Near East, and to remember that to-day we possess a knowledge of the life and thought of the "Bible-lands" extending over four or five thousand years, and that it is with but a small part of that area, and with only a few centuries of its lengthy history, that the Biblical student is concerned.

Accordingly, our approach to the Old Testament cannot be other than "modern." It must also be "critical"; and "criticism," it must be observed, is an attitude, an approach, rather than a system or philosophy. By the term "criticism" we mean the enquiry into the contents, qualities and character of our evidence, and into the various questions that arise out of it—questions of origin, date, authenticity and so forth. A distinction is often made between (a) Lower or Textual Criticism, that of the literary source, its phraseology, etc., and (b) Higher Criticism, that of the contents or subject-matter. But, in practice, questions concerning the verbal accuracy of a given source and questions concerning its subject-matter are not completely separable. The latter involve geography, archaeology, comparative religion, etc., and these in turn may influence our "Lower" or "Textual" Criticism. Other ways of classifying the varieties of criticism have been suggested; here it must suffice to say that "criticism," as such, is not censorious, negative, or destructive; that it is incomplete unless it becomes con-structive—i.e. synthetic rather than analytic—and that "criticism" is due to the effort to bring the object "criticised" into an intelligible relationship with ourselves, to understand and comprehend it—and also to know upon what evidence we base our views.

The use of such terms as "critical," etc., is not recent. In the seventeenth century we have the *Critica Sacra* of Cappellus (1650), the *Critici Sacri* of Richard Pearson (nine vols., 1660), and the *Synopsis Criticorum* of Matthew Poole (five vols., 1669). All such works, whether they use some form of the word "critical" in their titles or not, represent the learning of their day, though naturally they do not contain the more recent conclusions now called "critical," e.g. that the Pentateuch, as we have it, is neither by Moses

nor of his age, or that most of the Psalms are later than the
time of David. When adverse reference is made to modern
Biblical "criticism" and "critical" views, it is necessary
to remember that usually it is certain theories or conclusions
that are being singled out or stigmatised; the outlook of
virtually every modern writer on the Old Testament is
apt to be "critical," whether he accepts the so-called
"critical" theories or not. Nobody who studies the Old
Testament in the light of modern knowledge can help being
to some extent a "critic"; and to be able to realise that the
religious and other conditions amid which we study it differ
profoundly from those, say of the sixteenth century, and
still more, of course, from those of the Middle Ages, is to
take the first step in the modern and critical "Approach to
the Old Testament."

The Bible, though a unique collection of sacred writings
(Greek *biblia*), has never been regarded as outside or above
the "criticism" of the age. It is precisely because of its
uniqueness that the study of it must be as thorough as
possible. In these pages the Old Testament, the sacred
book of both Jews and Christians, will be treated by itself,
and the fact that the separation from the New Testament
can be readily made is not without significance. The Old
Testament is sometimes felt to be so essentially "Jewish"
as to be scarcely "Christian"; but we cannot forget the
Jewish origin of Christianity and the extent to which the
religious phraseology of the Old Testament has always
answered the needs of devout Christian souls. Moreover,
those who protest that the Jehovah of the Old Testament is
far below the level of Christian thought are apt to ignore
the many inspiring beliefs and ideas in the Old Testament,
and the fight of prophets and priests against the "lower"
elements in the old religion. The New Testament, or New
"Covenant" (διαθήκη, 2 Cor. iii. 14), is the beginning of a
new religion, a new stage in history; and the stormy vicissitudes of Christendom reflect the practices of "Christian"
peoples, even as the Old Testament, the literature of an
intensely active, if not elemental people, reflects the religion
of Jehovah in practice. Not inexcusably the intelligent

Oriental sometimes sees in the European Christ, as manifested in Christendom, a figure not unlike that which some Christians have seen in the "angry Jehovah" of the Israelites. To contrast the New Testament, and the *ideals* of a young religion, with the Israelites of the Old Testament, and their energetic life and thought, is misleading. None the less, the Old Testament did lead up, both to the New Testament and Christianity, and to Jewish Rabbinism and Judaism, and we have so to understand it that the significance of this bifurcation can be fully and fairly grasped.

In the pages that follow, our task will be to start, as we may naturally do, with the Bible in English, work from it in its present Western form to the land of its origin, and consider certain aspects of its contents. One fundamental principle will be steadily maintained throughout. Just as it is impossible to sever Biblical geography and history from the geography and history of Palestine and neighbouring lands, so the general principles and methods of Biblical research must not be severed from those in use in other research. It is sound method to avoid assuming processes other than those that can be illustrated elsewhere, so that, to take a simple example, it is useful to compare the vicissitudes of the English Bible with those of other Sacred Writings, or to observe how often the mistakes and errors of ancient scribes or copyists are of the sort still made by us to-day.

Much has been written on the history of the English Bible, but for the present purpose only a few details are necessary. The version named after Wycliffe (*c.* 1382) was the first translation of the Bible into a modern European language from the Vulgate, the Latin version in general use in the Middle Ages. The Bible, said Wycliffe, is man's supreme spiritual authority: "the Sacred Scriptures are the property of the people, and one which no party should be allowed to wrest from them." But his version adhered too closely to the Latin to be popular, and the revision of it, ascribed to John Purvey (*c.* 1388), was simpler. Purvey commented on the corrupt state of the Vulgate text and in the Psalter took note of the original Hebrew. Translations from the Hebrew came later, the three most influential being those of Germany (Luther's Pentateuch, 1523), England (Tyndale's Pentateuch, 1530) and France (Olivetan, 1535). Tyndale used both the Vulgate and Luther, though not blindly; and his version, the first to be made into English from Hebrew, has left its imprint upon all subsequent translations. He fashioned English religious phraseology, and in a number of cases the Revised Version of 1881 went back behind the Authorised Version and adopted and modernised his language. Coverdale's translation (1535)—popularly famous for its "triacle" (Jer. viii. 22) and "Tush!" (Ps. xiv. 1)—was the first translation of the Bible to include the Apocrypha, which, however, was isolated from the other books. But while his first translation was made from the Vulgate, and shows traces of the influence of Luther, his revision, the "Great Bible" (1539), claims to be truly translated "after the verity of the Hebrew and Greek texts."

Considerable progress was then being made in the study of Hebrew, and advantage was taken of this in the popular Geneva Bible of 1560, an independent revision of the "Great Bible" by the English Calvinist refugees at Geneva. To counteract its influence a revised edition of the Great Bible (the Bishops' Bible) was published by ecclesiastical authority (1568). Its editors were not indifferent to the diversity of readings "among the Hebrews, Chaldees (i.e. the Targums) and Greeks," but it did not mark any great advance in scholarship. Finally, with the Authorised Version (1611), appointed by James I to be read in the Churches, the English Bible definitely and for all time entrenched itself in the English-speaking world.

Meanwhile, Protestant enterprise had not been unchallenged by the Roman Catholics: they too produced English versions of the Scriptures. The Rheims New Testament (1582), characterised by a strongly Latin and theological style, influenced the Authorised Version, which, however, avoided its excessive Latinisms (e.g. Matt. vi. 11, "our supersubstantial bread"). The Bible of Douay (1609–10), one of the "English colleges beyond the seas," included the Old Testament. In their appeal to "the right well-beloved English reader" the translators extolled the Vulgate, "the authentical Latin," on the ground that it had not, like the Hebrew texts, been "foully corrupted" by the Jews. They made it their business to abolish renderings which they regarded as false and impious. As specimens of their Latinisms may be cited, from Ps. xxiii, "the waters of refection" (v. 2), "my chalice inebriating how good is it" (v. 5), and "dwell in the house of our Lord in longitude of days" (v. 6). The Douay Bible has been repeatedly revised.

As regards the Authorised Version, the revisers were chosen without regard to political party. They made a revision, utilising the best that could be found in earlier versions, rather than an independent translation. It was noteworthy for its supplementary matter: marginal notes, explanations of Hebrew or Greek words, headings of chapters and columns, and numerous references (which have since amounted to about 60,000). The influence of Luther's translation in German and of the Authorised Version in English has been incalculable; but while the former, written in a Low German dialect, moulded the German language, the language of the Authorised Version is, rather, the fruit of a long period of high literary culture. The Authorised Version of 1611 has more than held its own, in spite of the Revised Version. This was first mooted in 1856, begun in 1870, and published in parts: the New Testament, 1881; the Old Testament, 1884; and the Apocrypha, 1885.

For the study of the growth of a Sacred Book and its treatment, there is much that is instructive in the history of the English translation, and the following points may be singled out for special mention:

(1) Our knowledge of the origin of the different English versions is extremely unequal: even of the general history of the Authorised Version we know little, and of that of the Coverdale Version even less. The unequal preservation of material of historical interest, and the extent to which some is retained and the rest forgotten or lost, is always worthy of attention (cf. p. 192, n.).

(2) The Authorised and Revised Versions are the outcome of a lengthy process, the "composite" work of a Church rather than of a man. With their desire to be intelligible and to avoid difficult Latinisms and ecclesiastical terms they illustrate the various motives that influence the preservation and spread of a Sacred Book.

(3) New versions have constantly met with opposition. For some time Puritans preferred the Geneva Bible to the Authorised Version. At an earlier date, Jerome (A.D. 392–405) replaced the "Old Latin" version by the "Vulgate" which, it has been said, "almost created a new language," and helped to make Latin the language of the Church. But the Vulgate itself had to fight for recognition among those who regarded the old version as the true Word of God, though, after its position had been firmly established, it continued, in spite of numerous textual defects, to be the one legitimate version recognised by the Roman Church. Not entirely dissimilar, *mutatis mutandis*, must have been some of the vicissitudes in the growth of the Old Testament itself.

(4) In all versions slips and errors are to be found. In one issue of the Authorised Version in 1611 some twenty words of Exod. xiv. 10 were printed twice—a repetition like that in the Hebrew text of 2 Sam. vi. 3 f., which is found neither in the Greek translation (the Septuagint) nor in the corresponding passage, 1 Chron. xiii. 7. In the "Great Bible" of 1539, the Apocrypha by an oversight is called "the Bookes of Hagiographa." Well-known errors in English Bibles, for which the Hebrew Bible affords analogies, include "vinegar" for "vineyard" in the heading of Luke xx. (Oxford, 1716); "Rebekah arose, and her *camels*," for "damsels," Gen. xxiv. 61 (London, 1823); the omission of "not" in the Decalogue, Exod. xx. 14 (1631), and also in 1 Cor. vi. 9, "the unrighteous shall inherit the kingdom of God" (London, 1653), etc. The error "whom *ye* may appoint" (Acts vi. 3, for "we"; Cambridge, 1638) was ecclesiastically important. Again, in the edition of Cambridge, 1805, a printer's marginal note, that certain words were "to remain," got into the text of Gal. iv. 29 (". . . born after

the Spirit *to remain* even so it is now"); similarly, the intrusion of notes by ancient scribes or readers will account for certain perplexing passages in the Hebrew of the Old Testament. That improvement is not necessarily continuous is seen when Anah in Gen. xxxvi. 24 is wrongly treated as a woman in the Bishops' Bible of 1568 and 1572, but correctly as a man in 1569.

(5) Doublets and additions such as are found in ancient versions appear in the English versions. Coverdale, observing the existence of diverse readings, incorporated some (especially from the Vulgate) into the text in a different type, e.g. Joshua ii. 11, "as we heard these things *we were sore afraid and* our hearts did melt." The Prayer-Book Psalter contains several additions from the Vulgate (e.g. the last words of Ps. xiii., lxviii. 4, etc.). In particular, Ps. xiv., like the Septuagint, adds after *v.* 3 three verses from Paul's catena of quotations in Rom. iii. 10–18.[1]

(6) It is a very common failing of translators, both ancient and modern, to suppose that their original is necessarily complete, intelligible and translatable. Hence real difficulties are often slurred over and can be recognised only by resort to it. The end of 1 Esdras in the Apocrypha breaks off in the middle of a verse, as can be seen by comparing ix. 55 with Neh. viii. 12 f.; the Greek original has simply: "and they were gathered together . . .," but the English version endeavours to make an intelligible text by rendering "and for the which they had been assembled." In Gen. iv. 8 the Hebrew has "and Cain *said unto* Abel his brother, and when . . ."; both Authorised Version and Revised Version endeavour to avoid this awkwardness, but the Revised Version margin points out that many ancient authorities supply the missing words "Let us go into the field." In Gen. xxxv. 22 ("and Israel heard of it") the

---

[1] Here the Apostle, in harmony with ancient Rabbinic usage (cf. Mark i. 2 f.), joins passages with similar words or ideas from the Greek versions of Ps. xiv., v., etc., all of which are subsequently incorporated into Ps. xiv. Similarly, the Samaritan recension of the Pentateuch supplements passages in Numbers from the summary in Deut. i., where the Biblical writer is referring to passages in Numbers (or its sources), e.g. it adds Deut. i. 27–33 after Num. xiii. 33.

Hebrew breaks off abruptly: "and Israel heard . . . ."[1]
Similarly the conclusion of Zech. vi. 15 appears to be
missing; the rendering "*this* shall come to pass" obscures
the Hebrew, which has "it shall come to pass. . . ."

(7) Besides making efforts, more or less forced, to extract
some meaning from a passage which is imperfect or un-
translatable, translators sometimes deliberately alter, conceal
or distort the plain meaning of their original. The Authorised Version in 1 Sam. iii. 3 will not allow the plain statement (see the R.V.) that Samuel actually slept in the Holy
Place with the Ark; in 2 Sam. viii. 18 it makes David's sons
"chief rulers" (marg. "princes") instead of priests; and in
2 Kings xxiii. 7 the houses of the Sodomites, which were
really *in* the temple (R.V.), are explained to be outside, *by*
the temple.[2]

(8) An unedifying feature of the earlier English versions
was the presence of controversial matter in their Prefaces or
their marginal notes. These were not confined to one
religious party. Protestant notes and comments occur in the
Bibles of Tyndale and of Matthews (John Rogers, 1537).
The latter, the basis of the first English concordance (by
Marbeck, 1550), had various useful explanatory notes
(e.g. on the identification of Horeb with Sinai, Deut. i. 6,
on the meaning of Selah in the Psalms), and also purely
religious notes (e.g. on the meaning of "hate" in Deut. i. 27).
But not all were so edifying, and ecclesiastical, Calvinistic
and anti-Papal comments in the Great Bible and the Geneva
Bible led to retorts in the Rheims New Testament (1582).
The Bishops' Bible (1568) took a more dignified attitude, and
proposed "to make no bitter notes upon any text, or yet
to set down any determination in places of controversy."

---

[1] We learn from 1 Chron. v. 1 that Reuben was disinherited. A
statement to this effect has perhaps been omitted (contrast the last
words of Num. xii. 2 and what follows), and the narrator, or a later
compiler, gives, instead, a list of all the sons of Jacob.

[2] The "Sun" of righteousness (Mal. iv. 2) in many editions of the
Authorised Version follows the patristic exegesis, which referred
the words to Christ. The Revised Version prints "sun," but leaves
unchanged the possessive "his"; cf. also Ps. ii. 12 (A.V. "Son,"
R.V. "son").

The revisers of the Authorised Version (1611) agreed by
Rule 6: "no marginal notes at all to be affixed, but only for
the explanation of the Hebrew or Greek words which cannot
without some circumlocution so briefly and fitly be expressed
in the text." Thus were avoided such earlier notes as those
which pointed out that Exod. i. 19 "alloweth disobedience
unto the king," and 2 Chron. xv. 16 "taxeth Asa for deposing
his mother only, and not killing her." Examples of controversial treatment of history in the Old Testament will be
illustrated later.

(9) The chronological system of the Authorised Version
is based upon the work of Archbishop Usher (or Ussher),
which was first published in 1650–4, and appeared for the
first time in Bishop Lloyd's Bible (London, 1701). Although
his system has been rendered antiquated by modern schemes
of chronology based upon Assyrian and other monuments,
his date for the Fall of Jerusalem (588 B.C.) is only a year or
so too early. On the other hand, the collapse of the
Northern Kingdom is now known to have been more rapid
than he supposed, and the date of the Foundation of the
Monarchy should be 40–50 years later than his. Many
attempts have been made in the past to determine the date
of Creation. The various dates suggested range from
3483 to 6984 B.C. The eminent Cambridge Rabbinical
scholar, John Lightfoot, was more precise and fixed the
time of Creation at 9 a.m., October 23, 4004 B.C. The
figures in Genesis furnished by the Hebrew, Samaritan and
Greek differ considerably, and Usher's date, 4004 B.C., gave
currency to the old notion that the world would endure for
6000 years, 2000 of chaos (i.e. before Abraham), 2000 under
the Law (i.e. to B.C. 4), and 2000 under the Messiah. His
chronology has no greater authority than the Biblical and
other material (often discrepant) which he utilised; but his
novel scheme, once introduced into the Authorised Version,
became authoritative, and was sometimes treated as sacred
by people unaware of its late and somewhat arbitrary origin.

(10) Chapter divisions, in general, originated perhaps in
the thirteenth century, and it may be mentioned that even
in printed books the pages were not numbered before 1470.

Verse-division goes back very much earlier; but the separation of verses, as in the Authorised Version, seriously obscures the continuity of thought. The Revised Version has preferred the arrangement in paragraphs—except for poetical passages—and, in accordance with its principle of going to the original, reverts where necessary to the paragraphing in the Hebrew text. The headings of the chapters and the head-lines in the Authorised Version have served to facilitate the reading of the Old Testament and to guide the interpretation of its contents. Thus the headings to the Song of Songs represent a particular allegorical interpretation (see p. 26). The Revised Version omitted all headings, "as involving questions which belong rather to the province of the commentator than to that of the translator"; and, for very natural reasons, Jews have preferred the Revised Version, see e.g. Isa. ix. ff., Authorised Version headings ("Christ's birth and kingdom"). Stages in the transition from the Authorised Version to the Revised Version may be illustrated from the heading in Ps. cxlix., which in the Authorised Version in 1611 ran, "that power which he hath given to the Church to rule the consciences of men," the edition of 1762 omitted the last six words, and that of 1769 replaced "the Church" by "his saints."

Sufficient account has perhaps been given of the vicissitudes of a Sacred Book in relatively modern times; it now remains to observe that the Revised Version itself raises fundamental questions of translation. This version aimed at simplicity: there were to be no symbolical or allegorical exegesis, no chronological scheme, no headings or head-lines. It was not an entirely new translation, but rather a revision of the Authorised Version. The latter belonged to the "Revival of Learning," and was a considerable advance upon its predecessors. Among Christians Hebrew scholarship was for long indebted to Jewish methods and learning; and the Authorised Version betrays, in particular, its indebtedness to the exegesis of Rabbi David Kimchi (c. 1200), whereas Luther's translation was influenced by Rabbi Solomon ben Isaac of Troyes ("Rashi," died 1105). But after 1611 great progress was made in the independent study of Hebrew and the cognate languages, and of all the important ancient versions. Hence modern scholarship often goes behind the authorities upon which earlier translators relied, and recovers long-lost meanings or interpretations; thus Joseph's "coat of many colours" is "a long garment with sleeves" (Gen. xxxvii. 3, R.V. mg.).

The changes made by the revisers of the Old Testament were relatively fewer than those of the New Testament (see the Revised Version Preface). But their marginal readings are important. Of the revisers, some desired to depart from the Authorised Version as slightly as possible, others were more anxious to make full use of the results of modern philology and exegesis. Neither party predominated, and the rule was to place in the margin any renderings strongly supported but without the two-thirds majority of those present which was required at the final revision of the text. Where the Revised Version margin differs from the Authorised Version it represents an important new rendering, but one not sufficiently supported to be put into the text, and where it agrees with the Authorised Version, the preferred reading has won its place in the text, although a considerable body of opinion still clung to the Authorised Version. Hence any edition of the Revised Version without the marginal notes gives an imperfect conception of the revisers' intentions.

The Revised Version adheres to the Hebrew original more closely than its forerunners. To a certain extent it has modernised the English.[1] Many archaisms remain, including familiar words of Latin origin whose true meaning is often forgotten. Thus, a "solemn" meeting (Isa. i. 13, etc.) is one

---

[1] A further step in this direction was taken by the American Revisers (whose preferences are printed in the Revised Version) and by the American Standard Edition of 1901. In 1896 the Jewish Religious Education Board issued an Appendix containing alterations (a) where the Revised Version departed from the Hebrew text, and (b) where its rendering is opposed to Jewish traditional interpretation or dogmatic teaching, e.g. Ps. ii. 12, "worship in purity" (cf. Revised Version mg.), Lev. xxiii. 15, "weeks" for "sabbaths," and v. 40, "thick-leaved trees." Among more recent translations may be mentioned that of the Jewish Publication Society (Philadelphia, 1917), and that based on an emended text, published by the University of Chicago (1931).

that is fixed or stated (Lat. *solemnis*); "strange" gods, people, etc. are really "foreign"; and a "peculiar" people or treasure (Deut. xiv. 2) is "one's own" (*peculiaris*): in Mal. iii. 17 the American Standard edition reads "mine own possession." There are conventional renderings, e.g. to smite "hip and thigh," or "with the edge of the sword"; and some "hallowed mis-translations" in the Authorised Version are still cherished, e.g. "the desire of nations" in Hag. ii. 2 (Revised Version "the desirable things"). Now and then the Authorised Version is even to be preferred, as in Dan. iii. 21 ("hats," Revised Version, "mantles"), whence the Quaker George Fox had argued that men should not remove their hats in the presence of kings.

The English rendering of the Hebrew has a grandeur and sublimity of its own, though it sometimes reproduces the music of the original rather than its meaning.[1] Hebrew rhythm and parallelism lend themselves to reproduction in English, and, as Tyndale said, comparing Hebrew and English, "the manner of speaking is both one; so that in a thousand places thou needest not but to translate it into English word for word." The Revised Version, clinging as closely as possible to earlier renderings and phraseology, has retained religious terms which were tolerably familiar when the Bible was more widely known and expounded. But to-day both Authorised and Revised Versions stand in greater need of explanation than before, and new translations, more in accordance with modern speech, and more closely rendering what each translator takes to be the essential meaning of the original now find a public. Such translations are apt to lack the dignity of the familiar versions, or to restrict that exercise of the religious imagination which has been of such powerful influence in the past.[2] It is disputed

[1] Burkitt's warning that interest in the Bible may be more sentimental than intelligent should not be unheeded: "if the Bible were more read instead of being talked about, I fancy we should not hear quite so much about 'the noble English of our incomparable Version'" (*Journ. of Theol. Stud.*, XXIII, 24; cf. XXXVI, 243).

[2] For example, the "Day of the Lord" (Amos v. 18) will open up a much wider field of thought than such a paraphrase as "the Millennium."

whether a translation should aim at being literal—in which case it may be unintelligible; or whether it should follow Cardinal Newman's dictum: "in a book intended for general reading, faithfulness may be considered simply to consist in expressing the sense of the original." In any case, however excellent the translation may be, the Old Testament sooner or later needs interpretation.

It is arguable whether writings in any ancient, and, compared with Greek and Latin, relatively primitive language can ever be adequately translated into a modern European tongue. Some of the most familiar Hebrew terms have a connotation or range of meaning so wide that absolute consistency of rendering is undesirable: thus, the term "righteousness" sometimes means "rightness," and almost "rights." Many points of style are much more noticeable in the Hebrew than in the English. Thus, only by reference to the original can one fully appreciate the linguistic differences between Isa. i.–xxxv. and xl. ff., or avoid the common confusion of "captivity" with "exile," or see the connection between the "sojourner" or "protected client" (*not* "stranger," Exod. xx. 10, etc.) and the new relations heralded in the oft-misquoted Isa. xi. 6, where the wild beasts shall dwell with the lamb and the kid *under their protection*. In fact, the Old Testament reflects a world of thought and ways of thinking very different from our own. To understand it adequately requires not only an acquaintance with its original language, but some knowledge of ancient conditions of life and thought, and an ability to bridge the gulf between our ways of thinking and those of the ancient writers.

Finally, to understand the Bible requires an effort. It is not enough to suppose that the interpreter has simply to bring the Bible to men—men must also be willing to be brought to this ancient Book. We have to make some effort, to take a step towards it, to approach it with some preliminary knowledge about it: the true "Approach to the Bible" brings each nearer the other. It is then that we discover that the truest "criticism" of the Bible starts from what we have learnt from it.

CHAPTER II

The Hebrew Text and Canon

I. The Hebrew Text

In the previous chapter we began to go behind the English Old Testament; our next step is to consider its original language and contents. The Old Testament is written in Hebrew, with the exception of portions of the books of Daniel and Ezra, Jer. x. 11, and the name Jegar Sahadutha in Gen. xxxi. 47, which are in Aramaic.[1] The current form of the Hebrew Old Testament is called the Masoretic (or Massoretic) Text—the exact spelling and meaning are disputed—because we owe it to the old Jewish scholars who by their collection of "traditional" notes—the Mas(s)orah— gave it a fixity which distinguishes it from the New. They fixed and handed down the correct way of reading and writing MSS., they noted unusual spellings, they counted verses and letters, and discovered the middle verse, the middle word, and even (in Lev. xi. 42) the middle letter of the Pentateuch. These Massoretic Hebrew MSS. bridge the gulf between our printed Bibles and the actual original documents. In the Preface to the Revised Version the revisers make this important statement: "the Received, or, as it is commonly called, the Massoretic Text . . . has come down to us in MSS. which are of no very great antiquity and which all belong to the same family or recension. That other recensions were at one time in existence is probable from the variations in the Ancient Versions, the oldest of which, namely, the Greek or LXX (i.e. the Septuagint), was made, at least in part, some two centuries before the Christian era." What these words mean has now to be explained.

[1] The old name "Chaldee" is no longer used.

The Hebrew Bible was first printed by Jews in the last quarter of the fifteenth century. This Jewish edition was soon followed by the first Christian edition in the Complutensian Polyglot Bible, produced under the direction of Cardinal Ximenes (1514–17), which also contained the Targums (i.e. the Aramaic paraphrases), the LXX and the Latin versions. In other Polyglots, including Walton's famous Polyglot (1654–57), other versions were added. The Bomberg Bible (Venice, 1516–17) printed Rabbinical commentaries along with the text. Apart from inevitable typographical difficulties and the disturbing similarity of certain Hebrew letters—a common source of confusion from the earliest times—the treatment of the Divine Names in some of the early Hebrew editions deserves mention: Jehovah and Elohim (God) were spelt Y–h–*d*–h and Elo*d*im in order to avoid mentioning the name of God, a precaution that finds analogies at a much earlier stage in the history of the Hebrew text (p. 41).

As scholars began to study the Hebrew text, and to observe variations from it in the LXX and other versions (so e.g. Cappellus in 1634–50), they endeavoured to recover its earliest form. Exhaustive collations of MSS. were made, notably by Kennicott (1776, 1780) and De Rossi (1784–88), and it was discovered that the variations in the MSS. themselves, compared with those in the MSS. of the New Testament, were of the slightest significance. Moreover, the same errors, slips and peculiarities of writing, however trifling, reappeared everywhere: it might be a letter larger or smaller than the rest, a letter suspended or inverted, or one surmounted by a dot. Obvious mistakes were faithfully reproduced, and sometimes a marginal note stated that a word was to be read or written in this or that anomalous manner. Much was known of the extraordinary care taken by the Jewish scribes in copying Biblical MSS., and it was an inevitable conclusion that the remarkable similarity of all Hebrew MSS. must be due to their common ancestry. This was first guessed by Spinoza (seventeenth century); it was amply verified by the collations referred to, and was subsequently demonstrated on other grounds.

The oldest Hebrew MSS. are not very ancient. The earliest date that has usually been accepted is A.D. 916 (the Leningrad Codex of the Prophets); but there is a Cairo MS. of the Prophets of A.D. 895, and some fragments of undated MSS. may be earlier. All MSS. have the same ancestry, and their text, the "Massoretic Text," can be traced back as far as Jerome (c. A.D. 340–420), Origen (A.D. 185–255) and Aquila (first half of the second century A.D.). On the other hand, important variant readings are preserved in the LXX and other versions (notably the Old Latin), in the Hebrew Pentateuch used by the Samaritans, the "Nash Papyrus" (p. 38), the works of Josephus and elsewhere. Evidently this text must have been fixed somewhere about the beginning of the second century A.D., and it is not difficult to suggest the reason.

In the disturbance and anxiety after the Fall of Jerusalem in A.D. 70 the Jews would naturally desire to preserve their sacred books, even as Judas the Maccabee had done at an earlier date (2 Macc. ii. 14). Moreover, a new system of interpretation, a reaction from current allegorising, grew up at Jamnia (Jabneh), near Jerusalem, whither the Jewish elders had fled. The most prominent of these was Rabbi Aḳiba (died c. A.D. 132), a fervent supporter of the Messianic revolt of Bar-Kokeba against Hadrian. This system laid weight upon the merest word, however superfluous, even upon the presence and absence of single letters; nothing was meaningless. Thus, in Deut. x. 20, the accusatival particle *eth* (which otherwise means "with") was taken to imply that the Rabbis were also to be venerated "*with* the Lord." Such a system of interpretation naturally could not tolerate variant readings in any of the MSS.

At the same time, the Septuagint, the Greek version of the Old Testament used by the Greek-speaking Jews (see p. 25), gradually lost the esteem it had once enjoyed, and its numerous divergences from the Hebrew were frequently embarrassing. There appeared, then, another and strictly literal Greek translation by Aquila, a Jewish proselyte, a disciple of Aḳiba. His version was so extraordinarily literal that it has been styled "a learned and often ingenious crib"

(Burkitt). In Isa. vii. 14 he replaced the LXX "virgin" (παρθένος) by "young woman" (νεᾶνις), the word actually used elsewhere in the LXX to render 'almah (Exod. ii. 8, etc.), and thereby destroyed a favourite Christian argument against the Jews, who throughout preferred Aquila's version to the LXX. In fact, all disputes between Jews and Christians were complicated so long as the LXX differed markedly from the Hebrew, and the Hebrew MSS. differed among themselves. Hence, the Jewish situation after A.D. 70, the growth of a literal interpretation of Scripture, and controversies with the Christians, converge to suggest that the Hebrew text, as it has come down to us, was fixed probably at Jamnia, where also the "Canon" was determined (p. 25), about the beginning of the second century A.D.

We thus distinguish (1) the stage when the Hebrew text was settled and preserved by the Massoretic scribes (sōphĕrīm) from (2) the text in the Pre-Massoretic stage, when numerous important variants existed. Exactly how the text was fixed can only be conjectured; but when once this had been done, the most scrupulous care was taken to ensure the absolute uniformity of all subsequent copies.[1] Sooner or later divergent texts fell out of use, and earlier versions or paraphrases (such as the LXX and the Targums) were adjusted to the new M.T. (Massoretic Text) or replaced.[2] But variant readings did not quite disappear even in Jewish tradition, e.g. the Talmud has preserved the true reading in 2 Sam. xxi. 1 ("on Saul and on his house is blood"); and some MSS., as late as the twelfth century, read "ephod," as in the LXX, for "ark" in 1 Sam. xiv. 18 (mg.). Accordingly, the question sometimes arises whether noteworthy readings in a late MS.

[1] It is interesting to compare the early history of the Koran. For some time there were variant readings, which were the cause of bitter quarrels, until the Caliph Othman (A.D. 650–51)—scarcely twenty years after the death of Mohammed—was induced to establish a universally binding text. A "canonical" edition was prepared, of which four copies were made, and all other MSS. were then destroyed. These four became the ancestors of all subsequent copies.

[2] The LXX has come down to us through Christian hands, and has often been corrected to agree with the M.T.; hence the task of recovering even the original LXX is a difficult one in itself.

go back to the Pre-Massoretic stage or are later and secondary developments.[1]

At every step in the copying of MSS. there is the possibility of fresh error; but the Jewish scribes in their reverence for the sacred text went further, and even copied obvious mistakes, e.g. 1 Sam. xii. 15, where the M.T. has "shall be against you and against your *fathers*." Some slight errors are corrected by the marginal notes which distinguish what is "written" (*Kĕthībh*) from what should be "read" (*Kĕrē*). Even a simple misprint in 1 Sam. xvii. 34 (*zeh* for *seh*) in the Venice edition of 1525 was subsequently treated as unalterable, and in accordance with the old custom was corrected in the margin.

The lengthy history of the Hebrew Bible does not concern us further. It is only now that the effort is being made (by Paul Kahle) to replace the old "Received Text" by one based on MSS. some centuries earlier than those used by the great editors, Jacob ben Khayyim (Bomberg Bible, 1524–25), and Van der Hooght (1705). But even this new effort is only an attempt to recover the *best* Massoretic Text, fixed about A.D. 100; it is still necessary to go behind it to the Pre-Massoretic stage.

An instructive feature in the history of the Hebrew Bible is the repeated loss of old traditions and the growth of new ones.[2] A curious illustration of this is afforded by the story of the vowel-points. Hebrew writing, like that of most of

---

[1] See e.g. Burkitt, *Journal of Theological Studies*, XXII, 165–72 on a curious MS. in Trinity College Library, Cambridge, described by H. W. Sheppard; and J. Fischer, *Biblica*, XV, 50–93, on the Old Testament citations in the work of the Scholastic Odo (A.D.1140).

It may be observed that the Vulgate was based upon the Old Latin version which was taken from the Pre-Massoretic LXX, whereas the English Revised Version was made from the M.T., the relatively later text. In a few cases, as in 1 Sam. x. 1, the earlier reading of the LXX is to be found in the Great Bible of 1539 and in the Douay Bible of 1609, and the LXX of 1 Sam. xiv. 10 is preserved in the Wycliffe Bible, the Great Bible and the Douay Bible (since 1750). See G. B. Gray, *Mansfield College Essays* (1919), 109 ff. (esp. p. 118 f.).

[2] E.g. the origin of the "extraordinary points" in Ps. xxvii. 13, and elsewhere, was forgotten, and some of the Jewish explanations of peculiarities in the Hebrew are extremely fanciful.

the other Semitic languages, originally consisted solely of consonants, which, broadly speaking, were as easy to read as the vowel-less shorthand of the reporter. An early attempt to remove ambiguity was made by the insertion of "vowel consonants"—*matres lectionis*.[1] Vowels and accents were subsequently invented to express the exact pronunciation of words and their connection one with another. Such a case as the name Samson, which in the Hebrew pointed text is read Shimshon, illustrates the fact that the consonantal text is older than the vocalised one, and that when the vowel system was introduced the vowel of the first syllable of the name, which we derive from the LXX and the Vulgate, had changed from *a* to *i*. The full vowel system of the M.T. is probably not earlier than the sixth century A.D. Before that date we find allusions to ambiguities of pronunciation which would have been unnecessary had the text been vocalised; and, by the ninth century, a complete and highly complex Hebrew text, with all its vowel-points and accents, formed the basis of discussion in Jewish schools.

But just as the true story of the fixing of the M.T. was forgotten, so also the memory of the origin of the vowel system passed away, and after the Reformation a famous and not uninstructive controversy arose—"the Battle of the Vowel-points." There is always a desire to antedate one's valued treasures, and some writers ascribed the vowel-points to Ezra, some to Moses, and some even to Adam. The enlightened Rabbi Ibn Ezra and Raymond Martin (twelfth century) did not share such views as these, and Elias Levita (1468–1549) clearly showed that the vowel-points were evidently later than the Talmud. Luther, too, said: "I often utter words which strongly oppose these points, they are most assuredly not to be preferred to the simple, correct and grammatical sense." On the other

---

[1] To attempt an analogy: the English consonants L D S could be read in many different ways as the context might suggest. Next, by the introduction of the *matres lectionis* it could be made clear that L*DS must be "loads" and not "lads," L†DS "leads" (the verb, *not* the noun) and not "loads" and LD‡S "ladies" and not "lads," "lids," "loads," etc.

hand, later divines upheld their antiquity and sanctity, and an eminent Jew, Azariah de Rossi (1575), suggested as a compromise—which was readily adopted (e.g. by the elder Buxtorf, 1564–1629)—that the vowel-points communicated to Adam were subsequently forgotten; restored by Ezra, they again fell into oblivion, until they were once more recovered after the close of the Talmud.[1] Cappellus (1624), however, reaffirmed the "dangerous" views of Levita; but when he was supported by the French Roman Catholic, Morinus (1633), who used them to demonstrate the need of Church authority and tradition, Protestants were up in arms. At length, the Zurich Consensus (1675) asserted the doctrine of verbal inspiration, including the inspiration of the vowels and accents. But the wisest position was that of Brian Walton (1659), who denied that the late origin of the punctuation meant that the Roman Church alone could give the true sense of Scripture, and pointed out that the Protestant Divines had "involved themselves in extreme labyrinths, engaging themselves in defence of that which might be easily proved to be false, and thereby wronged the cause they seemed to defend." "The reading and sense of the text might be *certain* without *punctuation*," and therefore "the *Scriptures* did not at all depend upon the authority of the *Church*." This, said Walton, was the opinion of the chief Protestant Divines and the greatest linguists, who agreed that Scripture "was in itself a *sufficient* and *certain* rule for faith and life, not depending upon any human authority to support it." As an illustration of the combination of criticism and controversy "the Battle of the Vowel-points" is still of interest.

Although isolated portions of the Old Testament may come directly or indirectly from Babylonia or Egypt (p. 91), there is no evidence whatever for the supposition that we can regard it, as a whole, as of other than *Hebrew* origin. Recent discoveries of an ancient form of Hebrew in cuneiform in North Syria (p. 83) allow the supposition that parts of

---

[1] This is a type of argument that crops up elsewhere, e.g. among those who wish to maintain the antiquity of the Book of Deuteronomy, but believe that it was rediscovered in the reign of Josiah (p. 47).

the Old Testament might, for all we know, have been in this script, although, if they did not differ essentially from the M.T., there would still be the same Biblical problems. The oldest Hebrew records might have been written on ostraka (inscribed pottery sherds), on limestone or other tablets, on leather rolls, or on papyri. The writing was probably in some form of the old Hebrew (Phoenician or Canaanite) alphabet, later forms of which are preserved on Jewish coins as late as the Second Revolt (A.D. 132–35), and by the Samaritans. However, from about the sixth century B.C., with the spread of the "sister" Aramaic language and alphabet, a slightly different script came into use among the Jews of Elephantine in Upper Egypt (fifth century), in Palestine, and elsewhere, and from it is descended the now familiar "square" Hebrew character which, in turn, became the parent of the various cursive scripts of the Jews of the Dispersion. It is only in this "Aramaic" alphabet, and not in the old Hebrew (or Samaritan), that the *yōd* ("jot") is the smallest letter (Matt. v. 18). But there are variant readings in the M.T. and in the versions which presuppose the confusion of certain letters which are not at all alike in the "square" Hebrew, but closely resemble each other in the old Hebrew or in *early* Aramaic scripts (e.g. the words for "above" and "dew" in Gen. xlix. 25 and Deut. xxxiii. 13, respectively).[1]

There is reason to believe that in the oldest MSS. there was little or no space between words, clauses or even sentences. This agrees with Semitic papyri and inscriptions, where it is sometimes difficult to know how to divide up the letters, and it is confirmed by the re-divisions made by the Massoretes themselves, by the variations between the M.T. and the LXX (e.g. Jer. xxiii. 33, Hos. vi. 5), and also by the simple emendation of corrupt passages.[2] Yet an elaborate method of division is to be found in the old

---

[1] It should be noticed that "there is no ground for supposing (as is sometimes done) that in ancient times numerals were represented in Hebrew MSS. by the letters of the alphabet." S. R. Driver's warning (*Samuel*, p. 97 n.; Oxford, 1913) is still necessary.

[2] E.g. Amos vi. 12, where for the one word "cattle" (literally "cattles") we should read "plough with cattle the sea," *b–ḳ–r y–m*.

inscription of Mesha, King of Moab (*c.* 850 B.C.), where
words are severed by points, and clauses, etc., by perpendi-
cular lines. Why this useful device was not consistently
maintained it is difficult to say.

II. THE CANON OF THE OLD TESTAMENT

From a study of the variant readings in the M.T. and the
versions, and from the usage in ancient Semitic inscriptions,
it is possible to form some notion of the Hebrew Old Testament in its earlier Pre-Massoretic form. We have now to
go behind the contents and consider the stages in the growth
of the "Canon." It should, however, be observed that
strictly speaking, the conception of "Holy Scriptures"
(cf. 2 Tim. iii. 15) is older than that of a "Canon," and that
the Jews definitely settled their Sacred Writings about the
time that the M.T. was fixed, and therefore, before the days
of the Christian Canon.

The Hebrew Old Testament is divided into three parts:
the Law, the Prophets and the Writings. By the Law is
meant the Pentateuch, although the Hebrew word Tōrah,
like the Greek νόμος (e.g. 1 Cor. xiv. 21, John x. 34), could
be used generally of any teaching. The Prophets are
divided into the "Former Prophets," i.e. Joshua, Judges,
Samuel, Kings (excluding Ruth), and the "Later Prophets,"
i.e. our prophetical books (excluding Lamentations and
Daniel); and, according to Jewish tradition, Isaiah should
comes after Ezekiel.[1] All the books of the Second Division
are reckoned as "prophetical": Judges and Samuel were
said to have been written by the prophet Samuel, Kings
by Jeremiah, and Joshua himself could be called a prophet
(BS xlvi. 1). Not only are our "historical" books prophetical
in spirit, but the great prophets were men of action; they
found in history permanent truths; and not unnaturally
did a later age suppose that men who made history should
write it (cf. 2 Chron. xii. 15; xxvi. 22).

---

[1] Our so-called twelve "Minor" prophets bear an unfortunate
disparaging title. The position of Hosea (before and not after
Amos) may be due to the second verse, "the *beginning* of the word
of the Lord." Twelve is perhaps an artificial number.

The Third Division of the Hebrew Bible is called the Writings (*Kĕthūbhīm*), in Greek, Hagiographa. It comprises (*a*) the great triad, Psalms, Proverbs, Job; (*b*) the Megilloth or "Rolls," read in the Synagogue on festal occasions: Canticles (Song of Songs), Ruth, Lamentations, Ecclesiastes (Kōhéleth, the "Preacher") and Esther—the order varies—and (*c*) the narrative-books: Daniel, Ezra, Nehemiah and Chronicles. The natural order in (*c*) is inverted, for the Book of Nehemiah forms the end of a continuous record beginning with Chronicles and closes with a hint of the separation of Jews and Samaritans. But by placing 2 Chronicles at the end, the Jewish Bible closes on another note: the Exile is over, a new era has dawned, whosoever wishes may return to Jerusalem (2 Chron. xxxvi. 22f.). It is possible that the series Chronicles—Ezra—Nehemiah was divided and inverted so that there might be a more inspiring finale for the Jews than the last chapter of Old Testament history as preserved in Neh. xiii. No less fittingly do the Testaments of the Christian Bible end with Malachi and the imminent change, and with Revelation and the new aeon.

A threefold division of the Sacred Writings was known to the grandson of Ben Sira, the author of the Prologue to Ecclesiasticus (after 132 B.C.). He speaks of the Law, the Prophets, and "the others who followed upon them," or "the other books of our fathers," or "the rest of the books." But the contents of his Third Division are uncertain.[1] The Pentateuch was probably translated into Greek in the reign of Ptolemy II Philadelphus (283–245 B.C.), when many thousands of Jewish soldiers were settled in Egypt. The remaining books were translated gradually and by many translators who differed greatly in competence. In this Greek or Alexandrian Bible, Ruth is placed after Judges, Chronicles after Kings, and Lamentations after Jeremiah. This arrangement seems so natural that it is easier to suppose that the Hebrew order has been altered than that the Hebrew disarranged the Greek order. Moreover, Ruth

[1] Cf. Luke xxiv. 44, the Law, the Prophets and the Psalms (i.e. the first of the third group).

lacks the "Deuteronomic" style found in Judges and Samuel; internal evidence shows that Lamentations can hardly be by Jeremiah, who takes another attitude to Jerusalem; and it can be shown that Ruth and Lamentations were not translated into Greek by the translators of Judges and Jeremiah respectively. Hence it is probable, not only that the Hebrew order is the older, but also that the three Hebrew divisions represent the growth of three different collections, of which the Pentateuch was the first to become "canonical."

Josephus, writing towards the close of the first century A.D., speaks of the Scriptures as a well-defined collection of twenty-two writings (*c. Apion.* i. 7f.). The question of their authority was discussed at Jamnia. Doubts were felt at one time or another respecting Chronicles, Ezekiel, Jonah, Proverbs, Canticles, Ruth, Esther and Ecclesiastes. In Proverbs there were found to be contradictions (xxvi. 4f.), and in Ezekiel passages which conflicted with the Law (xlvi. 6, contrast Num. xxix. 2). Ecclesiastes, which, said Jerome, seems worthy to have been expunged, is refuted by the author of Wisdom (ii. 1–10); the "Wise" found that it was self-contradictory (i. 2 and vii. 3), but they accepted it because it began and ended with the words of the Law (i. 3; xii. 13). Canticles was a dubious book; it had been sung at banquets, and its fate was uncertain; but it was saved by giving it an allegorical interpretation. The heroine and Solomon were identified by the Jews with Israel and God—and by the Christians with the Church (or the Soul of the Believer) and Christ—and with typical Oriental hyperbole the "Songs of Songs" was even acclaimed a "holy of holies." It was decided that all the books, even Canticles and Kōhéleth (Ecclesiastes), "defiled the hands," that is to say, they made the hands that touched them ceremonially unclean—"tabu," to use an anthropological term; they were sacred, and those who handled them needed ceremonial cleansing (cf. Lev. vi. 27). The contents of the Hebrew Bible were thus settled in the course of the second century A.D.

There were other writings which came under suspicion and were rejected, namely, the so-called "apocryphal" and "pseudepigraphical" books. These are of such importance for the study of the Old Testament and of the period between the Old Testament and the New Testament that a brief reference must now be made to the chief of them. It will be convenient to start with the English Apocrypha. This collection we owe almost wholly to the LXX—the Bible of the early Christian Church. Here three main opinions found expression: (*a*) the writings are "apocryphal" (so Jerome), i.e. secret or esoteric, with a suspicion of being heretical; (*b*) they are "Scripture," i.e. "canonical" (so Augustine, Synods of 393 and 397); and (*c*) they hold an intermediate position, they are "ecclesiastical," and to be read for edification, though not canonical they are to be retained. The Roman Church (Council of Trent, 1546) followed the Greek or Alexandrian authority and anathematised those who did not accept the Apocrypha; but some later Roman scholars reckoned the apocryphal books of the Vulgate as deutero-canonical, and some included what the Council of Trent excluded (viz. 1 and 2 Esdras, Prayer of Manasseh). The Reformed Church, on the other hand, confined itself to the Hebrew Bible, and rejected the apocryphal books, which owed their status to the Roman Church, and seemed to support its authority.[1] However, in the Bible of 1534 the Apocrypha are "Books that are not equally esteemed with the Holy Scripture, but nevertheless are profitable and good to read" and they retained their place in English versions earlier than the London Bible of 1629.

There is no real gap between the Old Testament and the Apocrypha. Our Apocrypha includes Second Esdras, which is not in the LXX (though it is found in the Vulgate), but it ignores both its additional Psalm (a Psalm of David when he fought with Goliath) and the Third and Fourth Books of Maccabees. The opening book, 1 Esdras, is an incomplete fragment in Greek containing part of 2 Chronicles, the whole of Ezra and part of Nehemiah. It differs from the M.T.,

---

[1] E.g. Tobit might be quoted to support the belief in the intercession of angels, Ben Sira seemed to support the doctrine of salvation by works, and 2 Maccabees mentions with approval sacrifices for the dead (xii. 39 ff.).

partly in its readings and partly in its arrangement, and testifies to the late fluctuation of tradition. Josephus used it, and the Story of the Three Youths and the Praise of Truth (Ch. iii. f.) was especially valued by Christian writers, who accepted its canonicity.

The "canonical" Esther contains stories of the Persian age which are supplemented in the LXX by the additions that appear in our Apocrypha. But these stories are scarcely more important than those in the "apocryphal" books of Tobit and Judith; and, in fact, the "canonical" book of Esther is itself of slight religious value. It is a strange book: the names of Esther and Mordecai recall those of the goddess Ishtar and the god Marduk; and that of Vashti resembles an Elamite goddess! Its sacredness was questioned by Jewish scholars even to the third century A.D., and it was perhaps the popularity of the "Day of Purim" (ix. 32) that saved it. It was almost ignored by the Church. Not only does the book not mention the name of God—a Divine Providence acting on behalf of Israel does, however, lie behind the stories—its spirit is unethical, though the Alexandrian Jews by their additions attempted to introduce a religious note.

To the "canonical" Daniel there are three additions in the Apocrypha. The Book of Daniel is, in its present form, undoubtedly Maccabaean (cf. viii. 14), though it could be argued that some of its contents may go back earlier: the name, at least, is old (Ezek. xiv. 14; xxviii. 3). The "apocryphal" books of the Maccabees are indispensable for the historical background of the "canonical" book; and for its visions and for the spirit of the writer no less indispensable are the "apocalyptical" writings, which bear such ancient names as Noah, Enoch, Baruch, etc. Lines cannot be drawn between canonical, apocryphal and apocalyptical writings. The Epistle of Jude (v. 14 f.) cites Enoch i. 9, and the Book of Enoch was regarded as canonical by early Christians; but Jerome says that the Epistle was generally rejected simply because it quoted the "apocryphal" work.

The "canonical" Kōhéleth (Ecclesiastes) is doubtless as

late as the third century B.C.   Like the no less important
Alexandrian philosophical Book of Wisdom (which, as
Jerome knew, was sometimes ascribed to Philo), and like
the Psalms of Solomon (contained in some MSS. of the LXX
and originally composed in Hebrew) and the curious gnostic
(Jewish–Christian?) Odes of Solomon, it is associated with
a famous name.   What is now often known as the "Wisdom
Literature" comprises writings "canonical" (Job, Proverbs
and Ecclesiastes) and "apocryphal" (Ben Sira, Wisdom,
and the speeches in 1 Esdras iii. f.).   The Jews probably
rejected the Greek Book of Wisdom because the Christians
found therein evidence for their doctrine of the Logos; but
it is not easy to see why they also rejected Ben Sira's book,
the "Liber ecclesiasticus," *par excellence*, which like 1 Maccabees, was originally written in Hebrew.[1]

The Psalms of Solomon, which illustrate Messianic and
other Pharisaic ideas shortly before the rise of Christianity,
have been ignored; but the even later 2 Esdras (or 4 Ezra)
finds a place.   This book goes back in part to a Hebrew
original, and is of much value for the light it throws upon
one aspect of Jewish thought towards the close of the first
century A.D.   Written at a time when Judaism seemed lost,
and its step-daughter, Christianity, was making swift
progress, 2 Esdras—the last chapter of the Old Testament
we might call it—has a tragic interest (see p. 214).

The use made in the "apocryphal" and "pseudepigraphical" writings of honoured names—cf. also the
Assumption of Moses, the Martyrdom of Isaiah—was
entirely honest.   Thucydides puts into the mouths of his
historical characters sentiments which he honestly thinks
worthy of them; and in more modern times, though we no
longer publish, as did the pseudepigraphists, works of
Enoch, Baruch or Moses, yet in all good faith we at least
offer interpretations of the sacred writers and claim—
rightly or wrongly—to know what they meant!   The
ancient procedure finds an excellent illustration in the
"Little Genesis" or Book of Jubilees (150–100 B.C.), where

[1] To this literature belongs also the entertaining story of Aḥiḳar;
see p. 86.

the "canonical" narratives of the Patriarchal period are further developed and supplemented. The book, which is by a Pharisee, a staunch defender of Judaism against Hellenism, stands in the same relation to Genesis as Chronicles stands to Samuel–Kings. In each case the traditions and usages of the writer's day are carried back; and just as Chronicles ascribes to David the Levitical organisation of the post-exilic age, so the author of Jubilees teaches, e.g. that circumcision and the institution of the Sabbath dated from the very beginning of the world and that the Levitical law of purification after child-birth (Lev. xii.) was enacted after the creation of Adam and Eve. The writer claims to be inspired. His book opens: "as the Lord spake unto Moses on Mount Sinai when he went up to receive the Tables of the Law." He claims to know of "heavenly records" (iii. 10), of records handed down by the Patriarchs (xxi. 10), and words that had been guarded until the appointed time (xlv. 16, cf. Dan. xii. 4, 9).

It has been customary to read the Old and New Testaments in the light of each other; but a wider outlook is necessary. If we are to understand the Old Testament it is impossible to sever the later "canonical" books from the Apocrypha, the Pseudepigrapha, Josephus and the Alexandrian Philo. 1 Esdras is indispensable for the critical study of Ezra–Nehemiah, 2 Esdras (4 Ezra) dates after the rise of Christianity, and works like Enoch, Jubilees, and the Testaments of the Twelve Patriarchs, closely unite the course of Old Testament thought with the later currents among both Jews and Christians in the first century A.D.

In 2 Esdras (xiv. 21 ff.) there is a very curious tradition that has always attracted attention. It is related that the Law had been burnt but was restored by Ezra, who through the Holy Spirit dictated to five companions ninety-four books. Of these, twenty-four were for all to read, worthy or unworthy; but the remaining seventy were only for the wise, for in them is "the spring of understanding, the fountain of wisdom and the stream of knowledge." The importance of Ezra and the question of the seventy esoteric books must now be considered. From other sources we

know that the age of Ezra was a landmark.[1]   The canonical
books relate that he returned with the Law (Ezra vii. 14)
and made a new Covenant (Neh. viii. ff.).   It was an event
as epoch-making as the discovery, in Josiah's reign, of the
Book of the Law or Covenant (2 Kings xxii. 8–11; xxiii. 2–21).
It is generally supposed that the Book of Deuteronomy is
here referred to, and it is presumably the complete
Pentateuch that Ezra was believed to bring with him.
At all events, the Biblical account of Ezra's work on behalf
of Jerusalem and the Jews clearly represents it as a new
and decisive stage in post-exilic Judaism; and his insistence
upon the separation of the Jews from other peoples
(Neh. ix. 2) explains how it was that he became a hated
figure among the Samaritans.

A Talmudic tradition asserts that the Law had been
forgotten out of Israel until Ezra came and re-established
it.   There sprang up the tradition of a "Great Synagogue."
This was a council of elders who regularised religious
institutions (cf. Neh. viii. ff.).   It wrote Ezekiel, the Minor
Prophets, Daniel and Esther, and it endorsed the value of
Proverbs, Canticles and Ecclesiastes.   Tradition grew, and
at last it was even affirmed (by Elias Levita, 1538) that the
whole Canon was fixed by Ezra and this body.   This, the
orthodox theological dogma of the sixteenth and seventeenth
century, silenced protesting voices, excepting—it was said—
only of those *quibus pro cerebro fungus est!*   Thus, upon a
single figure and a single age were focussed processes that
extended over a number of years.   On the most moderate
estimate the older traditions imply that the Pentateuch,
as we have it, is in the form given to it by Ezra, in which
case his age would be the starting-point for the study of it.
But while conservative writers of to-day often hold that the
Pentateuch is of essentially Mosaic origin, though not without later changes—and a few writers still adhere to the view
that it was rewritten by Ezra—modern criticism treats the

---

[1] On his date, see p. 194, n.   To Ezra later tradition ascribed
the change from the old Hebrew to the Aramaic script (p. 23);
a certain deterioration of Hebrew style round about 400 B.C. also
has been felt by some modern scholars.

Pentateuch *in its present form* as not earlier than Ezra, while explicitly recognising that it is made up of sources, some of which are very much older (p. 49f.). In other words, behind these traditions relating to Ezra and his age (viz. in the books of Ezra–Nehemiah) are events of far-reaching significance for the study of the Pentateuch and the rest of the Old Testament. On the other hand, in 2 Macc. ii. 13–15, it is related that Nehemiah collected sacred writings about the kings and prophets, works of David (τὰ τοῦ Δαυείδ), and letters of kings about sacred books (cf. e.g. Ezra iv.ff.). This notice, whatever its worth, is isolated, and it gives Nehemiah a prominence which is elsewhere given to Ezra, who however is not mentioned, as is Nehemiah, in Ben Sira's list of famous men (xlix. 13).

Also, Judas the Maccabee is said to have collected writings which had been scattered during the persecution under Antiochus Epiphanes, when books of the Law or Covenant were hunted out and destroyed (1 Macc. i. 56f.). The circumstances of the Maccabaean revolt, the restoration of the Temple services, the strenuous reforms and subsequent proselytising measures certainly combine to make 164 B.C. another landmark in the history of the Old Testament. This date, which is long after the age of Nehemiah and Ezra, is some thirty years earlier than the grandson of Ben Sira (p. 25 above). It is noteworthy that the sage, writing about 180 B.C., counts himself among the great teachers of his people (xxiv. 30ff.; xxxiii. 16), and that the grandson is not conscious of any gulf between the Third Division of Sacred Writings and the work of his grandfather. On the other hand, the author of 1 Maccabees emphasises the difference between (*a*) the age of the great persecution (*c.* 166 B.C.) and after, and (*b*) the earlier days of the prophets.[1]

Josephus (*c. Apion.* i. 8), in his turn, draws the line between the sacred writers and the "post-prophetical" age after the reign of Artaxerxes; but when he proposes to begin his history where the earlier historians and "our

---

[1] iv. 46; ix. 27; xiv. 41; cf. also the Prayer of Azariah, *v.* 15 and Ps. lxxiv. 9.

prophets" conclude, he starts off with Antiochus Epiphanes
(*War* i. 6). The Jewish writing, *Seder Olam Rabba*, 30,
signalises the men who "prophesied by the Holy Spirit"
to the time of Alexander the Great (332 B.C.): "from that
time forward incline thine ear and hearken to the words of
the wise"; but in the Talmud (*Sanhedrin* 28a) it is said that,
"books like Ben Sira and similar books written from that
time onwards, may be read as one reads a letter." Here,
once more, the line is drawn not at Ezra and Artaxerxes
(? I or II), but later. Unfortunately, however, of the
history of the Persian and Greek periods there was the
haziest recollection; and the Samaritan schism itself was
evidently ascribed to the time of Nehemiah and Artaxerxes
(so Neh. xiii.) or to that of the Samaritan priest Manasseh
and Alexander (Jos. *Ant.* xi. 8). Of the famous names
mentioned in the ethical treatise *Pirke Aboth* only one
belonging to the third century B.C. can be found. Consequently, the loss of so much authentic history during the
periods which were of the first importance for the external
and internal vicissitudes of the Jews render it extremely
difficult to trace the steps in the growth of the Hebrew
Old Testament, although the age of Antiochus Epiphanes
and the Maccabees seems to have been of outstanding
significance.

Certain books undoubtedly became more sacred than
others; and Philo of Alexandria (middle of the first century
A.D.) uses those which we style "canonical" differently
from the rest. The Samaritans accepted only the Pentateuch, and the Sadducees also took a narrow line, giving
pre-eminence to the Law. At the other extreme is the view
in 2 Esdras which, as we have seen, sets seventy esoteric
writings apart from and above the twenty-four which "the
worthy and unworthy" may read (xiv. 45 ff.). For the
figure 24 (also given by the Talmud) Josephus (followed by
Jerome) gives 22. They can be obtained thus: the Pentateuch,
5; the Prophets, 8 (Talmud) or 13 (Jos.); the "Scriptures,"
11 (Talmud) or "hymns to God and the precepts," 4 (Jos.).
It is not difficult to combine Ruth with Judges, Lamentations
with Jeremiah, and Nehemiah with Ezra, and reach the

necessary totals; but we cannot prove, for example, that
Josephus included such disputed books as Esther and
Ecclesiastes.   Moreover, it is certainly not the case that
Jews, Samaritans and Alexandrian Greek-speaking Jews
possessed an absolutely identical Pentateuch; there are
differences as regards the chronological scheme in Gen. i.–xi.,
and the order of Exod. xxxv.–xl. in the LXX differs from
that in the Hebrew.   Nor can we be certain that the "Minor
Prophets," to which Ben Sira refers as a single work (xlix. 10),
exactly corresponded to what we have.

Of the seventy esoteric books in 2 Esdras—doubtless only
a round number—some no doubt survive in the various
apocryphal, apocalyptical and pseudepigraphical writings
known to us.   The fact that several of these have come down
in different versions testifies to their popularity.   The
literature, as a whole, is of great value for the light it throws
upon the diverse tendencies of thought among Jews and
also among Jewish–Christians during the transitional period
before Christianity and Judaism parted and hardened their
differences.   There was then little room for the literature;
it fell outside the development of the two religions.
Thoroughly "Jewish" though some of the writings were
in their esteem for the Law, to Christians the Mosaic Law
had not the value it had for the Jew; and, on the other hand,
some—like Enoch and Jubilees—tended to strike at the
uniqueness of Moses.   The Fall of Jerusalem, the tragic
position of the Jews, Jewish and Christian hostility, and the
desire to fix the contents and text of its sacred writings,
are enough to account for the way in which Judaism closed
its ranks, and, basing itself primarily on the Law, maintained
its individuality.

The Rabbis took a middle course between the Sadducaean
and Samaritan reliance upon the Law alone and the
extravagant tradition in 2 Esdras.   The Christians, for
their part, wavered between the Hebrew and the Greek
Bibles.   The "Canon" of the Old Testament might conceivably have been smaller; it might even have been much
larger.   It includes the pessimist Kōhéleth, but not the
finer Ben Sira.   It includes the uninspiring Esther, but

excludes the valuable historical book 1 Maccabees. The
opening book of the Apocrypha is of the utmost importance
for the study of the "canonical" Ezra–Nehemiah, and the
second one (2 Esdras) is as late as the rise of Christianity.
The continuity and the progressive development which can
be traced in the Old Testament as a whole are sadly disturbed
by some parts of it (e.g. Esther), and greatly illumined by
passages now "non-canonical" (Ben Sira). It is possible,
and indeed often helpful, to pass from the creative Hebrew
prophets to the great creative age of the New Testament,
but the development which proved to be so significant for
the history of thought can only be understood *historically*
when all the available evidence is utilised, whether
"canonical" or not.

CHAPTER III

Tradition and Criticism

I. THE VARIATION OF TEXT AND TRADITION

BEFORE the M.T. (Massoretic Text) and the books of the Old Testament were fixed there were numerous textual variants of greater or less importance. Many were slight, but there were others that seriously affected the meaning of a passage, or indeed, were so extensive that they represented varying or conflicting traditions.[1] All these variations are (a) between the Old Testament and other sources (whether versions such as the LXX, or other books such as the New Testament), or (b) within the Old Testament itself; and in the latter case they are found either in different books (e.g. Kings and Chronicles), or within the same book (which thus proves to be "composite"). The more important variations and divergences involve differing or conflicting traditions of certain features of the history and religion of Israel, and these it is the task of "Biblical criticism" to handle. In this chapter we shall notice variations of text and tradition, and then pass to certain aspects of the work of criticism. Moreover, since every reader is apt to approach the Old Testament with certain presuppositions and convictions, it will also be necessary to point out that besides the variation of text and tradition in the Old Testament, there have been and are significant variations of attitude towards the Old Testament itself.

The writers of the New Testament made free use of the Old Testament and sometimes show a knowledge of non-Biblical lore.[2] There are some well-known discrepancies

---

[1] The word "tradition" is used in these pages of material that has been handed down, whether orally or in writing.

[2] Cf., e.g. the references to Michael in Jude 9, the part played by angels at the Law-giving (Acts vii. 38, 53; Gal. iii. 19; Heb. ii. 2) and Noah as a preacher of righteousness (2 Pet. ii. 5; cf. Jub. vii. 20; Jos. *Ant*. i. 3 § 74f.).

between New Testament quotations and the Old Testament
(e.g. the number of men slain at Baal-peor is 23,000 in
1 Cor. x. 8, 24,000 in Num. xxv. 9). But sometimes the
New Testament version is not without Old Testament
support: thus the statement that Abraham had his vision
before he left Ur (Acts vii. 2, contrast Gen. xi. 31–xii. 4),
is supported by Gen. xv. 7; Neh. ix. 7. Similarly, the New
Testament statement that Jacob was buried at Shechem
(Acts vii. 15f.) is more in harmony with Gen. xxxiii. 19
(which tells of his purchase of land there) than with the
tradition that his grave was east of the Jordan (Gen. l. 10f.)
or with the other patriarchs at Hebron (*v.* 13), where
Abraham had bought ground.[1]

The once popular book of Jubilees adds several new
details to the Book of Genesis, e.g. Simeon's wife is of
Zephath (Gen. xlvi. 10 supplemented from Judges i. 17).
Its story of Jacob's war in Central Palestine (Ch. xxxiv.,
fuller in the Testament of Judah), is only a later form,
perhaps influenced by a recollection of the wars of John
Hyrcanus (134–04 B.C.), of the tradition of which there survives only an isolated reference in Gen. xlviii. 22 (the conquest
of Shechem). Its confused references to a war between
Egypt and Canaan (Jub. xlvi., mentioned also in the
pseudepigraphical "Testaments" of Simon and of Benjamin)
find their justification in the now solitary and tantalising
statement in Gen. l. 9f., of the powerful company which
went up with Joseph to bury Jacob. The Book of Enoch
contains a late and elaborate story which is connected with
the account in Gen. vi. 3f. of the descent of "divine beings"
upon earth (En. vi.–xi., cf. Jub. v. 1–11). It can hardly
have been spun out of the "canonical" account of the
Beginnings, but points to traditions a mere fragment of
which has been used by the Biblical writer to explain why
the Deluge was sent. Enoch, a famous figure in late
literature, did not gain renown merely from the verses in
Gen. v. 21–24; and of the redemption of Abraham (Isa.

---

[1] It is noteworthy that there are other novel details in Stephen's
speech (Acts vii. 14, the number of Jacob's family; *v.* 22, the wisdom
of Moses; *v.* 30, his forty years in Midian).

xxix. 22) only later sources preserve a tradition (Jub. xii.1f.).
Much old material has evidently been lost.[1]

Some interesting examples of textual variation are
afforded by the fragmentary "Nash Papyrus," the oldest
known specimen of Hebrew Biblical text; it was found in
Egypt, and is probably of the second century A.D. It
contains the Decalogue (in a form agreeing precisely with
neither Exod. xx. nor Deut. v.) and the Shema (Deut. vi. 4),
but with variants from the M.T. more numerous and
important than any preserved in Hebrew MSS. Thus, the
fourth commandment concludes: "the Lord blessed the
seventh day"; the fifth ends: ". . . that it may be well
with thee and that thy days may be long . . ."; and the
prohibition of adultery precedes that of murder (cf. e.g.
Luke xviii. 20). The Decalogue is followed by this introduction to the Shema: "these are the statutes and the
judgments which Moses commanded the children of Israel
in the wilderness when they went forth from the land of
Egypt." All the variants find their support in the LXX;
and as the latter contains others besides, the fragment is
not a Hebrew translation from the Greek, but evidently
represents a "Pre-Massoretic" stage of the Hebrew text.[2]

The importance of the LXX for the study of the Hebrew
text cannot be over-estimated; but it must be used with
great caution. It paraphrases, inserts explanatory words,
makes changes for theological or dogmatic purposes, and
softens strong anthropomorphic expressions (e.g. Exod.

---

[1] Other examples of variant, if not erroneous, tradition are to be
recognised when Josephus, who has a chronological system of his
own (*War* vi. §§ 269f., 435ff.), says that it was Pharaoh Necho who
carried off Sarah (*War* v. § 379) and that the Temple was originally
founded by the Canaanite Melchizedek (*War* vi. § 438).

[2] The introduction to the Shema may be an addition or inter-
polation. But if it is original, it has probably been omitted in the
M.T. on account of the popular tradition that the famous utterance,
the central tenet of Judaism, dated from the time of Jacob. Moreover, while the Shema ends in the M.T. with the word "one" (*ekhād*),
the papyrus adds the word "he" (*hū*): "One Lord is He." Here
decision is difficult. Tradition relates that the great Rabbi Aḳiba
died as he was lingering over the last word, and it is a nice question
whether it was the vital word "one" (as in the M.T.), or whether
he breathed out his soul with the word *hū*.

xxiv. 10: "they saw the place where the God of Israel stood"). Sometimes it misunderstands the Hebrew, so that where it seems to presuppose another reading, the question of its value has always to be determined. A comparison of 1 Esdras with the corresponding parts of the M.T. is instructive. Thus, in i. 29 the words "the *princes came down* against king Josiah" are a simple misreading of the original: "the *archers shot at*" the king (2 Chron. xxxv. 23). In *v.* 28 Neco has been misread as *nābhī'* (prophet), and the name Jeremiah has been added for completeness. Again, 1 Esdras i. 10–12 seem intelligible, but when we consult 2 Chron. xxxv. 10–13 it appears that the king's "command-ment" (*miṣwah*) was read as *maṣṣah* ("unleavened bread"), that "oxen" (*v.* 12 end) and "morning," which have the same consonants (*bāḳār* and *bōḳer*), have been confused, and that the Greek word for "good savour" rests ultimately upon an easy confusion of the Hebrew word for "pans" with the verb "prosper" and of the Greek εὐωδία and εὐοδία. Other examples could be given of the tendency of translators to misunderstand or mistranslate one or two words, and then to adjust the rendering of the whole passage to their initial error, a procedure which all teachers of foreign languages to-day could illustrate from their experience.

The LXX of 1 Esdras and Proverbs points to the existence of different arrangements or recensions of the original texts. The variations in the order of the prophecies of Jeremiah, as compared with the M.T., are especially noteworthy; neither the LXX nor the M.T. can be said to be intrinsically superior. But the LXX is shorter; and it seems more probable that the M.T. has been expanded than that the LXX has made omissions. In Jer. xxvii. 5–22 the LXX omits all reference to the restoration of the Temple vessels, a conception as contrary to the spirit of Jeremiah as the passage on the priests and sacrifices (xxxiii. 14–26), which the LXX also lacks. In 1 Kings it adds another account of Jeroboam from a lost Hebrew original, with the result that it ascribes to Shemaiah (cf. 1 Kings xii. 22) at Shechem in the days of Rehoboam what the M.T. ascribes to Ahijah at Jerusalem in Solomon's time (xi. 29ff.). Of the way in which David and Saul met there are two distinct accounts in 1 Sam. xvii. f.; and the LXX, by means of considerable omissions, attempts to remove the discrepancies.

So far we have been dealing with variations of text and tradition, discovered by comparing the M.T. with other authorities; we shall now give some simple examples of variation of interpretation for which the Old Testament itself supplies the evidence. Sometimes the meaning attached to certain words by the vowel-points differs from that plainly intended by the original writers. Thus, in the second commandment, the words "thou shalt not . . . serve them" (i.e. the foreign gods), are vocalised in an unnatural manner to suggest the interpretation "thou shalt not *be caused to serve* them," as though the commandment referred, not to apostasy, but to persecution and compulsion. In Exod. xxiii. 15 and elsewhere, the vocalisers wished to replace the too anthropomorphic expression "to *see* the Lord" by "to *appear before* the Lord." In Isa. xliii. 28 and lxiii. 3, 5 they turned statements referring to the past into prophecies of the future: the correct vocalisation involves the slightest of changes, and is tacitly made by the A. V. and R. V. margin in the former, and by the R. V. in the latter passage.

In these cases the vowel-points conceal the plain meaning of the consonants; in others they have been used to disparage heathen gods and cult objects, usually by substituting for the proper vowels those of the words "shame" (*bōsheth*) or "abomination" (*shikkūṣ*). This explains the spelling of the names Mōlech, Tōpheth, Ashtōreth, and also of Siccūth and Chiyyūn (Amos v. 26). Similarly in Jer. vii. 18 the word which should have been vocalised *malkath* (Queen [of Heaven]) is spelt *melēketh* (? "workmanship," cf. A.V. mg.).

In these operations the punctuators were merely extending the practice of the copyists, who had already substituted "shame" for "Baal" in the M.T., both when Baal stood alone (e.g. Hos. ix. 10), and where it formed part of a proper name, e.g. Jerubbaal (Judges vi. 32; 1 Sam. xii. 11) but Jerubbesheth (2 Sam. xi. 21). Saul's son Ishbaal ("man of Baal") is called Ishbosheth (2 Sam. ii. 8), and Jonathan's son, Meribbaal (? Meribaal, also "man of Baal") becomes

Mephibosheth (iv. 4). But in the little-read lists, 1 Chron. viii. 33 ff., the Baal names are preserved; and from 1 Chron. xiv. 7 it appears that David's son Eliada (2 Sam. v. 16) was otherwise—if not rather originally—known as Beeliada ("Baal knows").[1]

Scrupulous regard for naming the God of Israel accounts for such combinations as "God, thy God," Ps. l. 7, quoting Exod. xx. 2, the *Lord* [Jehovah] thy God; cf. also Ps. liii. with Ps. xiv., and Ps. lxx. with xl. 14 ff. In the Synagogues the divine name was replaced in reading by *Adōnāy*, the vowels of which, attached to the consonants J–h–v–h (Y–h–w–h), account for the European form Jĕhōvāh, from the fourteenth century onwards.[2] In the M.T. the oath "by the life of Yahweh and the life of thy soul" is slightly altered to suggest, "as Yahweh liveth and by the life of thy soul." To "bless" God is a euphemism for to "curse" (cf. Job i. 5 mg.), and in 1 Sam. iii. 13 (see mg.) the blasphemy of the priests, the sons of Eli, is obscured by an alteration of the text. In Judges xviii. 30, where Moses is named as the ancestor of the idolatrous priests of Dan, the half-hearted suspension of the letter *n* in the Hebrew text is to suggest that it was not MoSHeH, but MaNaSSeH— the renegade Samaritan priest is probably hinted at (Jos.

---

[1] The Greek-speaking Jews prefixed the feminine article to the name Baal which they read as "shame" ($αἰσχύνη$), and this word actually appears in their text of 1 Kings xviii. 19. A very interesting example of a change of text and of vocalisation is afforded by Nestle's suggestion (made in 1883, and now generally accepted) that "the abomination of desolation" (Matt. xxiv. 15), or rather "abomination that maketh desolate" (Dan. xii. 11) conceals the title "the Baal of Heaven," the Semitic equivalent of the Greek Zeus. With the first half may be compared the "abominable image" or "horrible thing" which the writer of 1 Kings xi. 5; xv. 13 refrains from naming, and the latter half is a recognisable alteration of the Hebrew word for sky or heaven (*shōmēm* for *shāmayim*). Much in the same way the name of the god Nebo is altered in Abed-nego ("servant of Nebo," Dan. i. 7); and in Num. xxxii. 38 there is a parenthetical warning that the names Nebo and Baal-meon are to be changed.

[2] Whatever the original pronunciation or form may have been (? Yahu or Yaho), the interpretation in Exod. iii. 14 f. (see mg.) justifies the form Yahweh which is favoured by most scholars, and used henceforth in these pages.

Ant. xi. 8). Finally, regard for the piety of David inserted the word "enemies" in 2 Sam. xii. 14, where the English version obscures the literal meaning: "thou hast blasphemed [the enemies of] Yahweh." There is another case of this in 1 Sam. xxv. 22 (see mg.).

Specially instructive examples of the variation of texts are afforded by the doublets or parallel passages, genealogical (1 Chron. viii. 29ff. and ix. 35ff.; ix. 1–34 and Neh. xi.), narrative (2 Kings xviii. 13–xx. 19 and Isa. xxxvi.–xxxix.; 2 Kings xxiv. 18–xxv. 30 and Jer. lii., cf. xxxix. 1–10); prophetical (Isa. ii. 2–4 cf. Mic. iv. 1–3; Jer. xlviii. f. cf. Isa. xv. f. and Obadiah), or poetical (2 Sam. xxii. and Ps. xviii).[1] In the account of the Tabernacle the instructions given to Moses (Exod. xxv.–xxxi.) and the subsequent operations (xxxv.–xl.) should be identical; but the M.T. is not of one piece, there are considerable differences between xxx. 11–16 and xxxviii. 24–31, and the order of the LXX is not that of the Hebrew. Above all, a comparison of 1 and 2 Chronicles with the parallel passages in Samuel–Kings brings to light numerous variations ranging from text to subject-matter or tradition. It shows how older traditions could be rewritten or supplemented, and how composite works were compiled. We read, e.g. in 2 Chron. xiv. 5 and xvii. 6 that Asa and Jehoshaphat removed the idolatrous high places, whereas xv. 17 and xx. 33 agree with 1 Kings xv. 14 and xxii. 43 that they did not. Not less instructive is the introductory historical survey in Deut. i. f. which refers to incidents recorded in Numbers, but not always identical with them.

Thus, a preliminary study of the Old Testament reveals many peculiarities which compel attention. The examples given may not perhaps appear to be of any very great importance when considered separately, but continued investigation has led to a keener analysis of its contents, and the persistent attempt to answer the questions they bring is "Biblical Criticism."

---

[1] Also, the lists of cities in Joshua xv., to judge from the numbers (*vv.* 32, 36), cannot be in their original form; nor is it easy to find thirty-seven heroes in 2 Sam. xxiii. (*v.* 39).

II. Biblical Criticism: Literary Analysis

It might almost be said that "Criticism" began with the prophets in that they did not hesitate to treat freely, where necessary, current beliefs and practices. We know what the Exodus meant for Israel; but Amos proclaims that Yahweh also brought the Philistines from Caphtor and the Aramaeans from Kir (ix. 7), and another prophet asserts that Yahweh, so far from being uniquely the God of Israel (e.g. Deut. iv. 32ff.), was also the God of those who knew not his cult (Isa. lxv. 1). Of the earliest history of Israel Jeremiah and Ezekiel have very different ideas; and the former did not hesitate to speak of the Temple and its cultus in a way that shocked and angered many of his contemporaries. Hosea (i. 4f.) condemns the blood shed by Jehu in his "zeal for Yahweh," and at the command of Yahweh (2 Kings ix. 6ff.; x. 16): even prophets who claimed to be Yahweh's mouthpiece were not necessarily genuine (see Deut. xviii. 22; Jer. xiv. 14, xxiii. 31). The story of the sacrifice of Isaac (Gen. xxii.) turns upon Abraham's readiness to perform a horrible rite which, according to the prophets, was not required by Yahweh (Mic. vi. 7f.), had never entered his head (Jer. vii. 31), or was, so to say, a divine penalty (Ezek. xx. 25f.). Moreover, the popular stories of the way in which men put Yahweh to the test (Gen. xv. 8; Judges vi. 36–40; note Isa. vii. 11f.) are entirely opposed to the stern injunction forbidding men to "tempt" their God (i.e. to put Him to the proof), Deut. vi. 16, cf. Ps. xcv. 9, etc. Modern "Criticism" simply follows in the footsteps of the men who did not believe that current traditions and convictions were necessarily unalterable.

The Old Testament was freely used by Jews and Christians regardless of the letter or context of a passage. On the one hand, Jesus himself, like other Jews, accepts the Biblical traditions (Noah, Sodom and Gomorrah, Lot's wife, etc.).[1] In his use of Ps. cx. (Mark xii. 35ff.) and lxxxii. 6 (John x.

[1] The reference to Jonah in Matt. xii. 40 is now taken to be a misleading gloss.

34 ff.) he characteristically meets his opponents on their own
ground, and brings home to them the implications of their
beliefs (cf. Nathan's condemnation of David, 2 Sam. xii. 7).
On the other hand, Jesus regards himself as fulfilling the
Scriptures, and as advancing beyond, and even superseding
them (Mark ii. 27, the Sabbath).   One of the old laws was
for the "hardness" of men's hearts (Mark x. 5), and "the
Law and the Prophets," which held good until John the
Baptist, now gives place to a new order (Luke xvi. 16).
It is unnecessary to pursue this further; scholars of different
shades of thought are agreed that the use of the Old Testament by Jesus and the writers of the New Testament
neither attests its literal infallibility nor excludes or even
discourages serious Biblical criticism.[1]

In striking contrast to the not uncommon insistence
nowadays upon the literal interpretation of the Old Testament are the allegorical methods employed alike by Jews,
notably Philo (early first century A.D.), and Christians,
e.g. another great Alexandrian, Origen (first half of third
century).   The latter ridicules the notion that the opening
chapters of Genesis are to be taken literally.   Writers who
were anti-Jewish (e.g. the "Epistle of Barnabas") and
those who, like Marcion, taught the worthlessness of the Old
Testament, naturally treated it with scant respect.   But
most of the early Christian writers took a sort of "evolutionary" view of it.   Thus, the writer of the Clementine
Homilies (iii. 47) believes that the laws of Moses are now in
a form far removed from the original; and Chrysostom
boldly recognises the slightness of the difference between
the rites described in the Old Testament and those practised
by the heathen, and argues that God intended to lead the
people gradually from their customs to "the high philosophy."   The merit of the Old Testament precepts, he says,
"lies in nothing so much as that we can now find fault
with them; their highest praise is that we now see them to
be defective."

[1] Cf. Paley, *Evidences*, Part III, Ch. 3 (cited by A. F. Kirkpatrick
The Divine Library of the Old Testament, p. 105 f.); Gore, *Doctrine of
the Infallible Book*, and *New Commentary*, p. 3 f.

The Neo-Platonist Porphyry (third century A.D.) held that the Book of Daniel must have been written in the time of Antiochus Epiphanes. Theodore of Mopsuestia (c. 400) went further; he rejected Chronicles–Ezra–Nehemiah, he denied the value of many of the titles of the Psalms, recognising—as did Calvin later—that several of them must be post-exilic, and he dated Ps. li. in the Babylonian exile. Especially interesting is the identification, by Jerome and others, of the law-book discovered in Josiah's reign with Deuteronomy—a view subsequently put forward afresh, and developed, when Biblical criticism was reborn in Western Europe (see below).

The Jews themselves were not unaware of real inconsistencies and contradictions in the Old Testament, e.g. Ezek. xlvi. 6 and Num. xxix. 2; the burial place of Aaron (Num. xx. 27f. and Deut. x. 6), and of such difficulties as the extent of the Flood.   More than one medieval writer saw that the list of the kings of Edom who reigned before Israel had a king (Gen. xxxvi. 31) must be later than the foundation of the monarchy, and that such details as the mention of Hebron (Gen. xiii. 18, see ₁Joshua xiv. 15), Dan (xiv. 14, see Judges xviii. 29), etc., must be post-Mosaic. Luther, while adhering to the belief in a verbally inspired Bible, denied the Mosaic authorship of the Pentateuch. He set the historical value of Kings far above that of Chronicles, and perceived that the prophecies of Jeremiah were not arranged in chronological order; he even held that there were later additions in this and other prophetical books.

Subsequently, it is true, Protestantism, with its doctrine of verbal infallibility, hindered the progress of criticism (cf. p. 2), but the men of the New Age had begun to take a historical view of the Bible and to read it in the light of their new knowledge of ancient history and religion.   Acute observations were made by independent minds, who helped to break down antagonism to the new study of the Bible, notably Hobbes in his *Leviathan* (Ch. 33; 1651) and Spinoza, *Tractatus Theologico-politicus* (Ch. 8f.; 1670–71).   The latter, for example, comments upon the discrepancies between the

chronological notices in Genesis and the narratives in which
they occur: thus, Isaac apparently lay on his death-bed
for eighty years, and Ishmael was seventeen years old when
he was carried by Hagar. More attention began to be paid
to duplicate narratives (e.g. Gen. xii., xx. and xxvi.) and
the evident use of different sources; Father Simon even
framed a theory of the composite origin of the Pentateuch
(1678). But it was not until 1753 that the decisive step
was taken, when the French Catholic physician Astruc
distinguished two main sources in Genesis, characterised by
the divine names Yahweh and Elohim. He had a forerunner in the German, H. B. Witter (1711)—only recently
rescued from oblivion—but it was Astruc who inaugurated
the new form of literary criticism.

Some of the more outstanding names and dates may be
mentioned. Astruc was followed by Eichhorn (1780), the
first to use the term "Higher Criticism." Two "Elohim"
sources were discerned by Ilgen (1798), and subsequently
demonstrated by Hupfeld (1853); thenceforth three main
sources of Genesis were generally recognised: the Jahvist or
Yahvist (J), the "earlier Elohist" (E), and the "later
Elohist," afterwards styled the Priestly source (P). Astruc's
clue had served its purpose and was now superseded. It
was found that there were other and more significant
variations than the two divine names; and as a matter of
fact it has proved much easier to separate the two "Elohim"
sources, E and P, than E and J. It is necessary to bear
in mind, therefore, that literary analysis does not depend,
as is sometimes wrongly supposed, merely upon the distribution of the names Yahweh and Elohim.

The "literary" analysis of the Pentateuch was carried on
side by side with the study of the religious history of Israel,
and De Wette marked another stage (1806) by showing that
Deuteronomy must belong to the age of Josiah (seventh
century B.C.), and that the profound differences between
Chronicles and the earlier and parallel narratives in Samuel–
Kings must be due to vital developments in the religion of
Israel. Scholars found it increasingly difficult to understand
the history and religion of Israel if the Pentateuch—

especially the middle books (Leviticus–Numbers)—stood at the head of it. Nor was Ezekiel's scheme of a reorganised priesthood under Zadok explicable (xliv. 6–15), seeing that it appeared to be already presupposed by the Mosaic Levitical institutions (p. 196). The Priestly source (P), it was shown, could be divided into narratives and laws, the latter of which, to judge from the religious conditions in Judah in Josiah's time, were unknown when Deuteronomy was "discovered" (so George and Vatke in 1835). The narratives of P, on the other hand, seemed to be the indispensable foundation or framework of the Pentateuch, and therefore earlier than the more popular narratives of JE. However, it was precisely P's narratives which were next demonstrated, especially by Bishop Colenso (1862), to be thoroughly untrustworthy; and as the characteristics of P became more clearly recognised (thanks to Nöldeke, 1869), it was found impossible to sever the two portions of P, as Graf had done in his admirable essays (1865, another important landmark).

Thus was introduced the sequence: the narratives of JE, D (Deuteronomy and the "Deuteronomic" editing in Joshua–Kings), and, after the time of Ezekiel (closely connected with the "Law of Holiness" in Lev. xvii.–xxvi. [H]), the post-exilic source (P).[1] It now became possible to attempt to sketch the religious history of Israel in its development from early pre-exilic times to the post-exilic age. This task was undertaken, notably by Kuenen (1869–70); and B. Duhm traced out afresh the theology of the prophets in a book that became a classic (1875). But it was Wellhausen's *Prolegomena to the History of Israel* (1878) that put the case for the new hypothesis so incisively and so fully that Old Testament scholars were forced to range themselves on the one side or the other, and that year may be said to witness the introduction of modern Old Testament criticism.

The literary hypothesis (i.e. of the sources JEDHP),

---

[1] That the traditional Law, Psalms and Prophets should be Prophets, Law and Psalms had been already taught by Reuss, as early as 1833, though his work was not published until 1879.

which is justly associated with the name of Wellhausen, rests upon the presence in the Pentateuch of numerous composite, duplicate or contradictory passages, differing in vocabulary, detail and spirit (e.g. the stories of Creation and Flood, Korah's revolt), and irreconcilable notices of the Festivals, the Priests and Levites, and the place of worship. It takes account of (*a*) the discrepancies between the pre-exilic history as told in Samuel–Kings and the narratives in Chronicles, (*b*) the close relation between the post-exilic history (Ezra–Nehemiah) and the middle books of the Pentateuch, and (*c*) above all, the contrasts between the prophetical books and the Law.[1] Only on the assumption that the great Prophets precede the Pentateuch as a whole in its present form is the relation between them and the Mosaic legislation intelligible. It is the supreme *religious* significance of the great reforming prophets that makes them as much a landmark in the history of religion in Israel as the Reformation itself has been in the West.

It is impossible here to comment upon the work done from various standpoints by men who proceeded upon the lines laid down by Wellhausen, Kuenen, Robertson Smith, and other outstanding scholars, and by those who were less attracted by the new literary problems, or even denied that they existed. Very noteworthy admissions and concessions have been made by "conservative" and even by strongly "anti-critical" writers; and since the current "literary hypothesis" involves the whole of the Old Testament, any new one that is framed to replace it must not be less comprehensive.

The hypothesis is essentially a *literary* one, and is based upon obvious cases of "compositeness" and of conflicting tradition. Compositeness is a very common feature in early writings. The once popular Gospel Harmony, known as the Diatessaron of Tatian, not only shows how passages from the Gospels could be welded together to form a single whole—though it is easily seen that the Fourth Gospel is distinct from the others—but it warns us that, even when

---

[1] The relative lateness of Isa. xl.–lxvi. was recognised by Döderlein in 1775 and Eichhorn in 1782.

we have before us a document that is demonstrably composite, there are limits to our powers of resolving it into its component parts. Moreover, it must be recognised that passages, late in their present form—e.g. the Book of Jubilees—may contain ancient tradition (see p. 37). In 1792 the Roman Catholic priest Alexander Geddes held that the Pentateuch was written in Palestine after the reign of David, but from material contemporary with or earlier than Moses. Similarly it is sometimes argued that although the Pentateuch did not reach its present form until Ezra's age, its contents are essentially Mosaic. It is a characteristic difference between Old Testament "critics" and their opponents that while the former will conclude that certain sources, documents or passages must be late in their present form, though they contain undoubtedly older material, the latter will maintain a conservative view, but admit that there have been additions and revision.

Literary theories of the dates of sources do not necessarily affect the value of their contents; hence they allow of views of Israelite history and religion relatively "conservative" or "advanced," as the case may be. Modern critics differ widely as to the extent to which they consider the accounts of some early period (e.g. the Patriarchs and the Exodus) to be trustworthy. It is a cardinal principle of criticism that every document represents in some way the circumstances and beliefs of its day; but it is as erroneous to suppose that a document must be of the same age as that to which its contents refer, as to imagine that what occurs in a late document applies only to a late age. The blood-revenge of the "ante-diluvian" Lamech (Gen. iv. 24) and Abraham's dealings with Sarah and Hagar (Gen. xvi.) are of course not exclusively of the particular periods to which they are ascribed; and many of the ideas and practices which occur only in P are by no means exclusively post-exilic and new.

In recent years Old Testament research has been entering upon a new phase. Much more is known now than was ever known before of the stage upon which the drama of Israel was played. The immense importance of the archaeological evidence that has come to light is recognised both by those writers who are chiefly concerned to find proof of the literal truth of Old Testament statements, and by those who are attempting to make a reconstruction of Israel's history that shall give due weight to all evidence from whatever source it comes. "Internal evidence" (i.e. that which is supplied by the Old Testament) and "external evidence" (i.e. that which is supplied by archaeology, the monuments, etc.) supplement each other. The second of these will be treated in due course; but before we turn to it, something remains to be said about the first.

At this point it may be useful to suggest how the reader can form a preliminary working notion of the "literary critical" position. The books Deuteronomy–Kings are closely interconnected and form a fairly continuous story. They contain much old material; but in their present form they are later than our Deuteronomy, and are, at least in part, post-exilic. This "Deuteronomic" version of Israel's history is distinctly older than the version set forth in Chronicles, and is part of the larger series Genesis–Kings, which is now in a later post-exilic form. Our ordinary ideas of Israelite history and religion are based, first, upon Genesis–Kings, which ceases abruptly in the middle of the Exile (viz. the release of Jehoiachin, 562 B.C.), and then, upon Ezra–Nehemiah, i.e. part of the very late post-exilic series Chronicles–Nehemiah, which, where it can be tested, is distinctly less trustworthy than the older series (Samuel–Kings). On the "critical" view, the Pentateuch in its present form stands at the head, not of Israelite national history, i.e. before the Monarchy and the first Temple, but of the late post-exilic Judaism not earlier than Ezra. At the same time, the study of the religious ideas of the prophets has immeasurably increased our knowledge of the periods from the Exile onwards. Criticism has enriched our knowledge of the centuries leading up to the rise of Christianity at the expense of the earlier patriarchal, Mosaic and pre-monarchical periods, and has associated the Old Testament more closely with the apocalyptical and pseudepigraphical literature which bridges the gulf that formerly seemed to sever the Testaments (pp. 30, 34 f.). The difficulty

of determining the history and religion of the earlier periods
and the extreme importance of the later ones are the two
most significant results of modern criticism.

III.   BIBLICAL CRITICISM: HISTORICAL ANALYSIS

Such then, in barest outline, has been the growth of the
"literary critical" view of the Old Testament. Leaving
entirely on one side the many complex problems connected
with it, we shall now proceed to approach Old Testament
history from another angle. It is clear, at the outset, that
this history forms a closely interconnected whole. From
the post-exilic age one can go back to the pre-exilic (e.g.
the return of the exiles, Ezra ii. 1), from the monarchy
to the period when "there was no king in Israel" (Judges
xvii. 6), from the "judges" of Israel to the entry of Israel
under Joshua into the land of their fathers, from the sojourn
of the Israelite tribes in Egypt to the descent of Jacob and
his family (Exod. vi. 14 ff. and Gen. xlvi. 8 ff.), and finally
from Jacob back to the call of Abraham. A characteristic
religious note runs throughout, from the earliest chapters
of Genesis onwards; and it is due to the writers who, like
all writers of history, had definite aims.

Some threads of history may first be noticed. (*a*) In one
distinctive series of passages (P), the god of the patriarchs
is El-Shaddai (Gen. xvii., cf. xxviii. 3; xxxv. 9–15; xlviii. 3–6)
until Elohim reveals to Moses his name Yahweh (Exod. vi.
2–8). (*b*) The account of the "judges" of Israel in Judges
ii. 6–xvi. is characterised by a "theory of cycles," alternate
periods of apostasy and penitence: oppression, deliverance
by a "judge" sent by Yahweh, his success, the peace enjoyed
by the land, his death and the subsequent relapse of the
people. To this, the "Deuteronomic Book of Judges,"
there is an introductory statement—the writer's "philosophy
of history" (ii. 11–19)—and the framework of the book is
easily recognisable by recurring formulae (e.g. iii. 12, 30;
iv. 1; v. 31). Similarly (*c*), the history of the kings of
Israel and Judah is embedded in a framework, with recurring
formulae. The monarchies are synchronised, the kings of

the schismatic North are condemned, and once the Temple
has been built (1 Kings iii. 2f.), worship at the local "high
places" is denounced (e.g. 1 Kings xiv. 23f.; 2 Kings xiv. 4).
After the sweeping reforms of Josiah (2 Kings xxiii.) no
occasion for blame is supposed to arise. These three
examples show that we have, not so much "objective"
history, as "subjective" history, that is, events selected
and treated in accordance with a definite aim and purpose
sustained throughout. There are other examples of connected narrative: the story of Joseph, and how God turned
the evil of his brethren into good (Gen. xlv. 7f.; l. 20); the
story of Bathsheba and the retribution that befel David's
family life (see 2 Sam. xii. 10–12); and the story of Ahab,
Jezebel and Naboth, and how the dynasty of Omri was
replaced by that of Jehu (1 Kings xxi. 17–29; 2 Kings ix. 36f.;
x. 30).

Next we may notice how history could be constructed.
For example, Samson *begins* (Judges xiii. 5) what is continued
by Samuel and Saul, and completed by David, namely, the
deliverance of Israel from the Philistines. Now, here it is
to be observed that although Samson appears among the
Israelite "judges," he is really a local hero, like Ehud
(Judges iii.). Israelite history is being illustrated by
traditions that are of local origin. Elsewhere, a writer
illustrates the hostility of the adversaries of post-exilic
Jerusalem between the reigns of Cyrus and Darius by a
record of the reign of Artaxerxes, i.e. *after* the time of
Darius (Ezra iv. 6–23). Again, the account of the journey
of the Israelites from the Red Sea to Sinai (Horeb) comprises
some narratives that, properly speaking, belong to a later
stage (note Horeb in Exod. xvii. 6) or presuppose the Law-
giving (Ch. xviii.). To take another striking example, the
closing scene of Elisha's life represents the dying prophet
as one who has been "the chariots and horsemen" of Israel
(2 Kings xiii. 14ff.). But since Elisha died in the reign of
Joash, some forty-five years after the accession of Jehu, it
is highly probable that some at least of the stories in
2 Kings iii.–viii. which tell of his influence *before* the rise
of Jehu, really belong to the stirring and calamitous days

of Jehu's dynasty, when Israel was so nearly wiped out by
the Aramaeans.   Finally, the national song of triumph,
"the Song of Hannah" (1 Sam. ii. 1–10), is as incongruous
in its present context as the psalm of thanksgiving ascribed
to Jonah (Ch. ii.); each, presumably, owes its presence to
apparently suitable allusions (v. 5 in each).[1]   In all such
cases we can distinguish between a writer's purpose or
theme and the way in which he carries it out by means of
incidents or materials which, strictly speaking, belong to
another context or date.   Thus, the purpose and the way
in which it is effected are two distinct things; even as,
among ourselves, a man's views or theories may be distinct
from—and not be so valuable, perhaps, as—the evidence
which he employs for his purpose.

When we examine the historical writings of the Old
Testament more closely we find three far-reaching interests
which have gone to shape them.   These are of such importance that they must be briefly outlined.   The first concerns
the priests.   The story in Judges xvii. f. casts a slur upon
the priesthood of Dan and its idolatrous cult.   Yet the
priests were descended from Moses (xviii. 30); and, according
to the original text of 2 Sam. xx. 18 (preserved in the LXX),
both Abel, an ancient and venerated city ("a mother in
Israel"), and the city of Dan near-by were famous for the
retention of old Israelite custom.   Similarly, a writer
justly condemns the cult of Shiloh, whose priesthood (under
Eli) traced itself back to the Levites chosen by Yahweh in
Egypt (1 Sam. ii. 22ff., 27ff.).   Now, it is said that the
priesthood of Dan lasted until "the captivity (or, rather
the exile) of the land," as long as the sanctuary existed at
Shiloh (Judges xviii. 30f.).   The natural presumption would
be, therefore, that Dan fell when North Israel was overrun
by Tiglath-pileser III in 734, or after the fall of Samaria
in 722 (see 2 Kings xv. 29; xvii. 6ff.; 1 Chron. v. 26).   But
when did Shiloh fall?   Although it had a prophet in
Jeroboam's day (1 Kings xiv. 4), it *seems* to disappear after
the Philistine invasion, the capture of the Ark and the

---

[1] Conversely, it is hardly necessary to point out how often the
titles and headings to the Psalms are entirely unsuitable.

death of Eli (1 Sam. iv., see *v.* 21 f.). Ps. lxxviii. 60 ff.
speak of the disasters when, as a punishment for the
idolatrous cults at the "high places," Shiloh and the rest
of the land were given into captivity, until Yahweh awoke,
overthrew the enemy, and, refusing the "tent of Joseph,"
chose Judah and Mount Zion. The verses describe an
overwhelming catastrophe. But if they really refer to the
days of Samuel, Saul and David, on the other hand, the
prophet Jeremiah (vii. 12; xxvi. 6) appears to allude to the
fall of Shiloh as a comparatively recent catastrophe (e.g. 734
or 722), and certainly not one that had occurred about
three centuries earlier. Hence one of the problems of Old
Testament history is, when did Shiloh and its priesthood
really fall? And the problem is not so unimportant as
might be thought.

Next, in place of the priesthood of Eli at Shiloh a faithful
priest is to arise, and a new priesthood shall serve a new
dynasty (1 Sam. ii. 35). The writer of this passage presumably has in view the supersession of Abiathar by Zadok
(cf. 1 Kings ii. 27–35);[1] although the degradation and
poverty of the family of Eli, announced in 1 Sam. ii. 36,
might seem to be explained by the abolition of the idolatrous
local sanctuaries, or "high places," by Josiah (cf. 2 Kings
xxiii. 8 f., and the Law in Deut. xviii. 6–8). On the other
hand, the promotion of Zadok reminds us of Ezekiel's plan
for rewarding the Zadokites for their faithfulness when the
other priests had led Israel astray after idols (xliv. 9 ff.);
although elsewhere (1 Chron. xxiv. 5) the priestly families
are divided between Eleazar (Zadok) and Ithamar (Abiathar).
These passages point to periods of hostility and change,
rivalry and compromise, though it is extremely difficult to
trace the vicissitudes (cf. p. 196).

Again, we read of the ritual error of the two elder sons of
Aaron (Lev. x. 1–7) and of the revolts against priestly and
Levitical privileges in the strange and composite story of
Korah (Num. xvi.). Here as elsewhere we have to recognise

---

[1] The name Zadok is closely associated with the Jerusalem priesthood; cf. also the names of Melchizedek (Gen. xiv. 18), Jehozadak
(Hag. i. 1), and the Sadducees.

how impossible it would be to sketch the course of Israelite history and religion if we supposed that every passage really illustrated the period to which it purported to refer. To Moses was ascribed the serpent which Hezekiah regarded as idolatrous (Num. xxi. 8f.; 2 Kings xviii. 4), and for the Golden Calf, another idolatrous object, Aaron was responsible, in spite of the curious wording in Exod. xxxii. 24 and 35 (see p. 154, n.). Quite another tradition knows that both Moses and Aaron were guilty of some grave fault, which, however, we can scarcely identify (Num. xx. 12). A keen interest in the fortunes of the priesthood is manifested in the very writing and compilation of the history; and post-exilic events—often illustrated in Josephus—show how bitter the priestly rivalries might be, and how easily these might affect what the different rival divisions might say—or write—concerning one another. The priestly factor in the growth of the Old Testament narrative is one of the most difficult of problems in the higher reaches of criticism.

The second important interest in the Old Testament history is the relation between Judah and Israel. There is an evident desire to exalt the first king of Judah over the first king of Israel: Saul is doomed before he has achieved the task for which Yahweh called him (cf. 1 Sam. xiii. 13f.; xv. 26; xxviii. 17; 2 Sam. vii. 15). There are two accounts of his election. In one he is raised up, the last of the "judges" as it were, to deliver Israel from the Philistines (ix. 16f.); in the other, Samuel is the last judge, he has defeated the Philistines and there is peace; the demand of Israel for a king is an affront to Yahweh (1 Sam. viii. 7; x. 19; xii. 17; cf. the answer of the "judge" Gideon, Judges viii. 23). Elsewhere Saul comes before us as the hero, the pride of the people, successful in his wars (1 Sam. xiv. 47 f.), and the dread of the Philistines (2 Sam. i. 19ff.). In the story as a whole our sympathy is claimed for David and for Jonathan; and at Saul's death the desperate situation of the country resembles that at his rise (1 Sam. xxxi. 7, cf. xiii. 7; 2 Sam. ii. 8f.). It is the *Judaean* David who overthrows the Philistines and captures Jerusalem (2 Sam. v.); although, according to another account, the *Ephraimite* hero Joshua had gained it for Israel (Joshua x.), and by the writer of 1 Sam. xv. 4; xvii. 54; xxvii. 10ff., Judah and Jerusalem were evidently supposed to be part of Saul's realm. Thus, allowance has to be made for the obvious anti-Ephraimite or anti-Israelite bias of the present narratives.

At the separation of the Northern and Southern kingdoms the North is represented as having thrown away its chances under Jeroboam (1 Kings xi. 37ff.; xiv. 7ff.); and after the fall of Samaria the South came to regard itself as the true representative of Israel. Yahweh was not with the North (2 Chron. xxv. 7; cf. xiii. 8ff.). On the one hand, it was said that (North) Israel had been carried away *en masse*—and many have been the speculations as to the fate of the Ten Tribes. On the other hand, there was still an "Israel" in the North. Even the later Samaritans, a Jewish sect, would claim or repudiate kinship with the Jews according to circumstances, and they desired to join in the rebuilding of the second Temple (Ezra iv. 2f.). The writer who sums up the fate of the Northern kingdom admits that they were not wholly heathen: their cult was a mixed one, they feared Yahweh, but served their own gods and retained the high places (2 Kings xvii. 32ff.). The inhabitants are reckoned as part of the original stock with whom Yahweh had once made a covenant, and in the New Testament the woman of Samaria speaks of "our father Jacob" (John iv. 12, cf. *v.* 20). There is, in fact, an attempt on the part of some of the Biblical writers to intensify the gulf between North and South, between the Samaritans and the Jews. Of the tribes of Israel, all that remained after the captivity of the Ten, at the fall of Samaria, were the two "sons," Judah and Benjamin. Yet, during the divided monarchy "Israel" and "Judah" were rivals, and in periods of friendship they would have been reckoned, not as "father" and "son," but as "brothers" (cf. the "brotherly" covenant with Tyre, Amos i. 9). Was Judah a "brother" or a "son" of Israel? One of the perplexing questions in Old Testament history is, what in any particular case, is the connotation of Israel? Does it mean all the tribes, "sons" of Israel, or the Northern ones, or only the Southern ones? See p. 71.

The third interest is to maintain the independence of
Israel: it it an anti-Canaanite feeling. We note, first,
that the lists in Chronicles, Ezra and Nehemiah represent
the priests and Levites of the pre-exilic and of the post-
exilic periods as an unbroken succession. This continuity
is emphasised by the remarkable statement that the families,
secular and other, who had gone into exile, returned each
to its own city (Ezra ii. 1). The writer's intention is to
ignore those who had remained behind in Palestine. These
would obviously have had another retrospect, another
"history" than those who had been in exile and returned.
Among the natives of Palestine were naturally some who
still worshipped Yahweh (Jer. xli. 5; Ezra iv. 3; Neh. ii. 20);
and it is impossible to understand the post-exilic conditions
unless we remember that the presence both of natives—
"Israelites"—and of families from exile meant the presence
of men differing in their convictions of what Yahweh had
done for them. The different sections would have, primarily
at least, different religious outlooks on the past, different
retrospects or "histories." As it is, however, what may be
called the "canonical" history has been given us by the
man who returned to Judah and Jerusalem and in due
course severed themselves from their Samaritan and other
neighbours of Palestine.[1] Due allowance has to be made
for this one-sidedness.

This difference of "history" may be supplemented by the
account of Origins in Gen. i.–xi., certain portions of which
exclude the tradition of a Deluge. Whereas Man is made
in the image of God (Gen. i. 26f.), the impious Nĕphīlīm
are the progeny of rebellious supernatural beings and human
wives (Gen. vi. 1–4). They were not destroyed by the
Deluge, for they are the giants encountered by the spies
(Num. xiii. 33, called Anākīm in Deut. i. 28). They are,
therefore, the "sons of Anak" who inhabited Palestine
(Joshua xi. 21ff.), the giants found in Hebron (Joshua
xiv. 15), whom David's heroes overcame in the wars for
the capture of Jerusalem (2 Sam. xxi. 18, 20, 22). They

---

[1] Priestly and other rivalries, inevitable in the circumstances,
can be discerned.

are also the depraved natives (cf. Gen. xv. 16), the tall, powerful, giant-like Amorites (Amos ii. 9). Whatever the name by which they were known, Biblical tradition asserts that these were the iniquitous native peoples driven out from before the Israelites (Lev. xviii. 24, etc.), heathens, but whose abominations were taken over by the Israelite invaders (1 Kings xiv. 24; cf. Judges iii. 5f.). Thus, the mythical origin of the Nephilim belongs to a fairly coherent series of traditions, but evidently very different from those of the origins of Israel and the ancestral patriarchs.

In its present position the fragment, Gen. vi. 1–4, serves to explain why the Flood was sent; but it obviously belongs to traditions which excluded the Flood.[1] Similarly what is said of Cain and the origin of human institutions (Gen. iv. 17ff.) is incompatible with the story of the Deluge. In other words, there were traditions of Origins in which the story of the universal Deluge found no place. Thus, *historical* criticism has to take account of different "histories," different outlooks or retrospects, the existence of which is perfectly intelligible when one considers the evidence for the mixed peoples of Palestine, the many stirring political and national changes, and the growth of the Old Testament into its present form.

A third and still more striking example of difference of "history" is afforded by the account of the Exodus, the entrance of the Israelites into Palestine, and their inter-marriage with the native inhabitants Judges iii. 6; Ps. cvi. 35ff.; Ezra ix. 12f.). The latter and the Israelites would naturally have entirely different traditions of their past. As the narratives now stand, the Israelite account of the descent of the *family* into Egypt and the exodus of the *nation* unites the Book of Genesis with the national history (Gen. xlvi.; Exod. i. 1–4, etc.). This growth of the family into a collection of tribes is of pivotal importance. For the sojourn in Egypt the chronology allows four hundred years (Gen. xv. 13), or four hundred and thirty (Exod. xii. 41; the Samaritan recension and LXX give half that figure),

---

[1] The story of the wickedness of Sodom and the extirpation of men (Gen. xix. 31) is also that of a more or less universal catastrophe.

and the genealogical lists (cf. Exod. vi.) assign only four generations from the sons of Jacob (Levi, Reuben and Joseph) to Moses, or five to Joshua. In contrast to these schemes, the narrative relates that Joseph lived to see the birth of the sons of the man to whom Moses gave Gilead (Gen. l. 23; Num. xxxii. 40). If so, Joseph and Moses overlapped, and when the former died and there arose the new king who "knew not Joseph," it is feared lest the Israelites—who need only two mid-wives—may become numerous and join the enemies of Egypt (Exod. i. 8 ff.). On the other hand, the tradition of an Israelite host 600,000 strong (Exod. xii. 37; Num. xi. 21, cf. details in Num. i.–iv., xxvi.) implies a nation of some two millions souls, and as Doughty once observed, a convoy of about 200 leagues in length. Whatever may be the best explanation of these details, it is now freely admitted, on various grounds, that not all Israel originally came out of Egypt. Hence the probability becomes stronger that there was a considerable native element among the Israelites in Palestine, and therefore, that there was much native tradition in which there would be no account of the Exodus and Conquest. Thus the question whether all Israel came out of Egypt, or only some portion, has far-reaching implications.

In fact, when one examines the traditions in Gen. xii.–l., it is found that most of them imply an entrance, a settlement, and a continuous occupation once and for all. That is to say, the Old Testament blends two quite distinct views of the origin of Israel: (a) the one in Genesis knows of the patriarchs settling in Canaan, of their Aramaean connections, and of a definitive conquest; the other (b) traces the national history back to Moses and the Exodus, when Israelites entered and conquered the land of their forefathers for the first time. Further evidence of the existence of two discrepant bodies of tradition can be found in the desire of the writers to associate laws and festivals, which naturally belonged to Palestine (and as such were of Palestinian or Canaanite origin), with the Exodus and the Wilderness life prior to the Conquest. This anti-Canaanite or anti-Palestinian spirit of certain parts of the Old Testament has left its mark upon the whole conception of Israelite history.

It will be seen, even from these bare outlines, that deeper examination of the Biblical history raises many very serious problems which students are obliged to consider when they attempt to frame their views of the history and religion of Israel. These problems constitute the difference between the ordinary Biblical literary criticism of the present day and "advanced" criticism, and it is only right to say that there is no agreement as to their solution. Scholars have naturally endeavoured to adhere as closely as possible to the main threads of the Old Testament narratives which knit together the Biblical history as a whole, even as P's narratives once seemed to be fundamental for the religious history of Israel (p. 47). But these narratives have been shaped by certain far-reaching *motifs*: Israel's indebtedness to her extra-Palestinian origin (the Exodus from Egypt) rather than to the "heathen" inhabitants; the pre-eminence of Judah and the Davidic dynasty over the "Israel" of the North; and the superiority of Jerusalem and its priesthood over other priests. Criticism has its limitations, however, and this is not the place to discuss how to "reconstruct" Biblical history. Fortunately, as will be seen in subsequent chapters, it is possible to make a preliminary study of the main features of Old Testament religion independently, although sooner or later it will be necessary for scholars once more to co-ordinate the historical problems with those of the development of the religion.

So far, then, we have worked back from the English Old Testament and have gone behind the Hebrew text, the "canonical" books, and the "canonical" history. It is easy to observe the development of tradition from Samuel–Kings to Chronicles or from Genesis to the Book of Jubilees, but it does not follow that even the earliest traditions that can be recovered in the Old Testament are in their original form. A fresh step has to be taken.

The Old Testament is the literature of a land from the history and religion of which it cannot be severed. The book itself takes a world-view as it passes from the Creation of Mankind to the choice of Abraham and of Israel.   Some of its most characteristic passages betray the consciousness of Israel's place in Yahweh's Universe.   Israel's sense of her own significance for man's history and religion requires that we place the Bible in a more universal framework, utilising not only the "external" evidence of modern research in the "Bible lands," but also the results of the comparative study of religions, in order that we may understand the place of Old Testament religion among the world's faiths.

CHAPTER IV

Land and People

I. Physical and Political Geography

Passing from the "internal evidence" of the Old Testament to the "external evidence" (p. 50), we turn next to the land of the Bible and its people, bearing in mind that we have to look upon Palestine as an integral part of a larger area, of whose history and culture extending over very many centuries we now possess a not inconsiderable knowledge.

At the eastern end of the Mediterranean, and lying between Asia Minor and Egypt, is a strip of coast-land, some four hundred miles long, whose inhabitants have played a part in history out of all proportion to its size. The land has been a bridge in war and in trade. It falls into two parts: the northern, Syria (probably a shortened form of "Assyria"), which in many respects would seem to be by far the more influential of the two, through its connections with Cyprus, Asia Minor and Armenia, and the southern, Palestine (derived ultimately from "Philistine") which, though the "least of all lands," overshadows its neighbours in importance. Palestine is reckoned at one hundred and forty to one hundred and fifty miles in length, and varies in width from twenty-three miles in the north to eighty in the south. It is about one-sixth the size of England, and classical writers ridiculed its insignificance.

The whole area in which Syria and Palestine are included is part of South-west Asia, it is the great "Arabian continent," commonly called "Semitic," after the descendants of Shem in Gen. x. But, while the "Semitic languages" (Accadian, Arabic, Hebrew, etc.) form a distinctive group, this sub-continent is, as regards people and culture, singularly varied. Asian, European and African peoples meet in it. On all sides it is exposed to the most varied influences, as is illustrated by the many invasions, by its archaeology, and by various elements in it of belief and custom which appear to be of foreign origin. But although there are found therein different physical types and evidence of inter-marriage with outside peoples, the Arab or desert stock predominates. Arabia, "fertile mother but poor nurse of men" (Sir George Adam Smith), must continuously send forth its half-starving children into the rich districts and towns, and this has given the history of the Brown Continent —as it is also called—a certain continuity. Arab tribes roam along the ancient routes in the desert, and from time to time there have been migrations of greater significance, like the entrance of Israel into Palestine.

The small land with which we are concerned lies on either side of the Jordan, which is part of that remarkable rift connecting the Sea of Galilee with the Dead Sea, the Gulf of Akabah, and ultimately with the East African lakes. The Transjordanian terrain, with its many ancient sites, was traversed from of old by an important trade-route (also followed in time of war, Gen. xiv.). This healthy and rich district unites the beautiful oasis of Damascus in the north with—in the south—Mount Esau (or Seir), or the Field (or mountain region) of Edom, an important area which links Egypt and Arabia. To the east it shades off into the desert, and it has always been exposed to the incursions of the "children of the East," who came, now as peaceful settlers, now as marauders, and who were ever a threat, save when the Romans could use them to ward off their still wilder cousins.

The Jordan itself, well called "the descender," flows between two ranges of mountains: as is well known, Lake Galilee is six hundred and eighty feet below sea-level, and the Dead Sea one thousand, two hundred and ninety feet. To the Damascene it is a poor river (cf. 2 Kings v. 12). It is useless for transport; but it serves as a barrier against dubious neighbours in Transjordania, and has several fords. On the west of the Jordan the "hill country" runs down, though with several breaks, from the Lebanons to the south Judaean *negeb* or dry region. Jezreel is essentially the centre of Palestine, a plain, or rather a series of plains, notorious for many great fights. After the strong city of Megiddo—already famous in Pre-Israelite times—near where the heavenly beings once aided Israel in their decisive defeat of Canaan (Judges v. 19 f.), is named one of the most impressive features of Hebrew eschatological expectation, the last great battle at Armageddon (Har Magedon, Rev. xvi. 16). The plain of Jezreel is bounded on the north by the well-watered and fertile region of Galilee, which, in spite of its mixed population (Isa. ix. 1), became the home of fiery Zealots and of the most orthodox Rabbis, as well as of the Founder of Christianity.

To the south of Jezreel lies a different type of country, the land of two rival kingdoms. The open region of Samaria invites foreign enemies and foreign trade; the town after which it is named occupies a strong site, and the mountains of Ebal and Gerizim, its highest points, would seem physically more prominent than even Zion. But as one passes south through the bare territory of Benjamin the terrain alters, and this fierce buffer tribe could attach itself with equal ease to its elder "brother," the Joseph tribes, or to the "house of David," as it did when the kingdom of Solomon was rent in twain. "Jerusalem, though strongly placed, and a good road centre for the southern sector of the highlands, could claim no special geographical advantage such as might make it the centre even of lesser Palestine" (Garstang). Comparing ill in this respect with Shechem and Samaria, Jerusalem, like Damascus, was one of the oldest of cities; and it served more suitably than e.g. Hebron, to connect the peoples of the north and of the south.

Physically, Judah is joined both to Egypt and to the deserts. Its external history was conditioned by these neighbours, and its internal physical features go far to explain the temper of its inhabitants. On the sea coast lies Gaza, a key-place which has been styled "the outpost of Africa, the door of Asia." It was the port for the trade between Arabia and the Mediterranean lands; and its persistent connections with Edomites, Nabataeans and Bedouins, and their movements in the road running east of the Jordan give this section of the country (South Palestine and Northern Sinai) an even greater importance than one would gather from the Old Testament.

The peoples of the coastland—Philistines in the south, Phoenicians in the north—were in constant intercommunication, and along the fruitful maritime plain ran one of the most famous of military roads. The plain is separated from the "hill-country" of Judah and Ephraim by the "lowlands" (Shĕphēlah), a fertile strip which invited both the Israelites of the inland mountain-range and strangers of the coast. Transverse passes, controlled by strong fortresses at their western ends, made the possession of the debatable Shĕphēlah a matter of the first importance for caravans and armies. Israel was impotent when the passes were held by her rivals or foes, and the people of the coastland cities were invariably those who would most endanger her spiritual independence.

As a land, Palestine is remarkably broken and varied; it is a land of extremes of climate and scenery—a world in miniature: "that it can ever belong to one nation, even though this were the Jews, is contrary both to Nature and Scripture" (G. A. Smith). The wealth and fertility of the land, and its entire dependence upon the "due measure" of rain (Joel ii. 23), made its inhabitants feel their weakness, and their practical needs gave shape and content to their religion. The cults are concerned to ensure the increase of man and nature; and appropriate rewards and threats hold a prominent place (e.g. Amos iv. 6–11; Deut. xi.). In contrast to its northern neighbour, Judah is more pastoral. On the east lies the wilderness and the Dead Sea; and the contrasts between the fertile tracts of Judah and the bare rock, between the luxuriance of the Jordan valley and the desolate wastes almost at the door of Zion, have deeply stirred the emotions, both of its old inhabitants and of modern travellers. Here were life and death, here too was the salt, at once a symbol of life-giving power and endurance (cf. the covenant of salt, Num. xviii. 19) and of everlasting destruction (cf. Jer. xvii. 6). Indeed, when we consider the effects of these contrasts upon an impressionable and highly-strung folk, and when we remember how all life depended upon the rains—which might bring devastation—and upon the sun—which might parch man and beast—it

is easy to see how a Nature-god could be regarded as both
benevolent and destructive.   In fact, it seems to have been
a Nature-religion that led the prophets to emphasize the
ethical attributes of their Yahweh, who could give both life
and death to his own people (cf. p. 145).

While the Dead Sea region had its legend of Lot's wife
and of Sodom and Gomorrah,[1] the traces and traditions of
former volcanic activity, and the periodical occurrence of
earthquakes, would well serve to arouse speculation.   Hence
it has been suggested that volcanic eruption in historical
times will account for the traditions of certain of the plagues
of Egypt, of the parting of the Red Sea, and of the burning
mountain of Horeb (Exod. xix. 16–18), and that to the
memory of an earthquake are due the more striking features
in the story of the fall of Jericho (Joshua iii. 16f.; vi.).

That the Old Testament, written in Palestine, should
accurately reflect local geographical conditions is only to
be expected.   But it does not follow that geographical
accuracy in itself guarantees the historical accuracy of any
narrative, or that the absence of it proves that the narrative
is a romance.   It is instructive to take note of the diverse
geographical horizons in different parts of the Old Testament,
e.g. Isa. i.–xxxv. and xl. ff., the Book of Ezekiel, the different
outlooks combined in the list in Gen. x.,[2] or the differences
between Ps. civ. and its Egyptian parallel (p. 140, n.).   It is
also to be observed that although the geographical features
support the tradition that Israel entered Palestine at
Jericho (Joshua vii.), some Biblical data suggest that
according to another and now lost tradition the passage
was made further north, towards the ancient shrine of
Shechem (Deut. xxvii. 1–3; Joshua viii. 30ff.).   If so, we
should compare the story of the entrance of the patriarch
Jacob towards the same city (Gen. xxxiii. 18ff.).

Incursions into Palestine were far from uncommon.   In
recent times one could trace in Transjordania the entrance
from the desert of nomads, and their transition from nomadic

---

[1] Of the other cities only the names survive (Deut. xxix. 23;
Hos. xi. 8).

[2] To P are ascribed *vv.* 1, 2–7, 20, 22f., 31f., the rest is J.

life to settled agricultural occupation. Just as the Kenites of the *negeb* were once found in the north (Judges iv. 11; v. 24), so even now Arab pastoral groups still move up from Beersheba to Jezreel. Desert tribes constantly press upon their settled kinsmen, and in turn may be pressed by new-comers, even as happened after the extensive Trans-jordanian movements of and after the sixth century B.C., when Nabataeans pressed upon Edom, and Edomites upon Judah. Taking advantage of a favourable opportunity, bands of Arabs crossed the Jordan in 1919–20 and moved into the plain of Jezreel; and, just as eager bands of Arabs were tempted in 31 B.C. to take advantage of the rumoured devastation of Judah (Jos., *War* i. 19, 3), so "in recent years the rumoured withdrawal of British troops from Palestine was soon followed by a mass raid of fanatical Wahābis who almost reached Ammōn" (Garstang).[1] To Gideon is ascribed the repulse of a great invasion of Midianites—the Amalekites possibly attacked from the south (Judges vi. 3f., 33)—but the Israelites themselves were closely connected with Midianites and Kenites (partly Amalekite in 1 Sam. xv. 6), and *their* successful invasion which, according to some hints, may have included an attack also from the south, is dated about only a couple of centuries earlier. After the Fall of Jerusalem in 586 B.C., Palestine was flooded by outlying peoples (Jer. xlix. 1; Ezek. xxxv. 10), and, earlier, in the time of Elijah and the Omri dynasty there are hints of invasions from the south (2 Chron. xxi. 16). Hence the Israelite invasion was by no means the only occasion when Palestine was likely to be deeply influenced by the people of the desert.

From the earliest times Palestine has been intimately connected with Egypt. Flight into Egypt for security or

---

[1] The early history of the Wahābis affords an example of militant nomads fired by religious zeal, fanatical in their asceticism, marching with their standards (cf. Num. x. 14ff.), and ruthlessly illustrating the "ban" (Deut. xiii. 16; cf. 1 Sam. xv.; Num. xxxi.). It may be added that one has only to see a moderate sized camp of some 4,000 men, women and children, crowded together in a space of 1 mile by ½ mile to realise (with Garstang) the impossibility of an Israelite host of 600,000 warriors journeying in the Wilderness.

for food is well vouched for. There were frequent close
relations between the two (e.g. in the anti-Assyrian and
anti-Babylonian alliances); and the Sinaitic peninsula itself
could fall within the borders of Egypt (cf. 1 Kings viii. 65).
There is abundant evidence for the influence of Egypt upon
Palestine and Phoenicia down to the time of Rameses III
(twelfth century); and the Amarna Letters (p. 94) vividly
depict the loyalty to Egypt of one section of the rulers
of Syria and Palestine about 1380 B.C., and enable us to
imagine what might be the feelings later, in the days of
Hosea (vii. 11; xii. 1), when counsels were divided. Egypt
continued to retain an hereditary interest in Palestine, and
when a Pharaoh hands over the important city of Gezer
to his son-in-law (1 Kings ix. 16), who was already in close
touch with Phoenicia and Edom, it is easy to see how
powerful would be Israel's political and commercial position.

Palestine tended to look to the South, Syria to the North.
A millennium separates the great wars between Egypt and
the Hittites from those between Ptolemies and Seleucids.
The conflicts are typical, for Hittites, Babylonia, Assyria,
Persia and Greece, in turn, all approached Palestine from
the north. After the division of the Israelite monarchy each
of the rivals was torn between the South and the North;
but under the Omri dynasty (North) Israel was closely
connected with Tyre and Damascus, and the capture of
Damascus in 732 B.C. by Assyria led to that of Samaria a
decade later. Indeed, one is struck by the importance of
the territory *north* of Jezreel. El-Ḳedah (Hazor) in the
basin of Lake Huleh, hard by a famous route from Damascus
to Egypt—the "way of the sea" (Isa. ix. 1)—must have
been, as Garstang points out, especially prominent (Joshua
xi. 10). Abel and Dan too, evidently meant more for old
Israel than our scanty evidence explains (2 Sam. xx. 18,
see p. 53). At its best, Samaria, or rather "the house of
Joseph," extended from Carmel on the coast to Manasseh,
across the Jordan—Manasseh being "older" than Ephraim
(Gen. xlviii.)—and had powerful connections with the
districts to its north.

On the other hand, the welfare of Judah depended on its

relations with the Philistines and Edomites.   How closely
the fortunes of the three were interlocked during the history
of the monarchies can be easily seen in the Old Testament,
where Chronicles can be used (with caution) to supplement
Kings.[1]   Edom and the Philistine coast were often allied,
and the prosperity of Judah presupposed some control over
the "treasures of Esau" (Obad. *v.* 6) and the coast trade.
Solomon's wealth and the wealth of the temple of Jerusalem
are more easily understood when—with Phythian–Adams—
we observe the traces of the mining industry in the (Edomite)
Arabah, south of the Dead Sea, its copper resources (which
could be traded for gold and ivory), and the turquoise mines
of Sinai, which were exploited by Egypt (until *c.* 1150 B.C.),
and later, no doubt, by the next ambitious power.   Hence
the connections between Judah and South Palestine were
of the closest; and there was a considerable infiltration of
Edomitic blood into the tribe.   Not only are Esau (Edom)
and Jacob (Israel) represented as "brother"-peoples, not
always at enmity, but, unlike Chemosh of Moab and Milcom
of Ammon, the national god of Edom is neither denounced
in the Old Testament, nor even named.[2]

That relations between Judah and her southern neighbours
frequently changed is easily understood; her relations with
her northern neighbours were not less unstable.   To whom
did Benjamin belong?   Late tradition locates part of
Jerusalem in Benjamin (Joshua xv. 8; cf. xviii. 16; contrast
xv. 63).   At the Schism, this tribe, named after the favourite
brother of Joseph, is reckoned to Judah (1 Kings xii. 21, 23),
or it is omitted (*v.* 20; cf. xi. 13, 32).   It has not always a
good reputation (esp. Judges xix. ff.); and perhaps the
little district of which Jerusalem could form part, lying as

---

[1] After David's conquest of Edom, we hear of Solomon's relations
with Tyre and with Ezion-geber, the Edomite port on the Gulf of
Akabah (1 Kings ix. 26f.).   Jehoshaphat held Ezion-geber (1 Kings
xxii. 47; cf. 2 Chron. xvii. 10f.).   Edom revolted against Jehoram
(2 Kings viii. 20ff.; cf. 2 Chron. xxi. 16).   Judah regained control
in the days of Amaziah and Uzziah (2 Kings xiv. 7, 22; cf. 2 Chron.
xxvi. 6f.), but lost it again under Ahaz (2 Kings xvi. 6; 2 Chron.
xxviii. 17f.).

[2] It was perhaps the "mountain-god" El Shaddai.

it did between the old political centres at Shechem and
Hebron, was of uncertain loyalty.

Close relations between (South)Israel and her neighbours
are expressed "genealogically" when Abraham, who, by his
concubine "Incense," is the "father" of sundry Arab tribes,
including Midian (Gen. xxv. 1ff.), separates near Bethel from
Lot (cf. the Edomite Lotan, xxxvi. 20), the "father" of
Moab and Ammon. Next, Hagar's son Ishmael, the
"father" of other desert tribes (cf. the Hagrites; 1 Chron.
v. 10), is sent away from Isaac (xxv. 12ff.). Finally, Isaac's
son Jacob parts from Esau (xxxvi. 7; cf. xiii. 6), the "father"
of the Edomite tribes. But all the non-Israelite names (Lot,
Hagar, Ishmael, Esau) are as closely interrelated as are
those of the Israelite "fathers" (Abraham, Isaac, Jacob,
Israel), and what might seem to be three distinct events in
Pre-Mosaic times may well be three different statements of
the ethnological relations between Israel and her neighbours.
Some desert tribes who are regarded as Aramaean belong
partly to the north (Damascus), and partly to the south
(near Edom). But all the desert tribes, whether Aramaean
or Arabian, readily pass from one district to the other, and
Israelite tradition connects the "fathers" with Aramaean
homes and wives.[1]

Hence, through Abraham and his "sons" the four groups,
Israel, Edom, Moab and Ammon, are very closely akin; some
relationship with Aramaean and other desert tribes is also
felt, and consequently the term "Israel" is really more
restricted than the rather ambiguous term "Hebrews." On
the other hand, Old Testament traditions repudiate kinship
between Israel and the Philistines, Canaanites or Phoenicians
in spite of the cultural relationships. Yet, Israel was more
closely related to the native inhabitants (Judges iii. 6) than
she wished to remember; and there were periods of alliance,
when covenants would be made, with "brother" Tyre
(Amos i. 9), or with the Philistines of Gerar (Gen. xxvi. 28;
cf. xxi. 32 ff.).

---

[1] See especially Deut. xxvi. 5 where the Israelite is to testify that
his "father" was an Aramaean, a nomad (see mg.; cf. also 1 Chron.
vii. 14).

Palestine, often torn by internal intrigue, readily became the pawn of the rival political groupings of the great powers of Egypt and South-west Asia; and in thus participating in a larger history the people of Palestine were brought into a larger world. This is very clearly seen in the Amarna Letters (p. 93 f.). The writers of Israel's history can, it is true, describe the Omri dynasty without any reference to the Aramaean coalition, then vainly attempting to stem Assyria's march upon Syria and Damascus; but the prophets have a wider horizon, as they survey Yahweh's dealings with their neighbours. Israel's strength waxed and waned. The diminutive Judah and Jerusalem of Nehemiah's age stand in contrast to the days when the rebellious city was a thorn in the flesh of the great powers (Ezra iv. 12–15); and what was subsequently achieved by the Hasmonaeans (p. 99) owed its inspiration to the fact that memories of past glory had not died out. Now and then we get glimpses of a larger Israel. One has only to look at a map of the tribes of Israel to see how the lands of Moab and Ammon coincided with the tribes of Reuben and Gad (or Gilead, Judges v. 17). Both Gilead and Bashan could be claimed as part of Israel's inheritance (cf. Mic. vii. 14); as also could Carmel, with its shrine to Yahweh (1 Kings xviii. 30)—corresponding to the sacred hill of Tabor at the eastern end of Jezreel—and much of the sea-coast (cf. Deut. xxxiii. 19; Judges v. 17). We have here a greater Israel, a Pan-Israel, one that could speak of "Israelites in Judah" (1 Kings xii. 17)—not the Israel of the rivalry of Israel *versus* Judah, or of ten tribes *versus* two (cf. 2 Sam. xix. 43), nor of the post-exilic age when Judah would claim to be the *only* Israel. The precise connotation of "Israel" is a perplexing problem (see p. 56).

Behind the "canonical" history are some great events of which only traces remain; in certain respects Israel had a bigger history and on a larger scale than the records have preserved. In some way the Pan-Israelite idea arose, it took root, and it continued to fertilise the imagination of a people whose history and physical constitution had been less coherent than it realised. But Palestine is a broken land, a land of tribes, unsuitable for political or religious unity; and the very fact that the world owes to such a land the conception of a single Israel and of a one and only God, of a Yahweh and his own "peculiar" people, makes the enquiry into the scene of this drama all the more absorbing.

II. Folk-lore and Archaeology

The more intensive study of Palestine itself has been devoted to the identification of places, the excavation of ruined sites, and the collection of native Palestinian tradition and folk-lore. Naturally this study is not pursued in isolation. The archaeological evidence, which ranges from architecture to pottery and flints, is co-ordinated with that of other lands; the beliefs and customs of the land are almost invariably discovered to have much in common with those found elsewhere; and ultimately it is possible to form a general picture of ancient and modern Palestine in which to place the Old Testament.

Western interest in Palestine is primarily due to the Bible, and the story of the growth and nature of this interest has some instructive features. Long ago Josephus told of the reputation which the temple of Jerusalem enjoyed; but it was not Jerusalem, the Jewish city, it was the Sacred Site of Christianity that soon began to attract pilgrims. With the triumph of Christianity under Constantine (A.D. 323–36) there quickly arose an enthusiasm for the Holy Land; but much of the past history had already been forgotten and a new and luxuriant growth of tradition began to spring up. Pilgrims demanded the exact locality of every scene in Scripture, and a scriptural reference for every interesting site, ruin or building. Rival sects cherished each its own favourite sites and traditions, and the not wholly pleasing story of the growth and vicissitudes of their numerous varied and often conflicting identifications and traditions is one to which the Old Testament itself supplies parallels. The mass of legends increased, till it reached its climax—it may be said—in that "apotheosis of scholasticism" the *Elucidatio Terrae Sanctae* of Quaresmius (1639). "In it," writes Bliss, "the traditions of the Holy Places, largely erroneous, which had been increasing for years, took on a stereotyped form which has enjoyed little variation since in ecclesiastical circles; the book is full of learning, but this is often learning running riot around matters essentially trivial." Hence it is not surprising that when scholarly research began, it found that the "Palestine of to-day is more a museum of church history than of the Bible—a museum full of living, as well as of ancient specimens of its subject" (G. A. Smith).

An interest in matters outside the sacred sites is to be found in the Dominican Felix Fabri (latter part of the fifteenth century). George Sandys (1610–11) proposed "to deliver the reader from many erring reports of the too credulous devotee, and too, too, vain-glorious." Attention was paid to the flora and fauna by the French physician Belon (1548), by Rauwolf (1573), and by the Swedish naturalist Hasselquist (1749–52), a pupil of Linnaeus who had once declared that the world knew less of the natural history of Palestine than of the remotest parts of India. Inscriptions were being copied in the seventeenth century, and notice began to be taken of matters of climate, physical geography, population, etc. Passing over many important names, we may say that a new period opens with the American Edward Robinson, who in his travels (1838–52), collected material from ancient and native sources, and compared modern nomenclature with the invaluable place-name lists of Eusebius and Jerome. He laid it down as a principle that "all ecclesiastical tradition respecting the ancient places in and around Jerusalem and throughout Palestine, *is of no value*, except so far as it is supported by circumstances known to us from the Scriptures or from other contemporary testimony." From his time onwards, Palestinian research was pursued unremittingly, until with such events as the foundation of the Palestine Exploration Fund, 1865; the corresponding German society, 1877; and the Dominican convent of St. Stephen at Jerusalem, 1890; it entered upon its present phase.

A deep interest has always been taken in Jerusalem and in other sites that struck the imagination of Christians;

and an immense amount of work has been done, ranging
in its motive from earnest attempts to "prove" or "confirm"
the Bible, to purely scientific endeavours to collect information.   The field of study now has three main sub-divisions:
(1) climate and meteorology, geology, the physical features,
identification of sites, routes and boundaries, political
geography; (2) native physical types, manners and customs,
folk-lore and traditions; and (3) surface ruins, excavation,
architecture, monuments, epigraphy (inscriptions and coins),
tombs, burial usages, etc.   These three sub-divisions
naturally overlap; and it is often possible, for example,
to traverse the centuries and by comparing ancient and
modern customs (e.g. games, toilet, funeral rites, etc.) to
learn much about both.

It is not to be supposed that the different forms of social
organisation and custom found among modern nomad,
pastoral or agricultural folk are identical with those of old.
Yet, in the modern ordeals, blood-feuds and ideas of law
and justice there is much that enables one to understand
ancient life more truly.   So, modern writers will comment
upon typical differences between the settled agriculturist
and the roving Bedouin, upon the latter's pride of race,
his love of genealogies—mere fabrications though they may
be.   The true Oriental is a born story-teller; but the
credibility of a tradition is never even considered by him
so long as it claims to rest upon unimpeachable authority.
Innumerable modern illustrations of age-long conditions
have been collected by travellers.[1]   They range from the
sad condition of the childless wife (1 Sam. i. 5 f.) to the way
in which the rafters sink in from slothfulness (Eccles. x. 18).
They save us from viewing eastern life through western
spectacles, and enable us to correct one-sided assumptions.
It is important, for example, to see the conditions under
which land is held at the present day, or to observe the
indifference of the aristocratic Bedouin to the useful art of
writing.   Hence, although the evidence of archaeology

[1] *The Land and the Book* by the Rev. W. M. Thomson, a keen
observer of the customs of a past century, deservedly became
classical (1857).

demonstrates the antiquity and frequent use of writing, it is quite another question whether the ability to read and write was necessarily more widespread than what it has been—at least until recently—in an illiterate Palestine.

The study of the nature and distribution of medieval tradition is supplemented by that of the innumerable traditions current among the modern inhabitants. The same tradition is associated with different names or it recurs at different places (e.g. the Flood). There are duplicate traditions of the same event, and one can often trace the rise of new traditions or the modification or reshaping of the old. When modern travellers find among the native inhabitants some Biblical tradition that seems ancient, it may turn out that, so far from going back twenty or more centuries, it is due to the influence of the Bible or of the Koran in medieval or later times. The traditional identi-fication of Mount Sinai is only post-Christian; and although there are some striking traditions of the Exodus in Northern Arabia, it is not certain whether they are really ancient and authentic. In general, the study of modern traditions, whether Biblical or other, throws light upon their typical vicissitudes rather than upon their ultimate origin.

Palestinian life has contributed greatly to our knowledge of inveterate religious ideas. One well known authority (C. R. Conder) tells of an image of the Virgin which could not be shown to anyone, for he who saw it would be struck dead (cf. Judges xiii. 22), and of a roof-top ceremony in Jerusalem, called the sanctification of the moon, which made him recall Jer. xix. 13; xliv. 17. Perhaps the most interesting evidence concerning ancient thought and practice that can be gleaned from modern life in Palestine is to be found at the local sacred places. Situated on a hill-top with a tomb, a tree or bush decked with rags, and often a well, the *kubbeh* or *makām* (lit. "place," cf. Gen. xii. 6, etc.) is the centre of everyday religious life. The place is an asylum; it must not be violated by strangers, and objects of value can be left there in security. Traditions justify its sanctity. The central figure is a saint or *weli*, generally with an orthodox Christian or Mohammedan name; but he is often known only by an epithet (e.g. protector, healer, rain-giver). His tomb will be visited by barren women, and the saint—who can assume human form—is regarded as a procreator: for it is a common belief that superhuman beings or disembodied spirits can unite with human beings (cf. Gen. vi. 2). There are "sacred" men; but their sanctity has not necessarily connoted ethical or spiritual worth, any more than in the days of old when prophets or priests were apt to indulge in ecstatic or licentious behaviour (pp. 168 ff.). The office of these sacred men may be hereditary; they (or the sheikh) guard the sanctuary, and perform sacrificial rites, the number and variety of which reveal an inveterate belief in the sanctity and efficacy of blood.

The local *numen loci*, who may be regarded as an ancestor, receives offerings; he rewards or punishes; he is the centre of the daily religious social life. He is near at hand and accessible, oaths are taken by him, so that although Islam has its Allah, the saint or *weli* is essentially the local god. Local cults of this kind are found almost everywhere. It is sometimes possible to trace back their history and perceive how the same sacred place has been successively appropriated by the adherents of different faiths. In this way a St. George in the Levant has replaced an Apollo of the Greek period, who in turn represents an earlier Semitic (Phoenician) Resheph; or the Virgin takes the place of some goddess of pagan times. Developments of this sort must have occurred earlier in the days of Canaanites and Israelites. It is with justice, therefore, that in the modern local saints and *welis* we may see the descendants of the local gods or Baals of old. There have, of course, been some profound and positive changes, but the evidence enables us to understand more intelligently the nature of ancient local cults, their persistence, the needs they supplied, and typical interrelations between local deities and the greater national deities or deity.

Of the entire history of Palestine as known to us the period covered by the Old Testament is only a small part. Accordingly we can approach the Old Testament with a knowledge of "the sort of thing" that we find in Palestine and the Near East, whether in Rabbinical (or Talmudical), medieval or modern times. The great historical periods did not leave things as they found them: Greek, Roman, Byzantine, Turk and Crusading waves swept over the land before the advent of the modern European; but amid conspicuous changes there is a certain permanence (p. 99 f.).

Turning from the people of Palestine to the work of excavation, we note, first, that there have not as yet been any very sensational discoveries. Much, however, has been achieved, and it illustrates ancient life, religion, arts and interests. Archaeology does not work blindly. Visible ruins and surface remains constantly invite the spade. The *tell* built and rebuilt and now ruined (Jer. xlix. 2; xxx. 18) marks the site of some ancient city, and it may happen that its name still survives on the spot or in a modern village near by. Potsherds on the surface will often afford a preliminary clue as to the archaeological possibilities. In Gezer a chance boundary-stone inscribed in Greek and Latin, and the heads of a couple of stones projecting above the ground, with a third lying close by, led ultimately to the discovery of a unique alignment of pillars, one of the most remarkable remains of the old religion. A temptation on the part of earlier diggers to look for the spectacular, and to lay bare high and low in the hope of finding inscriptions— thereby often destroying the evidence for the stratification of the débris—has given way to more methodical procedure; and the discovery of the importance of pottery types for determining the approximate date of the strata has turned excavation from an amateur's hobby into an arduous discipline. The pottery clue, first demonstrated by the veteran archaeologist Sir Flinders Petrie, does not stand by itself, and the excavator as he digs down is on the look out for all the hints furnished by scarabs, typical weapons or tools, the presence or absence of iron, inscribed objects, etc. Meanwhile so much has been done that it is possible to attempt a provisional archaeological history of Palestine.[1]

[1] *Canaan d'après l'Exploration Récente*, by Father Hugues Vincent (Paris, 1907), is still the great classical book on the subject.

There are of course pit-falls.   Disturbance of levels must always be reckoned with; and Professor R. A. S. Macalister found a Maccabaean coin in a neolithic stratum of Gezer. Working hypotheses are as necessary here as elsewhere. The excavator, says Garrow Duncan, "comes to a site with some knowledge of what he may expect to find, gathered from past history recorded: though it by no means follows that he may find what he expects.   He must not only see what he wants to see, but he must be prepared to give full value also to those details which appear somewhat un-expected and disconcerting."   That nothing is too poor or trivial is shown, not only by the clues originally provided by the examination of thousands of pieces of potsherd, but by the interesting historical possibilities suggested by the discovery of similar pottery types, or patterns, or weapons over extended areas.   Thus, important questions arise from a comparison of similar pottery found in districts as far apart as the Aegean and Susa, the Caspian and Egypt. Still, the appearance of Hyksos objects in both Cnossus in Crete and Babylon does not in itself prove that the Hyksos empire was so far-flung.   On the other hand, archaeological evidence accumulates for the importance of the Hyksos and earlier periods, and for the antiquity of Transjordanian sites.   Indeed, Pre-Israelite Palestine and Syria appear culturally so rich and important that their "Golden Age" might seem to have been over before Israel came upon the scene (p. 93).

It has been found that the entrance of the Israelites into Palestine evidently caused no set-back to its culture. Their settlement must have been gradual, as is suggested by the notices in Judges (Ch. i.), and not a sweeping and successful conquest, like that attributed to Joshua (Joshua x. f.).   By no means all the tribes invaded the land under his leadership.   In fact, the entrance of Israel is not necessarily a landmark for the archaeologist.   But the co-ordination of archaeological and Biblical evidence is always a delicate task.   For example, the marked absence of a certain datable type of pottery at Jericho led to the view that the city was destroyed *before* the appearance of Mykenaean pottery types, elsewhere ascribed to the Late Bronze Age (c. 1350–1200); and it is the selection of a particular chronological scheme which dates the Exodus of the Israelites four hundred and eighty years before Solomon (1 Kings vi. 1), and the capture of Jericho towards 1400 B.C. (Garstang). The depth and persistence of Egyptian influence during the period of the Israelite "judges" can be seen in Beth-Shan (the temples, etc.), and archaeologists think they can even recognise there and elsewhere a difference between the Israelite and the earlier religion. Traces of mercenary troops from the Mediterranean were also found in Beth-Shan, which suggest how their employment by Egypt—there and elsewhere—might have paved the way for the subsequent entry of the Philistines.

But the picture presented to us by archaeology is at present imperfect and disproportionate. The history of a *tell* cannot be safely determined from any partial excavation: further digging might reveal objects that would modify earlier hypotheses. The distribution of the sites excavated is also important: too little has been done in Syria, Transjordania and the Negeb. Archaeological material invariably stands in need of some *interpretation*; and the same evidence can be differently interpreted. Objects have sometimes been given a "religious" interpretation to which they were not entitled (e.g. as an altar, sacred pillar, or a cult-object); although it must be remembered, on the other hand, that practices—especially in agriculture—which might seem purely secular to us often had a religious significance.

It is interesting to learn that Shiloh is, archaeologically, a blank from the tenth to the sixth century; and that some considerable destruction of Judaean cities may be associated with the Babylonian period (c. 586 B.C.), and at no earlier or later date. But the temptation to connect purely archaeological evidence with the Old Testament easily leads to premature conclusions, and it is sometimes safer to dissociate archaeological periods and Biblical history. The excavations at Samaria do indeed indicate that this city was not founded before the age of Omri (1 Kings xvi. 24), and that its kings used ivory in their buildings (xxii. 39).

G

On the other hand, the generally admitted association of the Philistine invasion with the introduction of iron—which archaeologists date *c.* 1200 B.C.—does not simplify the Biblical evidence. For the entry of the Israelites—*as it is described*—belongs to a time when the Canaanites used iron chariots (Joshua xvii. 16; Judges i. 19; iv. 3), and iron objects were to be found in Jericho (Joshua vi. 19). Moreover, as regards the Philistines, the fact that their *name* persisted even in Maccabaean times (1 Macc. iii. 24; cf. BS 1. 26), and that they appear in the Old Testament as a "Semitised" folk, suggests that we must distinguish between the always mixed non-Israelite population of the sea-coast and adjacent cities and the "Philistines" of the Egyptian records, the invaders by land and by sea, of *c.* 1200 B.C., who gave their name to the region. Invaluable and indispensable though the evidence of archaeology always is—and much more is to be hoped for in the future—one must avoid promiscuous combinations of archaeological data and Biblical history: each must be independently tested.

CHAPTER V

Israel and the Nations

How modern research has succeeded in reconstructing the history and culture of what may be called the "Bible lands" is now an oft-told story, yet one that needs revision and supplement as fresh discoveries are made. Hence this chapter will confine itself merely to certain aspects of the culture, and to a brief résumé of the chief epochs of the history. At the outset, it is necessary to insist upon the essential difference between the "internal" evidence (i.e. the evidence of the Old Testament itself) and the "external" evidence (that of archaeology and monuments), for, whereas modern research must piece together the miscellaneous "external" evidence concerning the political, social and religious history of the ancient Near East, we have in the Old Testament continuous *written* histories with definite historical threads. The investigation of the nature and value of these threads is the task of Biblical Criticism (pp. 53 ff.); and the fact that the old writers have given us so elaborate an history distinguishes Israel from all her neighbours.

Archaeological evidence stands in need of some interpretation (p. 79 f.); but direct evidence is plentifully supplied by inscribed monuments, tablets, papyri, etc. The majority of these come from outside Palestine—which is really very poor in such material—and are written in scripts, the decipherment of which has been one of the romances of scholarship.[1] The clue has generally been a bilingual, i.e.

[1] The Palestinian records include the—strictly speaking—Transjordanian inscription of Mesha, King of Moab (c. 850 B.C.), the "Siloam" inscription relating to the completion of a conduit in Jerusalem (? time of Hezekiah), an old agricultural "calendar" found at Gezer, and various ostraka (inscribed sherds), seals and jar-handles. There are important inscriptions from North Syria of the eighth century and later; and a number of Phoenician inscriptions which, apart from a few of the twelfth to tenth century, are of the Persian age and later.

parallel versions in two languages, one of which is known. Thus, to take a very simple example, after the Phoenician inscriptions had been read it was soon found that in certain bilinguals the second language was Greek, and that ἔδωκεν was written in a *syllabic* script: *e–to–ke–ne*, and τυχαί *tu–ka–i*. Another bilingual in Greek and in Egyptian hieroglyphs contained the Greek names Ptolemaios and Kleopatra. This at once gave (in 1822) the Egyptian signs common to both names, *p*, *l*, *o*, *a*, and then, *m*, *s*, *k* and *r*—there were two kinds of *t*. The lengthy Rosetta stone (Greek and two styles of Egyptian) supplied more clues, and it was soon found that ancient Egyptian had as its last descendant Coptic, a language which itself was beginning to die out about three hundred years ago.

The decipherment of cuneiform was immensely more difficult. Trilinguals found in Persepolis in unknown "wedge-shaped" characters presumably related to ancient Persia, and one of the scripts was at once seen to be much simpler than the others. Certain recurring groups of signs contained, it was guessed, royal names and titles; and—to use symbols—the series *x* . . . *y* in one, and *y* . . . *z* in another presumably meant that *x* was the son of *y*, and *y* the son of *z*. Acting on this assumption Grotefend (in 1802) tried the names of various Persian kings in what he took to be their oldest form. Cyrus and Cambyses were ruled out, as the initial signs in the inscriptions varied; Artaxerxes was too long. The names proved to be Xerxes, Darius and Hystaspes. The work of De Sacy on the later Persian and Greek inscriptions and of Anquetil du Perron on the Avesta, the old sacred book of the Persians, brought fresh material, and at last the relatively simple alphabet and language of the Persians of the Achaemenid period were satisfactorily mastered. But the third script of the trilinguals, the Babylonian (or Assyrian), now called Accadian, was, as it seemed, much too complicated to justify the claims of the decipherers. It proved to be Semitic, and therefore was linguistically intelligible; but it was syllabic, and the same sign or rather group of signs often had different values! Gradually this writing too was conquered (notably by

Hincks and Rawlinson): when it was found, e.g. that the name Cyrus was spelt, in one case *ku–ras*, and in another *ku* followed by two unknown characters, it was obvious that these must be *ra* and *as*. Clues multiplied, and by 1857 it was clear that scholars could really decipher and translate cuneiform, and new worlds were opened out.

Immense interest was excited by Layard's spectacular discoveries in Assyria (from 1845 onwards). Then, popular enthusiasm was aroused when George Smith, in 1872, found among the tablets in the British Museum an Assyrian version of the Deluge. Later on, tablets referring to Sennacherib and Hezekiah were discovered. Among the more recent discoveries have been the tablets found at Amarna in Egypt (first published in 1896), which revolutionised our knowledge of the "Mosaic" age (see p. 94), the Code of Laws of Hammurabi (published in 1902), and quantities of Hittite tablets from Boghaz Keui in Anatolia (1906). Trained guessing, continuous checking, and the independent verification of results have solved the preliminary problems, though much still remains to be done. A few years ago there came to light the Hittite version of an Egypto-Hittite treaty 1272 B.C.), the Egyptian version of which had long been known; and, by an interesting coincidence, there was found among the papyri of a Jewish colony at Elephantine an Aramaic version of the Behistun inscription of Darius which had formed the basis of Rawlinson's epoch-making discoveries. Cuneiform writing in spite of its obvious intricacies was used for other languages besides Accadian, and since 1929 scholars have been at work on the interpretation of tablets from Ras Shamra in North Syria (of *c.* 1500–1300 B.C.) on which an old type of the Hebrew or Canaanite language is written in a cuneiform *alphabet*.

Although contemporary documents are more valuable than records selected, compiled and revised by later writers, they may still need "criticism." Of the Behistun inscription referred to, copies were sent throughout the Persian Empire, and the fragments of it found among the Jewish colony at Elephantine contain additions, omissions, and traces of rather divergent wording. Moreover, in 408 B.C., this

colony sent a petition to Bigvai (Bagoas), the governor of
Judah; duplicate copies were found, but they differ somewhat and contain errors. In fact, mistakes and omissions
not infrequently occur in ancient texts. Exaggeration is
of course not uncommon, and Egyptian kings, on their
monuments, have claimed as their own the same achievements as their predecessors. A stele of Esarhaddon
represents him leading Baal, king of Tyre, and Tarku
(Tirhakah) of Egypt, with a cord through rings in their
lips, though neither of them was actually taken prisoner.
Thotmes III, on the death of his powerful wife, Hatshepsut,
chiselled away her name and figure, and built masonry
around her obelisks at Karnak in order to suppress the
records of her fame. And later, during the efforts to
establish the cult of Aton in Egypt, the name of the god
Amon was deleted and replaced by that of Aton, and in
the subsequent reaction the process was reversed.

In history and myth the achievements of one king or
god are not rarely transferred to another. Different
versions are sometimes found, e.g. of the Babylonian myth
of Creation, or of the myth of the descent of the goddess
Ishtar into Hades. Even "compositeness" can sometimes
be recognised, as in the Babylonian account of Creation
and the Egyptian Book of the Dead. But although
Egyptian texts were often inaccurately copied, the ancient
scribes were on the whole faithful. Thus, Philo of Byblos, of
the time of Hadrian, quotes an earlier writer, Sanchuniathon,
as his authority on Phoenician cosmogony. He uses his
material to explain how the old gods were kings who had
been deified—this is the "euhemeristic" explanation of
myths—and he tries to show that Greek mythology was of
Phoenician origin. Yet, although Philo's cosmogony is in
a very late dress, some, at least, of its details appear to be
as old as the Ras Shamra tablets. Furthermore, lists of
antediluvian Babylonian kings used by the Babylonian
priest Berossus (c. 280 B.C.), contained data which were
already current about two thousand years earlier; e.g. it
appears that his statement that the shepherd Daos (i.e.
Tammuz) reigned 36,000 years rests upon extremely ancient

authority—though it is scarcely the more credible on that account!

In fact, characteristic of both Babylonia and Egypt is the persistence, with relatively little alteration, of writings of very high antiquity. Both lands had certainly arrived at maturity by about 2000 B.C., and subsequent developments are relatively slight. We are especially indebted to the men who copied tablets for Ashurbanipal (seventh century B.C.) for our knowledge of the earlier periods, and the intellectual life of which we gain a picture from them and from other scribes is one that underwent little change. Accordingly, the question will legitimately arise, when one is considering the Old Testament, whether here too the writings which refer to early times (e.g. that of the Patriarchs) are copies of ancient documents or at least are adequate witnesses for the Pre-Mosaic age.[1]

The most important myths of Babylonia and Assyria were current round about 2000 B.C. By that time astrology was well-advanced, and the literature, art and religion of the leading peoples of South-west Asia were completely established. As for Egypt, most of the literary works have come down to us in the form of school exercises. The Egyptians are characterised by love of life, sociability and a sense of humour. As early as about 2000 B.C. they were cultivating literature for its own sake. Reflecting upon human woes, a poet of the twelfth dynasty describes a man weary of life, discussing with his *ba* (? external soul), his desire for death. Another breathes the spirit of *carpe diem*: let a man "make a happy day" ere he goes where "none may take his goods with him and none that hath gone may come again." A Babylonian poem, certainly not later than the eighth century, is a precursor of Ecclesiastes: the righteous and the wicked meet with the same fate, and it is of no avail to serve the gods. Another, sometimes described as "the Babylonian Job," tells of a man, apparently

---

[1] Needless to say, every case has to be considered on its merits, and the general conclusion now reached is that the Biblical narratives have undergone much more development and change, owing to decisive religious developments, than the records of Babylonia or Egypt. See p. 100.

a king, overwhelmed by unmerited sufferings; he is unable to please the inscrutable god and is forsaken by his own god and goddess; but at last his sins and his maladies are removed, and he is restored.

One of the popular stories in Egypt, the so-called Tale of the Two Brothers has, among many *motifs*, that of the wife who tries to seduce her young brother-in-law, thus recalling the story of Joseph and Potiphar's wife. In the old tale of Sinuhe, an Egyptian who fled into Palestine, married a chief's daughter and fought the leader of a hostile band, we recall David's encounter with Goliath and his marriage with Saul's daughter. What was told of the birth of the mighty Sargon of Agadé finds parallels in the birth-stories of Moses, Krishna, Perseus and other figures. Myth and legend surround historical figures (e.g. Alexander the Great), and perfectly credible, if not genuine historical elements, attach themselves to pure creations of the imagination. Entertainment and instruction have been blended in the much-travelled tale of the sage Aḥiḳar, the noble vizier of Sennacherib and Esarhaddon: a story of ingratitude and its retribution becomes the vehicle for proverbial wisdom and appropriate fables. The tale was current in several versions—one was found among the Jews of Elephantine—and the hero is actually claimed by the pious Jew Tobit, as a kinsman of his (viz. Achiacharus, Tobit i. 21f.; xiv. 10).

The points of contact between the Biblical, Babylonian, and other accounts of Creation and of the Deluge, have frequently been discussed. Here it need only be remarked that in the different versions of the Creation and the primeval conflict, the Sumerian Enlil, the Babylonian Marduk, and the Assyrian Asshur are each in turn the central figure, while in the Old Testament, where Yahweh is naturally pre-eminent, there are sundry allusions (e.g. Job xxvi. 12f.), which reflect a knowledge of other versions besides the "canonical" account in Genesis. Similarly, besides the "canonical" account of Paradise, there are references in Ezek. xxviii. 12ff. to another more "mythological."[1]

One Sumerian tablet (of the nineteenth century B.C.)

---

[1] On Gen. vi. 1ff., see p. 57 f.

contains a more or less continuous account of creation, city-building and a deluge; the last-mentioned is followed by a sacrifice to the gods—though the sending out of birds, found in other versions, is wanting. Also, a tablet, apparently used for school purposes, seems to be based upon a deluge-story, for it includes the dimensions of a building of truly mythical size, and lists of animals, ending with dove, swallow and raven—the three birds sent out, according to the Gilgamesh epic, to explore the wastes. Certain beasts (e.g. the ox) are in sevens and others (e.g. the ass) are in pairs, and the tablet contains, on the reverse, a list of wines. Hence it is conjectured that in this particular Babylonian version the counterpart of Noah was the founder of viticulture, as Noah himself is said to be in Gen. ix. 20ff. As regard other points of contact, sometimes isolated elements recur, as when Yahweh's net (Ezek. xxxii. 3ff.) recalls the net which Marduk in the Creation-story threw over the monster Tiamat (i.e. the *tehom*, or Deep, of Gen. i. 2; Prov. viii. 27, etc.), or there are similar topics, as when the myth of Adapa explains how this hero just missed eating the food and water of life—how, in fact, man became mortal and lost his Paradise.

Advanced ethical ideas are common. In the Egyptian Book of the Dead is a list of offences which the deceased affirms before Osiris that he has *not* committed: he has not killed, or committed adultery, or stolen, or stirred up strife, etc. In Babylonia a sufferer will appeal to a priest, who enquires of him the offences of which he may have been guilty: e.g. has he committed adultery, murdered, or stolen, has he set the members of a family against one another, used false weights, said "yes" for "no" and "no" for "yes"? It would be easy to multiply examples of the most elevated sentiments; but it is necessary to remember that they are not of universal application. As early as the sixth dynasty (*c.* 2700 B.C.) an Egyptian official affirms his piety and justice: "I gave bread to the hungry, and clothing to the naked"; he relates that he was sent on an expedition to Nubia, and he continues: "I slew a great number there consisting of chiefs' children and excellent commanders. . . ."

Specially interesting is the Law Code of the Babylonian king Hammurabi (*c.* 2000 B.C.), the "shepherd of the people," whom the gods ordained "to destroy the wicked and evil, that the strong might not oppress the weak." The laws which he received from the Sun-god, the god of justice, range over a very large field and reflect a highly organised state. They concern such matters as property, runaway slaves, interest, debts, deposits, breach of promise, marriage, doctors, builders, collisions on the river, etc. Whereas in the Old Testament Yahweh stands behind Israelite law, here law is secular, and represents a more advanced stage of social development. Other laws (Sumerian, Hittite and Assyrian) have been discovered, and a comparison of the Old Testament with old Oriental usage yields many interesting results. Thus, the law of the goring ox appears in Hammurabi's code (§§ 250 ff.; cf. Exod. xxi. 28 ff.); and in this code a man whose wife is childless may have a concubine, who however, must not take advantage of her position (§§ 144 ff.; cf. Sarah and Hagar, Gen. xvi., xxi.). From other laws it is probable that when Rachel carried off her father's teraphim, the possession of the sacred objects entitled her to claim their owner's property (Gen. xxxi. 30 ff.).

Old Testament law is so much in harmony with Oriental custom that such cases as these do not prove either that Sarah and Rachel must have been acquainted with these particular laws or that their practices belonged only to the Pre-Mosaic age. There must have been much more law in Palestine than is preserved in the Old Testament: both the papyri of the Jewish colony at Elephantine and later Talmudic law refer to usages identical with or similar to those found in the ancient codes and presumably already known in ancient Palestine. In fact, the religious and humanitarian note in the Old Testament strongly suggests that protests are being made against the rigour and inflexibility of existing laws. But the laws in the Old Testament are unique in two respects: (*a*) Yahweh has a place held by no other god elsewhere, and crimes are regarded as sins against *him* (cf. Ps. li. 4), and (*b*) the laws are associated

with Moses and the Exodus and are part of the story of the
rise of Israel as a people.

The Old Testament also reflects protests against an older
religion.   Many lofty religious conceptions can be found all
over the Ancient East.   The old deities are no mean
creations.   They are often the good shepherds of the people,
and the protectors of the poor: men are the "flocks" of the
god, made in his own image, proceeding from his flesh.
If the god slays the wicked, says the Egyptian *Instruction
for Merikere*, it is "even as a man smiteth a son for his
brother's sake": that is to say, he must be equally fair to
all his children.   Here too we read: "more acceptable (to
the Sun-god) is one righteous of heart than the ox of one
that worketh iniquity."   Hymns of about 1400 B.C. to the
sun-god Amon and to his temporary rival Aton run along
monotheistic lines: the god is a deity of universal domain—
as befits a solar god—and giver of all life.   The Babylonian
sun-god is also the god of justice, who gives length of life
to those who are just, whereas "the seed of those who act
unjustly shall not flourish."   He hears the cry of the weak
and the helpless, and to him and to other deities appeal is
made for compassion and forgiveness.   The word of the
Babylonian moon-god Sin "brings forth truth and justice
that men may speak truth"; and one of the finest of
Babylonian hymns is addressed to the compassionate
goddess Ishtar (i.e. Astarte).

A vivid picture of temple, temple-cult and sacrificial
rites is furnished by the contemporary evidence of archaeology and the monuments.   But although there are numerous
similarities of principle, detail and phraseology, there are
many examples of national or regional differences.   So,
although Hebrew religion can be illustrated and supplemented by the much-discussed problem of
the origin of the Sabbath is still unsolved, though special
tabu days for the king are found in Babylonia: the 7th,
14th, 21st, 28th day of each month, also the 19th (the
49th from the beginning of the preceding month).

That good kings brought welfare to a people and bad ones
endangered their existence was very realistically believed.

By virtue of their pre-eminent position in the state and the religion—and the two were inseparable—much of the most striking religious ritual concerns them.   There are collections of royal proverbial wisdom.   There are also "prophecies" of misfortune and recovery: one in particular tells of the sufferings of the land and the rise of a new king Ameni (i.e. Amenemhet I) who shall deliver it.   The late "Demotic Chronicle," of the Ptolemaic period, looking back upon Egypt's struggles with the Persians, preserves a prophecy which is accompanied by a complicated commentary.[1] Babylonian and Egyptian literature includes royal hymns of praise to the national god, records of the achievements of the kings for or through their god, and praises of the king, who was commonly regarded as more or less divine.   Psalms, hymns and confessions written for the head of the state could naturally be adjusted to suit any individual; and what was addressed to the king in his divine capacity could also, with necessary adjustments, be addressed to his god, or, indeed, to any deity.

Interesting examples occur in the Amarna tablets, where the petty princes of Palestine and Syria, writing to their divine suzerain the king of Egypt (Amenhotep III or IV), call him their sun-god, their god, and their gods (a plural, like the Hebrew Elohim).   His breath or spirit gives them life; his name brings fear.   The king of Jerusalem cries: "see, the king has set his name in the land of Jerusalem for ever, therefore it cannot be deserted" (cf. Jer. xiv. 9); and, on another occasion, "the king my lord has set his name at the rising of the sun and at the setting of the sun" (cf. Mal. i. 11).   No one can escape the king for, says one writer, "my two eyes are upon thee; if we go up into heaven or if we descend into the earth, yet is our head in thy hands" (cf. Ps. cxxxix. 7f.).   The king *is* the sun-god or is *as* the sun-god; and his servants wait for his word, just as men wait for the rising of the sun in heaven.   One man writes: "to my lord I seek the way, from my lord I cease not" (cf. Ps. cxix. 15).   Another appeals to the king's prestige: "do not let it be said in future days thou wast not able to

---

[1] For a parallel, see the commentaries on Isa. xlviii.

recover [the lands taken by the enemy]" (cf. Num. xiv. 15f.).
One thrice-repeated sentiment runs thus: "I have looked
hither and I have looked thither and it is not light, but I
have looked upon my lord and it has become clear; and
although one brick may be shaken from beneath another,
yet will I not be shaken from beneath the feet of my lord"
(cf. Isa. liv. 10).   Much more could be cited to show how
Palestine and Syria of *c*. 1400 B.C. did address their overlord
whom they regarded as divine, and therefore how they
might have addressed a native ruler or god (see also p. 111).

It is often difficult to decide whether the parallels we
find in Egypt and South-west Asia are necessarily due
to borrowing.   Since they sometimes extend also to old
Greek literature, there may have been a somewhat similar
culture throughout the Ancient East.   Yet Palestine and
Syria certainly exerted a direct influence upon the life and
letters of Egypt in the nineteenth dynasty, and Semitic
influence on Egypt at earlier epochs may be suspected.
On the other hand, direct borrowing sometimes seems clear.
Thus, the collection of sayings in Prov. xxii. 17–xxiii. 11
is certainly connected with—or rather derived from—the
Egyptian "Teaching of Amenemope," which is not later
than the seventh century B.C.   Ps. civ. has close points of
resemblance with hymns to Amon and more particularly
to Aton.   The inscription which recounts the triumph of
Cyrus over Babylon finds noteworthy parallels in the
language of Isa. xliv. 27–xlv. 4; and not only does Marduk
in the former correspond to Yahweh in the latter, but
Marduk is elsewhere addressed as "He who passeth through
the heavens, who poureth out the earth, who measureth the
water of the sea" (cf. Isa. xl. 12).[1]

Palestine was always in close contact with the old Oriental
world, and the old Oriental religions with all their polytheism
and heathenism had reached maturity long before Old
Testament history begins.   The Amarna Letters suggest

---

[1] Parallels have also been found between Isa. ix. 21 and the legend of
Ir (or E)-barra (sea coast against sea coast, country against country,
etc.); between Ezek. xiv. 12–20 and the protest of Ea after the Flood
(that only the sinner should suffer for his sins); and between Job
xxvi. 12f. and the Creation myth.

that in the "Mosaic" age Palestinian thought, religious
and other, was firmly fixed; and it is certainly noteworthy
that phraseological parallels are often found in relatively
late Old Testament passages and not in the earlier
narratives (see above). But it does not follow, either that
Palestine first came under the influence of Oriental thought
at a late date, or that Israel was long in accepting the
influence of the older Palestinian or Canaanite thought; it
is, rather, that these earlier narratives arose among circles
that avoided it. There are, moreover, certain conspicuous
differences between Yahwism and the parallels in other
religions. Sometimes the Biblical writers are deliberately
repudiating the polytheism of the old myths, or they are
intentionally tilting at the deities and myths of their
opponents. Their ethical spirit, their humanism and their
earnestness, too, distinguish the Old Testament from all
other ancient writings; and, as the passion for ethical
monotheism shaped itself, Israel's life was subordinated to
her relationship with Yahweh in a manner that is without
a parallel.

An interest in past historical events can be found outside
Israel, and even a "Synchronous Chronicle" of Babylonia
and Assyria recalls, in its plan, the synchronous history of
the rival monarchies in the books of Kings. The history
of Israel cannot be viewed apart from the larger history
of Palestine and the neighbouring nations; but characteristic
of Israel is the fact that she underwent some drastic internal
changes, and that the religious significance of her history
was felt and expressed in a way that severs her from her
greater neighbours, although they, too, recognised that the
gods made history.

From these miscellaneous remarks upon the cultural
relations between the Old Testament, Palestine and neighbouring lands, we may turn to a survey of the chief historical
periods into which the general historical background to the
Old Testament may be conveniently divided.

(1) Palestine was inhabited by man many thousands of
years before the beginning of history, and already at the

close of the third millennium B.C. its connections are with Egypt and the Levant as well as with its eastern neighbours.

(2) The first decisive stage in the history is reached in the time of the first Babylonian dynasty, whose great law-giver Hammurabi reigned somewhere about 2000 B.C. The twelfth dynasty of Egypt (the Middle Empire) is roughly contemporary. This was the Golden Age of both lands; and the inclusion of Jerusalem in a list of Egypt's foes indicates that it was already a considerable city. The view that the Amraphel of Gen. xiv. is Hammurabi and that the account of Abraham's war with Chedorlaomer has some historical foundation in this period is open to doubt; but it is not improbable that the compilers of Hebrew history believed that to it belonged the first of Israel's ancestors, who came from Babylonia and visited Egypt (Gen. xi. 31; xii.).

(3) This great age was brought to an end by the invasion of Babylonia and Egypt by the Kassites and the "Hyksos" respectively. The latter probably came from Syria and the North, and Palestine now became an integral part of a powerful state, some of whose kings bear Semitic names. The Hyksos conquest made a lasting impression upon Egyptian tradition, and since Josephus (first century A.D.) has to refute garbled stories of the Hyksos and the ancestors of the Jews, it is not unlikely that the descent of Abraham, and later of Jacob, into Egypt and the Exodus of the Israelites had long been associated in Hebrew tradition with the inroad of these "shepherd kings" and their expulsion.

(4) At all events, the expulsion of the Hyksos and the rise of the eighteenth dynasty (1580 B.C.) mark the beginning of a very important period. Egypt followed up her victory over them and extended her conquests into Palestine and Syria. Palestine definitely became part of the Egyptian Empire, and close relations were established between Egypt, the Levant and South-west Asia. The times of Amenhotep III and IV (1411-1362) stand out conspicuously by reason of the "Amarna Letters." They are written in Accadian, the language of intercourse over nearly the whole area, and

throw vivid light upon the political and other conditions of an age that may justly be called international. In particular, they tell of revolts in Palestine and Syria, and of persistent attempts of the disaffected to throw off the yoke of Egypt with the help of *Khabiru*, Amorites, and Hittite invaders from the north. The fact that in the nineteenth dynasty (1346–1210) Egypt had to fight to re-establish her position in Palestine, and, in fact, was quite ready to make a treaty with the Hittites (1272), indicates that her hold over Palestine was weakening, and that the internal situation underwent considerable change.

Meanwhile the cult of the sun-disk, Aton, had become prominent in Egypt, and Amenhotep IV (Ikhnaton) is famous for his violent efforts to destroy the old national religion of Amon-Re. The new monotheistic cult had its centre in Akhetaten, the modern el-Amarna. It aroused the supporters of the old régime, and in the reaction which followed the king's death, they destroyed his city and endeavoured to blot out his name and record. The modern discovery of the city and its archives made known to the world the significance of what may be conveniently called the "Amarna Age," and Ikhnaton's "heresy," the much-praised beauty of his wife Nefertiti, and the treasures of the tomb of his successor Tut-ankh-Amon (1360) have combined to focus attention upon what may well have been also "the age of Moses."

The cult of Aton and the repeated emphasis upon "Truth" in Ikhnaton's inscriptions are not the only noteworthy features of the age. In Northern Mesopotamia lay the important State of Mitanni, ruled by an Indo-Iranian aristocracy in close relationship with Egypt. Other Indian or old Iranian elements can be found in that area, and they have left their traces as far south as Palestine. This early intercourse of the Mediterranean States with the forerunners of the Achaemenids and Parthians allows us to see that the Iranian or Persian factor in their history has been a significant one. And to this it must be added that the deities worshipped in the Amarna Age include the great ethical gods Varuna and Mitra, both of whom become prominent

again in the Persian period.   The former then reappears in
the figure of the Zoroastrian Ahura-Mazda—in India
Varuna came to occupy a secondary place—and the latter
was destined to become subsequently a rival to early
Christianity.   Thus, both in Egypt and in Mitanni there is
evidence for striking religious conditions round about
1400 B.C., and it is natural to suppose that Palestine itself
was not unaffected.

Although the Exodus of the Israelites from Egypt and
the conquest of Palestine cannot be identified with the
movements of the Khabiru (? Hebrews) and the invasions
from the north to which the Amarna Letters testify, it is
not improbable that the Hebrew writers knew that there
were big movements about that date, and that they
associated with them their national traditions.[1]   But the
external evidence throws no light upon early Israel; only
the stele of Merneptah (1221 B.C.) mentions Canaan,
Ashkelon, Gezer and Israel among the enemies of Egypt
whom he subdued.   Frankly, it is not easy to correlate the
books of Joshua and Judges with the Amarna Letters and
the abundant evidence for the strength of Egyptian power
in Palestine: much of the early history has been forgotten
or obscured by the Hebrew historians.

On the other hand, Israelite tradition itself places the
Israelite invasion in the Iron Age, i.e. about 1200 B.C.
(p. 80), and not only is this the age of movements in the
Levant in which the Philistines took part, but the Biblical
traditions definitely associate the rise of Israelite independence with the overthrow of the "uncircumcised" aliens.
The period from about 1400 to 1200 must have been of
great moment for the rise of Israel.   So much is now known
from the archaeological evidence and from the Amarna
Letters, the Hittite tablets, and the new tablets from Ras
Shamra, that the entire period—which can still be called

---

[1] They may have had some sort of comparative chronology,
cf., e.g., the note on the relative antiquity of Hebron and Zoan in
Num. xiii. 22.   If the Exodus was four hundred and eighty years
before the commencement of the Temple (1 Kings vi. 1), the date
(c. 1450) is, all things considered, tolerably near the events of the
Amarna Letters.

the "Amarna Age"—stands out as a mighty landmark in universal history and religion. Of the native deities of Palestine and Syria, and of the religious and other conditions of a land, half Amorite, half Hittite (cf. Ezek. xvi. 3), there is now so much contemporary material that an enquiry into what the land had to offer to Israelite invaders is not less important—and, in the opinion of the present writer, far more practicable—than any attempt to discover what their religion then was. Here, as elsewhere, archaeology and the monuments have placed old problems in a new light.

(5) From the Amarna Age we pass to that of Israelite independence. It was at a time when the surrounding powers had fallen (Crete, the Hittites) or were weak (Egypt, Babylonia, and Assyria), and when the menace of the Philistines had been broken, that the smaller peoples seized their opportunity to assert themselves. Later Israel looked back to the united monarchy under David and Solomon as to a Golden Age. Apart from the stele of the Moabite king Mesha, useful contemporary evidence is practically non-existent. We have to rely almost entirely upon the Old Testament for information concerning this heroic age: the schism, the rival monarchies of Israel and Judah, and the rise and fall of the house of Omri. The last was a dynasty so powerful that Assyria continued to call the Northern Kingdom after its founder's name. With the rise of Jehu (841) begins the Assyrian period.

(6) Assyria's designs upon the Mediterranean States opened with the expeditions of Ashur-nasir-pal (876). His successor Shalmaneser III was confronted by an Aramaean league under Hazael of Damascus, of which Israel was a prominent member. This league broke up, apparently at the rise of Jehu (841); and after fierce Aramaean attacks upon Israel and strife between Israel and Judah, the Hebrew monarchies enjoyed independence and power under the two great contemporaries, Jeroboam II of Israel, and Uzziah or Azariah of Judah (middle of the eighth century). The space devoted by the Biblical writers to the work of Elijah and Elisha suggests that they realised the significance of

the years of the decline of the dynasty of Omri. But it is noteworthy that they do not mention Assyria. The reigns of Jeroboam and Uzziah must have been far more important than the scanty Biblical records suggest; and fortunately the Assyrian records throw welcome light upon Palestinian history. They describe the steady westward pressure of Assyria, the fall, first of Damascus (732 B.C.) and then of Samaria (722), an attempt to capture Jerusalem (700), and the invasion of Egypt. For a time Assyria held Egypt and South-west Asia, and the extent of her influence is illustrated by archaeology (e.g. two cuneiform tablets at Gezer). But her supremacy was short-lived, and the brilliant reign of Ashurbanipal—to whose antiquarian interests we owe so much of our knowledge of early Babylon —was followed by the rapid downfall of Assyria, general unrest among the desert peoples, the invasion of Palestine by the Scythians, and the rise of the Medes.

(7) In 612 B.C. Nineveh fell to the Chaldaeans, or Babylonians, and their Median and Scythian allies. Egypt under Necho sought to revive her old empire, but the battle of Carchemish (605 B.C.) gave the legacy of Assyria to Nebuchadrezzar. With him we enter on the Chaldaean or Neo-Babylonian period. Judaean intrigues, the first exile in 597, the Fall of Jerusalem, and the second exile in 586, put an end to the Southern Kingdom. The Biblical writers, who had already ignored Samaria after 721 B.C., leave a gap in the history and pass on to the next period (below). Yet, from various sources it can be seen that the years after 721 were vital for the internal history of Palestine. Colonies were settled in Samaria by Assyria, tribes from outside entered the land, and, as we learn from a number of passages in the Prophets, there were important sociological changes (Jer. xlix 1; Ezek. xxxiii. 24; xxxv. 10; xxxvi. 2–5; Zeph. ii. 8). The general upheaval encouraged simpler conditions and more primitive ideas; and the disappearance of political emnity between north and south would facilitate a *rapprochement* between the people of the once rival States. Moreover, while in both Babylonia and Egypt this was a period of the revival of the past, the question is a vital one how far the

Judaism or Mosaism that is about to become prominent
in the next period can be viewed as a mere revival of the
old, or as some combination of old and new (see p. 194 f.).

(8) We now come to another great landmark in the
history of thought (p. 192). New political situations arose.
Circumstances had brought together Egypt and Greece
(in the "Amarna Age" it had been Crete); the Median
power passed to the Persians, and Cyrus, capturing Babylon
(539 B.C.), inaugurated the Persian or Achaemenid period.
The march of Persia upon Greece brought together the
East and the West. Her repulse and final defeat in 478
led up to the time when the tables were completely turned
by the eastern conquests of Alexander the Great (332–31
B.C.). Under the Persians the Jews were specially favoured,
and the rebuilding of their temple (516 B.C.) and the reorganisation of their religion, as described in the books of
Ezra and Nehemiah, make the Persian Age that of the
inauguration of Judaism.

Very little is known of the internal history of the Jews
beyond the fact that the cleavage between the Jews and
Samaritans—strictly a Jewish sect—evidently followed upon
a season of less hostile relations. Contract-tablets of the
reigns of Artaxerxes I (464–24) and Darius II (424–04) from
Nippur, on the River Chebar (Ezek. i. 1), contain many
Jewish names, and testify to the prosperity of the exiles.
The papyri discovered in the island of Elephantine, opposite
Syene or Assouan (first published in 1906), tell of a flourishing
military colony of "Aramaeans" or "Judaeans" (Jews),
whose temple, dating from before the time of Cambyses,
was destroyed by Egyptians in 411 B.C. They testify to
the conditions prevailing among the Jews outside the home-
land (see p. 150), and it is the more regrettable that
quantities of the papyri were carelessly lost or wilfully
destroyed by natives before the value of their contents had
been recognised. If only some of the sacred literature of
these Jews had been recovered!

(9) The Greek period of Jewish history (331–63 B.C.)
falls, after the death of Alexander the Great (323), into two
parts, the Ptolemaic and the Seleucid (from 201 B.C.

onwards). The darkness of Jewish history is suddenly lit
up by the books of the Maccabees and their account of the
valiant repudiation of the attempt of Antiochus Epiphanes
forcibly to Hellenize the Jews. The re-dedication of the
desecrated temple of Jerusalem in 164 was followed by the
Jews' attempts forcibly to Judaize their opponents, and at
last in 142–1 they were strong enough to gain their independence. Under the Hasmonaeans (142–63 B.C.) the new
Israel entered upon an age of expansion and recovered some
of her ancient glory. But the instability of the State was
soon apparent, and when Pompey entered Jerusalem and
the Jews became tributary to Rome (63 B.C.), we reach the
last act of the drama.

(10) The Roman and later periods naturally lie outside
the historical background of the Old Testament. But as
we peruse the Bible, book by book, and form our ideas of
the religion and its development, it is not a little astonishing,
directly we pass outside it, to observe the persistence of
features that take us back to the early days. Thus,
Palestinian (non-Jewish) coins of the first century A.D. bear
such devices as twin-pillars, comparable to Jachin and Boaz
(1 Kings vii. 21), horned altars (*ibid.* i. 50; ii. 28), portable
arks or coffers, and sacred stones. If "El Shaddai"
denotes a mountain god, it was from an Arabian mountain-
god, symbolised by a stone, that the notorious emperor
Elagabalus (A.D. 218–22) took his name. Old Oriental
deities survived, with their old names (Bel, Astarte, Tammuz,
etc.), or under other names, as when the war-god Resheph
was Hellenized as Apollo. The names of Hadad and Baal,
already familiar in Palestine in the Amarna Age, were still
honoured; and there were famous Baals of Baalbek (Helio-
polis) and of Damascus. At Baalbek licentious rites lasted
until the middle of the fourth century A.D.; just as human
sacrifice had long persisted among the Phoenicians and
Carthaginians, who justified it by the myth that the god
Kronos had sacrificed his only (or beloved ?) son to his
father.[1] And this Kronos appears on coins of Byblos of

---

[1] On the other hand, Gen. xxii. had previously replaced the
human sacrifice by an animal victim.

the second century B.C. with three pairs of wings, like the seraphim of Isaiah's inaugural vision (Isa. vi. 2). The emperor-cult is as conspicuous in the latest period as the worship of the divine king had been, long before, in the Amarna Age—though it has undergone some noteworthy changes—and there is even a sort of solar monotheism which recalls the reformed religion of Amenhotep IV, Ikhnaton.

In short, the religious development which is reflected in the Old and New Testaments becomes far more striking when we view it against the background of the lengthy religious history of Palestine and the surrounding lands. We have to approach the study of the Old Testament with a complete recognition of the mixed character of the population of the land, and of the many changes in its fortunes, and of the influences from outside, which must have drastically affected the course of life and thought. In the nature of the case it is not to be expected that the study will be an easy one.

CHAPTER VI

The Religion of the Old Testament

WE are apt to treat the Bible as a single book and forget the drama of history that lies behind it. Even if we recognise the historical differences between the Old Testament and the New and appreciate the drama of the rise of Christianity, we often overlook the significance of the stirring history from Pre-Mosaic times to the monarchy, from the prophets to the catastrophe of the Exile, from the post-exilic reorganisation to the Maccabaean revolt and its sequel. The value we attach to the Bible is based— whether we know it or not—upon the outcome of sweeping events, of periods of peace and war, of life and death. Of that greater history in which Biblical history must be placed we now possess some knowledge, and from what is known of the world's religions we can more vividly appreciate the nature of Biblical religion. Indeed, it is only as we cease to isolate it that we realise that the part this religion has played in human history, as compared with other religions, cannot be fortuitous.[1]

Even the fact that the three great religions, Judaism, Christianity and Islam were born in the same quarter of the world, viz. in South-west Asia, hardly seems accidental. In this area we find the usual realistic and practical types of thought that recur among primitive and ancient peoples. But everywhere the content of thought is shaped by everyday interests, by particular local, social and political circumstances, and this corner of Asia is, speaking broadly, the meeting-place of continents, and therefore, more fitted than any other region to stimulate life and thought. Moreover,

---

[1] It is particularly instructive to contrast the progressive history of Yahwism in Palestine with the fate of the monistic idealism of Ikhnaton and with that of the fine ethical religion of the Indian god Varuna (p. 94 f.). The oldest of the Indian hymns have a sublimity of expression that reminds one of Psalms and Job.

the effect of desert and of nomadic or semi-nomadic conditions in an area exposed to so many external influences has
throughout been an important factor in the growth of
religion. The austerity and monotony of desert life, in
contrast to the variety of settled town life, inevitably leave
their mark upon a people's ways of thinking. The nomad is
thrown back upon himself and, not being tied to any one
spot, is self-centred, and carries about with him his best
and his worst. His is a certain elemental simplicity.
Some of the most striking ideas in the Old Testament are
derived from semi-nomad and pastoral life—the tent
(2 Sam. xx. 1; Ps. lxi. 4 mg.; Isa. xxxiii. 20), the shepherds'
abode (Exod. xv. 13), and the god or king as a shepherd
(Ezek. xxxiv. 11 ff.). But desert influence upon Palestine
was not, of course, confined to any one period, and consequently it would be a mistake to suppose that such
phraseology was due wholly to the entry of Israelites in
the days of Moses and Joshua (p. 67).

A Christendom scarcely able to live up to its highest
ideals cannot condemn the rude standards and outspokenness
of ancient peoples who were below their best. The Old
Testament is the record of a very human folk. Here and
there we meet with what is crude and coarse (Gen. xix 8;
xxxviii.; Exod. iv. 24–26; Judges xix. 26), with deception
and lies (1 Sam. xxvii. 10–12; Jer. xxxviii. 24 ff.; Gen. xx.
12; cf. xii. 13, 19). In the life of Jacob there is a shrewdness
which befits his name; and although "Jacob"—the name
Jacob-el is also found[1]—has recently been explained to
mean "he (the god) watches over or guards," the "sup-
planted" Esau knew better (Gen. xxvii. 36). The old
writers do not always conceal the faults of their heroes—
even of Moses and Aaron (Num. xx. 12). The fanaticism
of Simeon and Levi is now condemned (Gen. xxxiv. 30;
xlix. 5–7), and now extolled (Judith ix. 2; cf. also Exod.
xxxii. 26 ff. with Deut. xxxiii. 8–11). Hosea denounces
Jehu's sanguinary zeal for Yahweh (2 Kings x. 10 ff.).
David's treatment of Joab and Shimei provoked no comment
(1 Kings ii. 5 f., 9); but the story of his high-handed conduct

[1] It is the name of a Hyksos king and of a place in Palestine.

in the matter of Uriah and Bathsheba—contrast Joseph in
Gen. xxxix. 9—is so written as to show explicitly how his
exhibition of Oriental tyranny marred the rest of his life.
Much more might be said; but, in estimating the men of
the Old Testament, one must remember the conditions
against which the best minds had to contend—this applies
equally to what Mohammed could achieve—and the more
highly appreciate the courage of the prophets in their
demand for God's own righteousness.

Israel was not blind to her faults, and the late *Testaments
of the Twelve Patriarchs* (Judah, Ch. 17) specially condemns
the love of money and of women.   In fact, the wealth of
the temple of Jerusalem, the frequent harsh treatment of
the poor (e.g. Neh. v. 5), and the striking financial promises
and threats of Deuteronomy (xxviii. 12 and *v.* 44) point to
an Israelite type other than that which identified the
"merchant" with the "Canaanite" (see the R.V. mg. in
Zeph. i. 11; Zech. xiv. 21; Prov. xxxi. 24).   A strong vein
of physical and sensuous imagery runs throughout the
writings; cf. the simile of a woman in travail, Isa. xiii. 8, etc.,
and of birth, Isa. xxxvii. 3; lxvi. 9 and Hos. xiii. 13.   The
union of Yahweh and Israel is represented as a marriage
union (p. 120); hence apostasy is "faithlessness" (Jer. iii. 20),
and "whoredom," especially in Hosea and Ezekiel; and the
latter's allegories (Chs. xvi., xxiii.) depict Israel's gross
ingratitude with Oriental vividness.   But while this idea
of a marriage union encouraged licentious rites, as symbolical
expressions of that union (hence, e.g., the necessity of the
prohibitions in Deut. xxiii. 17f.), it also encouraged conjugal
fidelity, by associating the marriage covenant among
Israelites with Yahweh's covenant with his people (cf. Mal.
ii. 10–16).   Indeed, the very passion which found an outlet
in sensuous "sacred" cults and human sacrifice forced the
earnest enquiry, what did God really require of men and
among men (Mic. vi. 8)?   Religion had tolerated the
"sacred" men and women (Gen. xxxviii. 21 mg.), but
religion also served to beautify the family life, always
characteristic of the Jews.

Among the Israelites warfare was "sanctified" (Jer. vi.

4 mg.), and was only made the more fierce by the deadly
khérem or ban (Isa. xxxiv. 5 mg.; cf. Deut. ii. 34). But
religion, which could encourage a terrible fanaticism (Num.
xxxi. 3, 15 ff.; Judges xxi. 11; 1 Kings xx. 42), could also
soften the bitterness of war (2 Kings vi. 21 f., contrast
1 Sam. xv.), and encourage the hope of a world at peace
(Isa. ii. 4). Strong in their loves as in their hates (cf. Jer.
xvii. 18; xviii. 21 ff.), these men of old are characterised by
an insistent earnestness and passion. It is not only "like
people, like priest" (Hos. iv. 9), men are like the gods they
worship (ix. 10; cf. Ps. cxv. 8; cxxxv. 18); and one, though
only one side of their character, is revealed in the conception
of an explosive or demonic Yahweh who manifests his
"sacredness" by destroying Gog (Ezek. xxxviii. 16–23), by
killing Uzzah for his well-meant anxiety to save the Ark
(2 Sam. vi. 6 ff.), or by threatening to make an end of a
"stiff-necked" people (Exod. xxxiii. 3). Many passages
could of course be set against these, and a selection that
gives only one side gives a very imperfect notion of the old
religion.

The God of Israel was above all, but yet He was effectively
in the midst of men. The relations between Yahweh and
Israel were so real and intimate that the Israelite could feel
the dangerous majesty of his God and yet glory in the
relationship. He could take it for granted, abuse it, and—
as is psychologically intelligible—suffer mental anguish in
consequence. The realism of the old religions of the East
accounts for the extremes of pride and humility, of abase-
ment and of egotism, and even of megalomania. From the
heights of confidence men leaped to rash over-confidence and
fell into the depths of despair. From the tremendous reality
of this *our* God, and of this *His* and therefore *our* world,
men passed into gross "this world-ness" and materialism;
and modern writers acquainted with Oriental life emphasise
its paradoxes and extremes, the sublime and the spiritual
mingling with the coarse and the cruel, and an utter self-
consciousness which when not guided aright engenders in
the individual a profound dissatisfaction that finds the cause
everywhere but within himself.

To know that "His thoughts are not your thoughts" (Isa. lv. 8 f.) betokens a consciousness of God's "otherness"— of the transcendence of Israel's immanent God; and it is because we actually pass in history from the heights of such a passage as this to the varied life and thought of the post-exilic age (Chap. xi.) that we cannot treat the whole of the Old Testament as of one stamp. Not Old Testament religion as a whole, but the ethical and spiritual ideas that we trace therein, give it its permanent value in human history; and when we say that we owe "ethical monotheism" to the Hebrew prophets, ethical righteousness without religious principles is as incomplete as is a monotheism without definite ethical principles.

"Hebrew," says Sir George Adam Smith, "may be called primarily a language of the senses. The words originally expressed concrete and material things and movements or actions which struck the senses and started the emotions." Metaphors and symbols abound, sometimes in a welter of confusion (Isa. xi. 10; xxviii. 18). But they were hardly recognised as such, and the true interpretation of such pictures as Joel's locusts (? invaders) is often elusive. The heart *is*—not, is *like*—water; the moon *is* blood(-like); the life is not *in* the blood, but it *is* the blood, as truly as an idol was taken to be a god and not merely the embodiment of a god. Likeness and identity are one: Jezebel calls Jehu "thou Zimri" (2 Kings ix. 31), and one could speak of a "[very] David" (Ezek. xxxiv. 23; xxxvii. 24), or "Elijah" (Mal. iv. 5). Hence it was easy to attribute to Daniel or to Enoch what a veritable Daniel or Enoch might have said (p. 28 f.); and we can understand why, in the books of Isaiah, Jeremiah and Ezekiel, there are passages, not written by these prophets, but in harmony with their style or thought.

Hebrew has no empty or abstract terms. A "house" is, rather, a "household" (Gen. vii. 1; Deut. xxv. 9; cf. Neh. vii. 4), hence the word-play on Yahweh's house or temple and David's household or dynasty in 2 Sam. vii. 5, 11, 27. As distinct from the empty space and time of the philosopher, "land" (*ereṣ*) is especially the land as inhabited, and "for ever" (*lĕ'ōlām*) means "permanently" rather than "eternally." Life and death are no mere physical states (p. 139). Names connote both the label and the packet, so to say; and importance is attached to the knowledge of a name (Gen. xxxii. 29; Judges xiii. 18), and to the change of a name (Gen. xxxv. 10), for the name is, as it were, an integral part of a man's nature and has a power of its own (Isa. xxx. 27). Instead of indirect address the Hebrew demands. the *ipsissima verba*. The use, in the sense of meditate, think, intend, of such words as *hāgāh*, *zāmam* (properly to croon, recite, etc.) "illustrates the Oriental's difficulty to think except aloud" (G. A. Smith). Yahweh's purpose is generally expressed in his own words (Gen. xviii. 20f.; Exod. xiii. 17; cf. Naaman in 2 Kings v. 11). Thought is activity, see Jer. xxix. 11; Ps. xl. 17; Prov. xxi. 5; note especially Joseph's words to his brothers: "ye thought (planned) evil against me, but God thought it for good" (Gen. l. 20). To "remember" implies action, and words for love, hate, anger, covet or desire, cover the practical results of these feelings. "Knowledge" involves also the power to act in accordance with it, whence the "knowledge of Yahweh" means, or rather, should mean, conformity to his will. To "judge" is to pass sentence and carry it out (cf. 1 Sam. xxiv. 15 mg.), and the "judges" of Israel (Othniel, Ehud, etc.) were more than dispensers of justice. The words "save" and "salvation" imply practical deliverance, and "peace" is more than a mere passive state. Hebrew thought is throughout practical and realistic.

Yahweh's feelings—e.g. his hatred of Esau—were manifested in the fate of Edom (Mal. i. 2f.); cf. also Joab's words to David, 2 Sam. xix. 5–7. As a general rule, prosperity and good fortune were regarded as signs of divine benevolence, and misfortune and sickness had, equally, some supernatural cause. Hence, the healing of sickness and the forgiveness of sin are one (Isa. xxxiii. 24; Ps. ciii. 3; cf. Mark ii. 1–12). The vicissitudes of history can be treated as reflecting the religious character of an individual or a people. Thus, in the "Deuteronomic" Book of Judges (p. 51) Yahweh sends harsh foes when the people forsake him after the death of a "judge"; and the writer of Chronicles explains the fortunes of Judah by the religious conduct of their kings (2 Chron. xii. 2; xx. 37; xxi. 10, etc.). It was considered possible to ascertain the cause of all misfortune (Joshua vii.; 1 Sam. xiv. 37f., see p. 152): it might be an ethical fault (the forswearing of an oath), or a ceremonial or ritual short-coming (the breaking of a tabu)— contrast the more ethical offences in Amos i. 3–ii. 5 with the wholly ritual offence of the sons of Aaron in Lev. x. 2. The fault might be an offence against Righteousness or a violation of the god's "Holiness" or "Sacredness." The tendency to associate misfortune and evil of all kinds with a supernatural cause was inveterate; and what the Old Testament typically associates with the worship of Yahweh was, in Palestine and elsewhere, otherwise associated with divers gods or demons. Traces of the "lower" forms of belief are not wanting in Yahwism itself (p. 124).

The primitive mind sees *ends* not beginnings; or rather, the consequences are immediately seen in the act itself, and preludes and sequels are not necessarily severed. The word for iniquity (*'āwōn*) means also the consequent punishment (Gen. xx. 9; 2 Kings vii. 9); cf. similarly the word "sin" (*khattāth*) in Zech. xiv. 19 mg. To "deal wisely" is to "succeed" (Joshua i. 8 mg.; cf. Job vi. 13 mg.). Righteousness brings its reward, and the "right[eous] acts of Yahweh" are those that repay men their rightful due (Judges v. 11). To "eat bread" is to earn a living (Amos vii. 12; cf. Mic. iii. 5, 11); "work" and "effect" are one (Isa. xxxii. 17), as also are "toil" and "wages" (*pĕ'ullah*). The word to "re-compense" or "re-tribute" (*gāmal*) also means to do that which will be re-paid. A "covenant" (*bĕrīth*) includes also the resultant harmony (Hos. ii. 18; Isa. xxviii. 15), to "redeem" (*pādah*) includes the redemption, and to "cover" or "wash away [sin]" (*kipper*)—the meaning is not certain—involves the subsequent reconciliation or at-one-ment. How readily men saw things un-analysed and in a complementary relationship or correlation is seen further when the word for client or sojourner (*gēr*) can also be used in Arabic of the patron or protector, and

Allah is the *jār* of the righteous.   The common word *ba'al*, lord, seems primarily to involve a dependent, just as the seigneur (senior) necessarily involves a junior, and the teacher a pupil.   The recognition of reciprocity occurs on a larger scale when we note (*a*) the original complementary character of tribal rights and duties; (*b*) the conception of reciprocity between gods and men, and (*c*) what corresponds to the conception of the conjoint Transcendence and Immanence of God (cf. Isa. lv. 8f., p. 179).

Another characteristic of Hebrew thought is the fusion of prelude and sequel or of purpose and result—illustrated among us in the homely complaint that children do things to annoy their elders; e.g. men make idols "that they (themselves) may be cut off" (Hos. viii. 4; cf. Jer. vii. 18; Mic. vi. 16; Isa. xliv. 9).   The consequences, which are represented as purposes, are inevitable but undesigned, for retrospect always tends to arouse convictions of intention, destiny, or fate.   In the New Testament the statement that things happened "that the Scriptures might be fulfilled" can mean that what happened did in fact—though not in intention—"fulfil" the Scripture quoted; and "fulfilment," in general, connotes not only the accomplishment of what has been foretold, but also the completing or supplementing of what went before (cf. 1 Kings i. 14; A.V. mg.).

It is an unhistorical view of Old Testament prophecy which supposes that the prophets consciously spoke for a distant future far outside their own horizon and that of their hearers (p. 172).   There is, to be sure, a fundamental interconnection between the Old Testament and the New Testament; but since both Christianity and Judaism can look back upon the Old Testament and find, on retrospect, each its own preliminary stages, it is necessary to bear in mind that the "fulfilment" or development was not precisely the same as regards the two religions.

Nothing is more common than the recurrence of similar *types* of situation, event or personality, so that a certain resemblance can be found between them and a progressive development traced.   The old-fashioned "typology" of a past age—e.g. the sacrifice of Isaac as a "type" of the death

of Jesus—has now given place to an objective historical and
psychological comparison of the "types," "patterns" and
resemblances, with results that are extremely interesting
for the study of different sorts of development.   In looking
forward, the prophets were determinists and optimists.
They knew that ultimately, at least, there would be a
better age, a glorious Israel, an all-powerful Yahweh, a
Messiah—but as to what precisely should be the constitution
of such an "Israel," Jews and Christians would give different
replies.   Apart from specific concrete hopes the prophets
had fundamental convictions of a Divine Righteousness, or
Rightness, that *must* manifest itself in the long run.   Confident specific expectations, on the one hand, and confidence
that Israel's God must be both Righteous and Holy, on the
other, represent respectively the more concrete and the
more dynamic outlooks upon the future, and the certainty
that the latter outlook was justified and must be "fulfilled,"
brought courage when specific expectations were dis-
appointed.   There were definite, tangible, hopes which men
sought to realise; there were inevitable truths that could
not but realise themselves in *some* form.[1]

Early thought was concrete, material, realistic.   The life
or soul is located in, if not rather identified with, blood,
fat, or oil.   Supernatural power or influence can have its
abode in trees, stones or water, in hair, clothing, etc.   There
are well understood ways of conveying such power—by
transferring clothes or personal objects, by touching, kissing,
or anointing.   In like manner, ideas, instead of being stated
as abstract principles, are embodied in narrative, e.g. the
story of Abigail and David (1 Sam. xxv.) illustrates, *inter
alia*, the soft answer that turns away wrath (Prov. xv. 1).
The permanent value of Old Testament narrative consists
in the beliefs and ideas that inform it, and that made and

---

[1] Cf. the remark of A. B. Davidson (*Theology of the Old Testament*,
p. 379) on the "day of the Lord."   It was connected with many
different things, "the prophets are in the dark as to the time of that
day, but they are in no ignorance of the principles of it."   The fact
is of great philosophical importance, for a deeper knowledge of God's
Universe tells men of fundamental essential processes rather than of the
form they have taken in the unknown past or will take in the future.

still make history. They may lie before us on the surface, or they may be recovered by modern "criticism." Israelite character shows itself in the way the history is written, and the writers felt that Yahweh had manifested *his* character in history. The "holiness" of Yahweh, shown in history, must be imitated by men (Lev. xi. 44), i.e. manifested in *their* conduct; and "righteousness," which was *his* attribute, must no less be that of his people.

The same concreteness of early modes of thought explains the symbolical acts of the prophets. Yahweh will break Egypt "as a potter's vessel is broken," declares one prophet (Isa. xxx. 14), and another breaks a bottle: "thus shall I break this people and this city" (Jer. xix. 11). But at a lower stage of mental development pottery is ceremonially broken, as a piece of "magic," in order to make a curse effective. Ezekiel realistically symbolises the siege of Jerusalem (iv. 1 ff.). But among many peoples there are imitative ceremonies before war which do not merely strengthen the *morale* but are regarded as ensuring success, for "well begun is half done." There is a note of reality about such acts, and the gulf is not a wide one between actions which enable men to visualise and "realise" utterances, and the "magical" belief that the acts themselves are effective. It is not difficult for us to understand the psychological efficacy of various ordeals (e.g. read Num. v. 19–22), or the power of the spoken word, notably, of course, in blessings and cursings (as in the story of Balaam, Num. xxii. ff.); and men have always found it easy to believe that sacrificial rites are effective in themselves (cf. the warning Prov. xxi. 27).

Yahweh, like other gods, was believed to possess human feelings (anthropopathism), if not human form (anthropomorphism). But in every case of what may be called "anthropism" it is useful to ask whether the human language is an unavoidable "accommodation," as when a god is said to love or to be angry. Sometimes the language may derive ultimately from image-worship; so, possibly, when a letter is brought before Yahweh for him to see and hear (2 Kings xix. 14–16; cf. 1 Sam. x. 25; also Joshua xxiv. 26 f.).

On the other hand, the institution of the "divine kingship" may lie behind the phrase, to "lift up" a man's face (Mal. i. 8). In the Amarna Letters the divine Pharaoh is said to "cast down" the face of a man; and the phrase to "seek the face" is used by the Amorite Aziru in his letter to the divine Pharaoh and by the Psalmist in his address to Yahweh (Ps. xxiv. 6; xxvii. 8, etc.).[1] Gods eat and drink (Deut. xxxii. 38; cf. Lev. xxi. 6; Ps. l. 13), and Yahweh enjoys a "satisfying odour" (Gen. viii. 21). They sleep and must be awakened (cf. Ps. xliv. 23)—by trumpets (Num. x. 9f.); and when aroused they glory in a fight (Ps. lxxviii. 65; cf. Isa. lxiii. 1–6). If they are tired they must rest (Exod. xxxi. 17; contrast Isa. xl. 28). Anthropic also is the appeal to Yahweh's prestige (Exod. xxxii. 12; Num. xiv. 16; Joshua vii. 9), and his care for his own Name (Ezek. xx. 9; cf. Deut. xxxii. 27).

Anthropism as such is not "primitive." It is capable of expressing lofty sentiments. It has its strength and its weakness. Thus, as regards sin and forgiveness, Yahweh may "visit" a sin upon a man or pass it by (Mic. vii. 18). He may not remember it (Hos. viii. 13; Isa. xliii. 25), he may forget it (Amos viii. 7; ? Job xi. 6 mg.). He may cover it up and not reckon it as iniquity (Ps. xxxii. 2). A bribe blinds the judge (Deut. xvi. 19; cf. also Gen. xx. 16); but Yahweh is too pure to gaze on evil (Hab. i. 13). Indeed, sin is something which a benevolent deity might "wink at" (cf. Acts xvii. 30). When sin thus becomes a personal matter between the god and the offending individual or nation, there is a risk that the tendency will arise to attribute favouritism or arbitrariness to God, or for a people to expect special treatment (note the warning of Amos iii. 2). Moreover, the victims of a man's sin are not necessarily taken into account. Ezekiel (Ch. xviii.), one of the two great prophets of individual responsibility (p. 118), teaches that at any point in the life of an individual or of a family there can be an immediate passage from a state of righteousness to one of wickedness, or the reverse. The past is wiped out and has no effect upon the new state.

---

[1] For other examples, see p. 90 f.

Ezekiel is characterised by his insistence upon Yahweh's holiness.   As a priest he would be familiar with the ritual occasions when a man passed from the condition of ordinary everyday life to a state of ceremonial purity and back again (cf. Exod. xix. 10 f., 14 f., 22; 1 Sam. xxi. 4 f.).   But here sin is regarded as a matter of status rather than of ethical misbehaviour, as was the prevailing teaching of the prophets (p. 188).   Further, when ideas of group solidarity prevail, the acts of a man do not concern himself alone, they affect the rest of the group and its subsequent fortunes: others profit or suffer through him, as the case may be (p. 118).   This is also true of a group of nations, and Israel came to feel that she had some significance for other peoples because her Yahweh was God also of all peoples (pp. 155 ff.).

Ideas of right and wrong take a less personal form when wrong-doing, however unintentional, more or less automatically and inevitably brings retribution upon the offender, if not upon the group of which he is part.   Here there is, as it were, an impersonal process.   Speculation swings between conceptions of a personal God who repays and some more automatic requital.   From an early date in the history of religion these two beliefs struggle for mastery: the belief in a personal relation between gods and men and one that implies an inevitable impersonal and automatic process.   The ethical monotheism of Israel sought to combine the two by its conviction that a personal ethical Yahweh *must* inevitably punish offenders, even his own people: he is bound, as it were, by his very righteousness.

Anthropic religion can both stimulate religious reflection and misdirect it.   The consciousness of God's holiness carries with it that of His relation to Man: "holiness means kinship to the worshippers and their god" (Robertson Smith).   The experience of a *personal* relationship with an unseen Supreme Being evoked the conception of a *personal* God; but in framing appropriate symbolism based upon purely human relations, it was found, for example, that marital imagery had its dangers, and Rabbinical Judaism

avoided it.[1] The concept "God" must always have a
meaning, a content. Everything has depended upon the
character attributed to Him, and in and behind the Bible
are the efforts to formulate and purify men's ideas. *What*
was God? How could an Oriental people, accustomed to
arbitrary personal rule and to extremes of temper, think
of a God who was not a man that He should change (Num.
xxiii. 19; 1 Sam. xv. 29), but who might change His purpose
as regards His people? Israel solved this problem when
the name Yahweh—whatever its original form and meaning
may have been (p. 41, n. 2)—is supplemented by the words
"I will be that I will be" (Exod. iii. 14 mg.): that is, Yahweh
will be—what he proves to be. At times Yahweh might seem
negligible (Zeph. i. 12), like the helpless deities of Israel's
neighbours; but by maintaining the conviction that Yahweh
was always the Holy and Righteous One of Israel, Israel
both preserved and developed her ethical monotheism.
Whatever Yahweh did would prove to be righteous, i.e.
right. It was Israel's consolation that there is a one and
only God, a loving God, whose actions would sooner or later
be found to be intelligibly just. From Ethical Monotheism
the road led to the conviction that God's Universe, too,
must be intelligibly right; although it did not lie within the
power of Israel to take those forward steps which, through
the influence of Greek thought, led ultimately to the science
and philosophy of the West.

Anthropism is world-wide. By uniting God and Man it
has led Man to know more of his nature, his powers, and
what God requires of him. By uniting Man, God and His
Universe, it made Man feel his supremacy over all other
life (Gen. i. 26ff.), his inferiority only to the superhuman
(Ps. viii.), and his nothingness before a God whose "otherness" was an experience no less real than the experience of
intimate relationship. Indian religion might affirm that the
soul of Man is, in the last analysis, one with the soul of the
Universe; but the religion of Israel was not pantheistic but

---

[1] Even personal names expressing the kinship of Yahweh and the
Israelite ceased to be made when the difference between God and
Man was more keenly felt.

theistic; and Man was what he was—or rather would be what he was meant to be—only through his relationship with God. Israel took no interest in the cosmos as such—but only in its *personal* significance for the individual—and to her is due the imperishable truth that men are to search for the ultimate principles in the facts of human development no less than in the "outside" physical world.

Religion, as we have it in the Bible, has, throughout, the closest points of contact with other religions. Yet it is unique. And in a sense it is a torso, in that, long before its earliest recoverable form, it had had a history; and the tendencies of modern thought suggest that in coming to understand it better, this age is contributing to its further development. What, then, is there in Old Testament religion, besides its realism and its anthropism, that is so dynamic?

CHAPTER VII

The God, the People and the Land

THE Old Testament (or "Covenant") and the New Testament
are linked together by the presence in both of similar
fundamental ideas. In the one we find Israel and her
covenant with Yahweh, in the other, the new Israel and a
new covenant (Heb. xii. 24). From the links between
Israel, the land of her fathers and Jerusalem, we pass, in
the New Testament, to profounder conceptions of the home
of this new Israel and of a Heavenly Zion. Deep-reaching
ruling ideas are interconnected: Israel and her God, His
rule or kingdom, the kingdom of Heaven, the body of Israel
united by their God and His Anointed King, the ideal
"Body of Christ," the Fellowship of Saints. Here are
specially developed forms of what can be found in other
religions, for ultimately we deal with the conception of a
group, its constituents, function, coherence and binding
principles. This complex of ideas involves conceptions of
the group and its god, the specific "father" relation between
a god and the group, the "sonship" of the group, and the
"brotherhood" of its members. Hence the group-idea has
many forms and ramifications. It is capable of the pro-
foundest developments; and although it is world-wide, it
is the particular history of it in and behind the Bible that
makes Biblical religion unique. It will be helpful to think,
first, of a triangular relationship between Yahweh, Israel
and Palestine, since, in course of development, ideas of
God are purified, and the Israel of history and her land are
replaced by Man and the world in which he finds himself,
and there is a new triangular relationship, namely, God,
Man and the Universe. To put it otherwise, our conceptions
of Man, God and the Universe find an early and peculiarly
pregnant expression in Israel's old-time convictions of herself,
her God and her land.

At the outset it is to be noticed that a group can so regard itself as a unit that a personal name may have a collective meaning. Israel says to Sihon "let *me* pass through thy land" (Num. xxi. 22; cf. "thy brother Israel," xx. 14; also *v.* 18). Jacob says, "I am few in number."[1] More explicitly one speaks of the "house" of Joseph (cf. Joshua xvii. 16f.), Ephraim (Judges x. 9), David (2 Sam. vii. 26), etc.; and the Assyrians long continued to call Samaria "the house of Omri" after its founder.   So, a group is named after its founder or ancestor—or conversely, a fictitious group-ancestor is invented, e.g. Eber for the Hebrews (Gen. xi. 15), and Anak for the "sons of Anak" (i.e. giants).   In the stories of Jacob (or Israel), Esau (or Edom), etc., there is a mixture of tribal and individual elements which requires careful discrimination (cf. p. 70). For example, the social difference between Sarah and Hagar or between the Aramaean wives of Jacob and his concubines (Gen. xxx.) seems to indicate differences of status between the tribes or clans who are their "sons" (xxi. 10; xxv. 12ff., cf. *v.* 6).   Similarly, the story how Reuben lost the birth-right (1 Chron. v. 1f. and refs.) describes the secondary position of this tribe, rather than accounts for it.   The genealogy of Caleb as part of the tribe of Judah in 1 Chron. ii. 18ff. appears likewise to point to clan and not individual movements and relations.   Above all, when we observe the identity of the *family* of Jacob–Israel which went down into Egypt (Gen. xlvi. 8–27) with the tribes and clans of the *people* Israel (Num. xxvi. 5–51; cf. 1 Chron. ii.–viii.; Exod. vi. 14ff.), we have to enquire whether the traditions of the original entry of the "patriarch" Jacob–Israel into Palestine echo traditions of the entry of the Israelite nation itself (p. 128, cf. p. 58f.).

When a group feels its solidarity, the offence of any one constituent endangers the whole. Thus, all Israel is endangered by the offences of Benjamin (Judges xx. 13), or of the eastern tribes (Joshua xxii. 13ff.), or of Achan (vii.

---

[1] Gen. xxxiv. 30; cf. further, Judah's invitation to his brother Simeon (Judges i. 3), and the Danites' words to Micah (*ibid.*, xviii. 23 mg.).

11 ff.).   Or vengeance is taken for the offence of an individual upon his whole family or household (1 Sam. xxii. 16; Gen. xii. 17; cf. xx. 18; 2 Sam. iii. 29; xxi. 6; Jer. xxiii. 34). Against this custom there are famous protests, by Abimelech (Gen. xx. 4), Moses (Num. xvi. 22) and David (2 Sam. xxiv. 17); and the Deuteronomic law (xxiv. 16; cf. Amaziah in 2 Kings xiv. 5 f.) is directly aimed against an inveterate practice which never quite died out.   But if the sins of a few fall upon the many, conversely the many may be saved by the merits of a few.   The presence of ten righteous men would have delivered Sodom (Gen. xviii. 22 ff.; in Jer. v. 1 one would suffice), and a powerful intercessor can take upon himself the consequences of a people's sin (Exod. xxxii. 32 f.; cf. 2 Sam. xiv. 9), and pray on behalf of them (1 Sam. xii. 19, 23; Isa. xxxvii. 4).

Hence, special individuals, such as the "Servant of the Lord," can save their people (Isa. liii. 4–6), though, in other circumstances, not even Moses or Samuel (Jer. xv. 1), or Noah, Daniel and Job (Ezek. xiv. 14) can mediate. Accordingly, a group may be represented by pre-eminent individuals who have greater powers and responsibilities than the rest.   Emphasis is laid upon the functions of the prophets (Ezek. iii. 17 ff.; xxxiii. 1–9); they are the nation's watchmen (Isa. lvi. 10).   The sins of the priest imperil the people (Mic. iii. 12); and the king, who in the pre-exilic religion of Israel was evidently the head of the cult, wielded a power more "mystical" than that of modern rulers or leaders (cf. p. 162).   Not only does the anointed king represent the kingdom (e.g. Isa. x. 5 ff.; Ezek. xvii. 22–24; xxviii.–xxxii.), but a people could figuratively be called "king" or "anointed" (Ps. xxviii. 8).   This corporate way of thinking is of fundamental importance in Biblical and early religion.

In general, the individual felt himself bound up with his group and its traditions.   But in the stormy history of Israel there came a time of change and disintegration, marked by ideas of individualism and individual responsibility.   Men resented the notion that they should suffer for the faults of others; they complained: "the fathers have

eaten sour grapes and the children's teeth are set on edge"
(Jer. xxxi. 29f.; Ezek. xviii. 2ff.; cf. Lam. v. 7).   This the
prophets deny: everyone suffers for his own sin; Yahweh's
relation is not with the national group as a whole, or through
its representative royal or priestly head; but it is immediate,
with every man.   "All souls are mine," each man shall be
judged according to his ways (Ezek. xviii. 4, 20); there shall
be a New Covenant written in men's hearts (Jer. xxxi. 31ff.),
and Yahweh's word shall be nigh unto every man (Deut.
xxx. 11–14).   But men cannot have it both ways.   If there
is no corporate responsibility there can also be no corporate
merits; men can no longer profit from the righteous deeds
of others, each man is to be judged by God in and by himself.
Consequently, individualism and freedom from collective
responsibility have their disadvantages, and as the years
pass, the old group or national idea reappears, though in a
new form.   Even Jeremiah's New Covenant was to be a
national covenant, like the earlier one; and once more the
individual lives as an integral part of his community, sharing
its weal and woe, participating in its gains and losses.   Yet,
in the individualism of Jeremiah and Ezekiel there had been
a great break in the development of thought; and although it
is natural to associate the break with the sweeping changes
round about the time of the Exile, the actual historical
circumstances which led to the new reorganisation of Israel
and its new consciousness of solidarity are extremely
obscure (pp. 180, 192f.).

Besides the feeling of group unity or solidarity there is
also a unity in time, betokening a consciousness of a continuity of tradition.   Thus, Yahweh's dealings with and
promises to the patriarchs ensure the welfare of those who
regard themselves as their descendants; and for Yahweh
to "remember Abraham, Isaac and Jacob" is to help the
people of the Covenant.[1]   In like manner, Yahweh's
promises to David benefit the people (Ps. lxxxix. 49; cxxxii;
Isa. lv. 3).   Yahweh remembers wrong-doing to the third
and fourth generation, but keeps his covenant to a thousand

---

[1] Cf. Exod. xxxii. 13; Isa. xli. 8; Lev. xxvi. 42, 45; Ps. cv. 42;
Ezek. xxviii. 25; xxxvii. 25, etc.

(Deut. v. 9; vii. 9). Certain animosities become almost "canonical" (Amalek, Deut. xxv. 17–19); and while the worst effects of some religious or political acts may be more or less self-evident (Jeroboam, 1 Kings xiv. 16; Manasseh, 2 Kings xxi. 11 ff.), it is due to ideological rather than to historical continuity when later generations link together the Fall of Man and the persistence of sin (Wisdom ii. 24), the First and the Second Adam (1 Cor. xv. 22), and the Old Jerusalem and the New (Rev. xxi. 2). However familiar this interconnection of Biblical ideas may be to us, the internal history of Palestine was at times so broken, and so much of ancient tradition has been lost, that such continuity of thought as we do find is the more striking. Whereas Ezekiel could conceive an abrupt break with the past (p. 112), the dominant conviction was one that united past and present and future, and saw a unity and continuity in history—and it was this that preserved Israel as a people and as an "idea."

Old Testament religion is concerned with Yahweh, Israel and Israel's land. People and land are essentially one (cf. Hos. i. 2), each is Yahweh's "inheritance" (1 Sam. xxvi. 19; cf. Zech. ii. 12), and Israel is sown or planted (Hos. ii. 23; Amos ix. 15) in a land which Yahweh gave his servant Jacob (Ezek. xxviii. 25). Yahweh dwells in the midst of it; it is "sacred" or "holy," and the people, too, must be "holy" (Deut. vii. 6, etc.).[1] Israel, being holy or sacred, is inviolable, like the first-fruits that belong to Yahweh (Jer. ii. 3); and Yahweh will punish all who harm his people, his inheritance.[2] There is a strong sense of soil (Prov. x. 30): the land is inalienably Israel's (Lev. xxv. 23; cf. the denunciations, Isa. v. 8; Mic. ii. 2; Ezek. xlvi. 18). Bloodshed and sin "pollute" it (Jer. ii. 7; iii. 9; Num. xxxv. 33; Lev. xviii. 25, 28), and Yahweh in his just anger "polluted" his "inheritance" when he handed it over to

---

[1] Lev. xvii.–xxvi., an independent collection of ceremonial and moral laws and exhortations, is known by scholars as "the Law (or Code) of Holiness," because of the stress laid upon Yahweh's holiness which must also be imitated by his people.

[2] Jer. xii. 14; cf. Gen. xii. 3; Zech. ii. 8; Ps. cv. 14 f.; Judith xvi. 17.

Babylon (Isa. xlvii. 6). Food eaten away from it is "unclean" (Hos. ix. 3; Ezek. iv. 13; cf. Dan. i. 8), for other lands are ritually "unclean" (Amos vii. 17)—cf. Joshua xxii. 19, where the land of Yahweh's tabernacle is contrasted—and David, driven out from Yahweh's inheritance, must worship another god (1 Sam. xxvi. 19f.). Naaman must take away with him Israelite soil in order to worship Yahweh fitly in his own land (2 Kings v. 17), and strangers entering the sacred land must learn the "cult" of "the god of the land" (xvii. 26f.).

Israel is "Yahweh's people" (Num. xi. 29; cf. Moab, the "people of Chemosh," Jer. xlviii. 46); his name is "called upon" her (Num. vi. 27; contrast Isa. lxiv. 19). Indeed, the name of a people and that of a deity may be identical (e.g. Gad, Edom), and an Arabian tribe in the seventh century B.C. is called "Ishtar of the Heavens" (i.e. the Queen of Heaven, Jer. vii. 18). Yahweh is the spouse of Israel (Jer. iii. 14, xxxi. 32; cf. Isa. liv. 5, Ezek. xvi., xxiii.); he has betrothed her to himself (Hos. ii. 19f.), and taken her under a covenant (Jer. xxxi. 31f.). For her apostasy she is divorced (Jer. iii. 8; Isa. l. 1), and during the Exile is barren and childless (Isa. liv. 1, 6; cf. lxii. 4f.). Israel is also his first-born (Exod. iv. 22; cf. Ephraim, Jer. xxxi. 9; Hos. xi. 1–3). The Israelites are his children: "my children whom thou didst bare unto me" (Ezek. xvi. 20f.; cf. also Hos. ii. 1f.). Yahweh is the parent (Deut. xxxii. 6, 18f.), and it is he who can close or open the womb (Gen. xx. 18; 1 Sam. i. 5f.; Isa. lxvi. 9).

Yahweh sends or withholds rain and all the gifts of nature, for he is the cause of all fertility (Lev. xxvi. 19f.; 1 Kings viii. 35f.; Isa. i. 19; Jer. v. 24; Ezek. xxxvi. 29f.). His people's cause is his own, he "sends" them to battle (1 Kings viii. 44), and they fight "the wars of Yahweh" (1 Sam. xviii. 17; cf. Num. xxi. 14; xxxi. 3). In the old religions the gods maintain treaties and covenants, and false oaths and broken covenants are religious offences (Saul and the Gibeonites, 2 Sam. xxi. 1f. [see Joshua ix. 15ff.]; Zedekiah, Ezek. xvii. 11–19). Law and justice are secured by chosen "divine" representatives (*Elohim*, see Exod. xxi. 6 and xxii.

9, 28 mg.), or by sacred oaths of purgation (Exod. xxii. 9; I Kings viii. 31f.), ordeals (e.g. Num. v. 21), or lots (Joshua vii. 19; cf. I Sam. xiv. 40ff.).[1] Yahweh also reveals his will by the prophets (Amos iii. 7), or by such things as censers and rods (Num. xvi.f.). Thus men can rely directly or indirectly upon Yahweh (e.g. Ps. xx. 7); but "confidence" must not be "carelessness" (cf. Isa. xxxii. 9 mg.), and men must learn to know when to leave their cause to Yahweh and when to avenge themselves (I Sam. xxv. 26 mg.).

Yahweh is the god of the children of Israel. But a non-Israelite could be affiliated or adopted. There were specific ceremonies of recognition (Gen. xxx. 3; l. 23); and circumcision of the male, a necessary rite before a man could marry an Israelite woman (cf. Gen. xxxiv. 15), became indispensable for the new-born babe of Israel, and the token of Yahweh's covenant (Gen. xvii.). To be uncircumcised was to be outside the pale, and on entering the "sacred" land all Israel must be circumcised (Joshua v.). The position of a woman was secured, either by her husband, while he lived, or by the fact that she was the mother of a son: thus a distinction is drawn between the married sister of a priest and a sister who is unmarried, or widowed, or divorced and childless (Lev. xxi. 3; xxii. 12f.). By an interesting fiction a childless man could take a concubine by whom his wife could be "built up" (Gen. xvi. 2; xxx. 3 mg.), or the widow of a childless man could be taken by his brother or the next-of-kin and the children reckoned to him (Deut. xxv. 5–10, the Levirate marriage).

As a member of a group a man had both privileges and responsibilities: in I Sam. xxx. 24f. it is discussed whether those that take part in a fight should share the booty with the non-combatants (cf. similarly, Num. xxxi. 27ff.). Theoretically all Israel are holy, a people of priests (Exod. xix. 6; cf. Isa. lxi. 6); but in practice the priests form a special class. There are stories of fierce jealousy about

[1] See Prov. xvi. 33: "the lot is cast into the lap, but the whole decision thereof is from Yahweh" (cf. xviii. 18). Hence the guilty Achan is exhorted to confess (Joshua vii. 19) since otherwise the implication is that the lot-taking which was controlled by Yahweh (*vv.* 13–15) was at fault.

sacred rights in Num. xvi. (cf. also xii. 2). Even the
aspiration that all Yahweh's people might be prophets
(Num. xi. 29) would in practice be embarrassed by the
frequent difficulty of distinguishing between the true
prophets and the false (p. 170). But there is, especially in
Deuteronomy, a strong democratic note, and the community as a whole is enjoined to recognise its common
responsibility.[1] In fact, Yahwism, at its best, is the religion
of a people, and the Bible is, in a sense, the story of a people's
complementary duties and rights.

Religion unites the people. The "holy seed" should not
intermarry with another people: indeed, they should destroy
them, or at least not "seek their welfare."[2] Nehemiah
(xiii. 23ff.) demands, not only purity of blood, but also
purity of language. Theoretically, at least, all the first-
born are Yahweh's (Exod. xiii. 2; xxxiv. 19f.); but the
Levites are taken instead of them (Num. iii. 12). His also
are the first-fruits (cf. Jer. ii. 3); for everything is his and
men do but repay what he has given them (Deut. xxvi. 10;
1 Chron. xxix. 14f.). Only in a "sacred" state may men
perform "sacred" duties, whether sacrificial or military.
Certain tabus must then be observed (1 Sam. xiv. 24;
xxi. 5f.; 2 Sam. xi. 11): shoes must be removed on sacred
soil (Joshua v. 15), and special clothing may be necessary
during a temple-ceremony (cf. 2 Kings x. 22). Family
sacrifices (1 Sam. xx. 6), common meals and festal occasions—
especially agricultural festivals—kept alive the group-
feeling; and traditions told how all Israelites had a common
ancestry and a common history. This sense of solidarity
was the ground of all ethical appeals (Mal. ii. 10; Neh. v. 5;
Job xxxi. 15); and the story of the covenant between
Yahweh and his people (Jer. xxxi. 33; Zech. viii. 8; cf. Hos.
ii. 23), how it was instituted, broken and restored, how it
was the beginning of Israel's history and was to be the
hope of the future—all this was founded upon Israel's

[1] Cf. xiii. 9, xvii. 7, xxi. 18–21, also Num. xv. 35, Josh. vii. 25,
Judges xx., cf. vv. 23, 28.

[2] Ezra ix. 2, 12, 14; cf. Ps. cvi. 34f.; cf. also the stipulations
concerning Ammon, Moab and Edom (Deut. xxiii. 2–8).

experience of the relations between herself and Yahweh. Nor is this all, for this relationship between Israel and Yahweh rested upon that between the people themselves: what God was for Man might depend upon what men were for one another.[1]

Behind the history of Israel lie periods of disintegration and of fresh reorganisation (p. 180), and what the best minds of Israel spiritualised goes back to cruder ideas of the relationship between gods, men and their land. The function of the deities in furthering the increase of man and nature is, elsewhere at least, often understood more physically. Man and nature are closely akin, if not one, so that, whereas in the Old Testament sin disturbs the land (Isa. xxiv. 5; xxxiii. 9), and it is Yahweh who punishes men by sending drought (Jer. iii. 3; l. 38; cf. v. 24f.), more realistic ideas closely connect wrong-doing and nature (cf. Gen. iii. 17f. and Rom. viii. 19, 22), and the rejuvenation of nature and national restoration (cf. Isa. lv. 12f.). In general, either the social order and the order of nature were linked together through an ethical and omnipotent Yahweh, Lord of the Universe, or, in more elemental fashion, all life and growth, human and other, were regarded as being in some way immediately interconnected. Even sacrificial ceremonies were essentially practical (p. 151), and licentious rites were not mere sexual license but served some religious purpose (p. 103).

The relationship between Yahweh and Israel was definitely not an identity, as it might seem to be when a group bore the name of a god (e.g. Gad); yet it was so close that at times Israel's misfortunes reflect upon Yahweh, and to wrong Israel was to wrong him. The highest thought had to contend with the dangerous conception of an almost automatic relationship, as though Yahweh were "immanent" in Israel or existed for her. It was as difficult for Israel to conceive of *her* Yahweh as a Being apart from her, as for the

---

[1] The conception of *khésed*, "leal love" (G. A. Smith), "charity" (in the undebased sense of the word), that is, of the bond joining God and men, is one of the most characteristic contributions of Israelite religion to humanity.

earnest theist of to-day to imagine the nature of *his* God before the dawn of Man and the emergence of human personality.

Yahwism, when looked at in the light of the modern comparative study of religions, is seen to stand between crude and primitive ideas of the relationship between gods, men and their land, and more refined and philosophical enquiries into the problems of the relations between God, Man and the Universe. In the Old Testament is Israel's attempt to answer still unanswered questions; in it are traces enough of less developed ideas alien to Yahwism, and also of pointers towards conceptions which Judaism itself failed to assimilate and develop. To Israel mankind is eternally indebted for a few centuries of history during which her best minds took over an older inheritance, remoulded it, and gave it a form which subsequently helped to make Western thought what it became.

Palestine was a land of mixed peoples, and Old Testament history and religion extend over some busy ages. Hence Old Testament religion inevitably contains "higher" and "lower" ideas, ideas of permanent worth and ideas more in harmony with earlier or transient conditions of life and thought. The Yahwism of the Old Testament is, therefore, no simple religion, and it is impossible to give a simple account of it. In this chapter we have been considering certain features of the practical religious life in Israel in all its realism, we have next to leave the visible work-a-day world and consider the not less real realm of the Unseen.

CHAPTER VIII

The Unseen World

From the typical practical interrelations between Yahweh, Israel and the land of her fathers, we turn to Israel's relation to the Unseen World. Yahwism grew up in a world of gods and spirits richer than the Old Testament allusions suggest. We do indeed read of hairy satyrs (Lev. xvii. 7; 2 Chron. xi. 15 mg.), and of a nocturnal demon Lilith (Isa. xxxiv. 14; cf. Apocalypse of Baruch x. 8); and the word used in Accadian of a protective being is applied in a derogatory sense to the gods of the heathen (Deut. xxxii. 17; Ps. cvi. 37). But the results of excavation (charms, scarabs, figurines of tutelary deities) show that Palestine was not so different from her neighbours as the Old Testament might suggest, and numerous passages in post-Biblical literature prove that Jewish monotheism never succeeded in driving out Yahweh's rivals and foes.

Even in the Old Testament Yahweh is not quite alone (p. 143). He sits enthroned, surrounded by his court of divine beings, his angels or messengers (Ps. ciii. 19, 21; Job i. 6; ii. 1; iv. 18), later called "watchers" (Dan. iv. 17). He has his council of holy ones whom he consults (Ps. lxxxix. 7; Zech. xiv. 5), his mighty ones (Joel iii. 11), an armed "camp" (Gen. xxxii. 2), the "host of heaven," with a heavenly leader (1 Kings xxii. 19ff.; Joshua v. 14). These last are the stars (Job xxxviii. 7) who are worshipped by the heathen (Deut. iv. 19; xvii. 3), and take sides and fight like the men on earth (Judges v. 20). The "we" in Yahweh's mouth (Gen. i. 26; iii. 22; xi. 7; Isa. vi. 8), and the picturesque description of Moses as the steward of his household (Num. xii. 7) can be claimed as further evidence that Israel's Yahweh was by no means necessarily thought of as ruling alone in solitary grandeur. But in the Old Testament all supernatural beings are subordinate to Yahweh (Neh. ix. 6), and "the adversary" (Satan, Job i. 6; Zech. iii. 1f.) who

opposes or accuses men, has not yet become the tempter,
the prince of evil, the opponent of God, as in dualistic
religion (cf. Wisd. ii. 24; p. 205). Yet there are heavenly
beings who have impiously descended and mingled with
the daughters of men (Gen. vi. 3), and others who are foes
of Yahweh and liable to condemnation (Job iv. 18; Ps.
lxxxii. 6f.; Isa. xxiv. 21f.).

When we ask *where* Yahweh was supposed to dwell, we
raise ultimate questions of men's conceptions of God. The
Biblical narrative elaborates the view, not so much that
Yahweh was worshipped almost from the beginning of man's
history (Gen. iv. 26), or that he was the God of the fathers
(e.g. Exod. iii. 15), as that the Yahweh who revealed himself
at Horeb at the beginning of Israel's national history had
been previously known to the patriarchs in Palestine as
El Shaddai (Ex. vi. 3). Yahweh is especially associated with
Sinai or Horeb, the "mount of God" (iii. 1; cf. xix. 18;
xxiv. 9f.), and thither Elijah fled when Yahweh's altars
in Palestine were destroyed (1 Kings xix. 8–10, 14). And
just as it is said, later, that the Law was given by angels
(p. 36 n.), so certain passages state that it is not Yahweh but
his angel who goes with Israel—it is substantially Yahweh
himself (Exod. xxiii. 20ff.)—or that he sends his Face or
Presence (xxxiii. 14ff.; cf. the "angel of the Presence,"
Isa. lxiii. 9). Moreover, the Ark is addressed as "Yahweh,"
and is not less powerful than he is (Num. x. 35f.; xiv. 44f.;
cf. 1 Sam. iv. 3–8). In fact, the journey of the Ark and its
varying fortunes (cf. 2 Sam. vii. 7; xi. 11), until at length
it is installed once and for all in the new temple of Jerusalem
(1 Kings viii. 1–11), is one of the leading *motifs* in the story
of early Israel. The Pillar of Cloud and Fire was another
visible representative or embodiment of Yahweh (Num.
xiv. 14). Thus, emphasis is laid upon the way in which
Israel was supernaturally guided, not by Yahweh, but by
some divine representative.[1] On the other hand, a series
of striking poetical passages tell of the triumphant journey

[1] Of the pressing invitation to the father-in-law of Moses to serve
as a guide (Num. x. 29–32) we only know that, later on, he is actually
found with the Israelites in Palestine (Judges i. 16; iv. 11).

of Yahweh himself from Edomite or other parts of South
Palestine (Deut. xxxiii. 2; Judges v. 4; Hab. iii. 3; Ps.
lxviii. 7).

The Israelites, entering into what was said to be the
land of the fathers, found themselves among a polytheistic
people.   They intermarried with them and worshipped their
gods (Deut. vii. 3; xii. 2; Judges iii. 7; Ps. cvi. 36ff.).   The
"Song of Moses" vividly depicts the decay which followed
when the people forsook Yahweh and adopted the cults of
the land (Deut. xxxii., esp. *vv.* 15ff.); and recent excavation
has illustrated their nature.   Even in Jeremiah's time the
prophet could complain that each city had its own god
(ii. 28; xi. 13).   Such deities were local or regional; and,
in general, it was believed that men who were outside the
realm of their god were removed from his care (cf. David,
1 Sam. xxvi. 19; Cain, Gen. iv. 14), and that, e.g., gods of
the hill-country would be helpless in the plains (1 Kings
xx. 23, 28).   Each people had its own god, who would not,
normally, trespass on another's domain (esp. Judges xi. 24).
That there were clan or family cults, such as are found elsewhere, may be inferred from the family sacrifices (1 Sam.
xx. 6; cf. i. 21), from the story of Gideon (Judges vi. 25;
cf. viii. 27), and possibly from the reference to the "fear"
of Isaac (Gen. xxxi. 42), i.e. the god feared by him or his
"house" (Amos vii. 16).

Now, although a god might be definitely associated with
a certain place, it did not necessarily follow that he could
only be found there.   Personal religion finds God in a man's
heart; institutional religion defines the place, the conditions
and the circumstances in which He may be found.   Elijah,
in a Phoenician town, prays to Yahweh (1 Kings xvii. 20);
and although it is at Bethel that Jacob finds Yahweh, he
looks for and receives his help in another land (Gen. xxviii.
20ff.; cf. xxxi. 11, 13, 42).   Men located Yahweh in the
far-off unknown and inaccessible sky or in some definite
place, here and now, especially on some elevated spot.
There were some famous holy mountains (Carmel, Tabor,
Ebal and Gerizim, Zion); and the name El Shaddai (Exod.
vi. 3), traditionally explained as "God Almighty," most

K

probably designates the god so named as a "mountain god."
But, of all the sacred places, Shechem was especially famous,
as a rival to Jerusalem; and we are told that the semi-
Aramaean *family* of Jacob put away their foreign objects
of cult there (Gen. xxxv. 2, 4), and that it was at Shechem
that the *children* of Israel, after their entry into Palestine,
agreed to renounce the gods they had hitherto served
(Joshua xxiv.).   The two stories, which are evidently not
unrelated, testify to the sanctity of the place before Jerusalem
became the central sanctuary of Israel (cf. also I Kings
xii. 1, 25), although Jerusalem itself was an important city
even in Pre-Israelite times.

All the land of Israel was Yahweh's, but Mount Zion, the
great Judaean sanctuary, was pre-eminently his.   It was
Yahweh's holy mount; and although the whole land was
holy, Jerusalem and its environs enjoyed a peculiar sanctity.
On the Mount of Olives was a shrine (2 Sam. xv. 32); at
Gibeon was an ancient "high-place" (I Kings iii. 4).   The
exact site of the priestly city of Nob—if not the same as
Gibeon—is unknown, but another priestly city, Anathoth,
lay near, and it is thought that Beth-Lehem was named after
a god (Lakhmu).   Tōpheth had the worst of reputations
(Jer. vii. 31), and both the vale of Rephaim ("the shades")
and that of Hinnom (? "slumbering")—whence comes
ultimately the name Gehenna (vale of Hinnom)—seem to
have been connected with rites for the dead.   As for
Jerusalem, "the city of righteousness" (Isa. i. 26),[1] its
temple was in keeping with what is known of other ancient
temples.   The sun-cult—cf. the horses of the sun in the
temple (2 Kings xxiii. 11) and Yahweh's heavenly chariots
(Hab. iii. 8; Ps. lxviii. 17)—the cherubim and seraphim,
the pillars Jachin and Boaz, the serpent Nehushtan, the
"brazen sea," and much else that it contained, represent
Non-Israelite, or at least Pre-Israelite ideas.   It is unnecessary to dwell upon the reforms attributed to king
Josiah in 621 B.C. (2 Kings xxiii.) or upon Ezekiel's programme (see xliv. 6ff.): they combine to emphasise the gulf
between the actual religion of Jerusalem before the Exile

[1] See p. 54, n.

and the more spiritual ideals of reforming prophets and priests.

It is well known that in the religion of Israel cosmic myths, not unlike those found in Babylonia, were associated with Yahweh (Isa. li. 9; Ps. lxxiv. 12–15; lxxxix. 9f.).   In ancient times the temple where the great god dwelt often had a sort of cosmic significance; and Josephus knows of the cosmic value of the tabernacle, and of the temple of Jerusalem (*War*, v. 5, 5).   The temple was comparable with the cosmic temple of Sidon, of which Phoenician inscriptions tell us; and, like the temple of the Babylonian Bel at Nippur, it united earth and sky.   When Ezekiel (xlviii. 35) concludes his sketch of the future with the words "the name of the city from that day shall be, 'Yahweh is there,'" it must be remembered that the presence of the God of Israel, the God of the Universe, in his temple in Jerusalem, was understood in an extraordinarily realistic way which the Western mind does not easily apprehend.

The sun-god (Shamash) and the storm and war-god (Hadad or Baal) were already well-known in Palestine in and about the fourteenth century B.C.   There was a Baal *of* or *in* the sky, and current tendencies towards a sort of monarchical monotheism prevailed by the side of the belief in deities who were on earth (p. 143).   That Yahwism should have taken over older ideas is only to be expected.   In popular Israelite belief Yahweh might come down from heaven (or the sky) and see for himself conditions on earth (Gen. xviii. 21; Exod. iii. 18); or he had his own messenger or angel, who was essentially his personal representative (p. 160).   But, in any case, the conviction prevailed that Yahweh was or would be effectively among his people (Hos. xi. 9; Isa. xii. 6; Ezek. xxxvii. 28; Joel ii. 27).

The height of religious expression is reached when Yahweh is said to be over sky (or heaven) and earth, and these are his throne and footstool respectively (Isa. lxvi. 1).   He may be said to "fill earth and sky" (Jer. xxiii. 23f.); but even the highest heaven cannot contain him (1 Kings viii. 27; 2 Chron. ii. 6; vi. 18).   Yet, although he is in the sky, he can be approached through his temple in Jerusalem, for his eyes, his heart and his "name" are there (1 Kings ix. 3). When men resort thither to his altar he will hear them (viii. 31 f.), and those afar off can spread out their hands and pray towards Jerusalem (viii. 29, 31), or have their windows opened in the direction of the holy city (Dan. vi. 10). Such ideas as the "name" or the "presence" of a deity may seem to us to be purely "spiritual"; but it is to be observed that among Israel's immediate neighbours certain specific deities were called "the Name of Baal" and "the Face (or Presence) of Baal" down to the Christian Era. The Ark was certainly more than a symbol, for "the God of heaven and earth dwelt on (or between) the cherubim" (2 Kings xix. 14 f.); and in Isaiah's vision of Yahweh enthroned in the temple (vi. 1) it was the very presence of a sublime and pure Deity among a people of unclean lips that filled him with fear.

Thus, the temple is the abode of Yahweh (Ps. xlvi. 4; lxxvi. 2) because he is effectively there, or he is represented in some intelligible manner by the altar or the Ark, or even by his anointed king (see p. 161). A difficult passage in the account of the dedication of the temple (1 Kings viii. 12 f., fuller in the LXX) locates him in the dark inner shrine, the Holy of Holies (1 Kings vi. 16; cf. Ps. xxviii. 2):—

> "The Sun hath Yahweh set in the sky,
> He himself hath resolved to dwell in thick darkness.
> Build my house a lofty mansion to me,
> A place to dwell in for all time."

If this rendering is correct, Yahweh is dissociated from the sun and sun-cult, as in Deut. iv. 19, where he allows other peoples to worship sun, moon and stars, but is himself the only god of Israel. The conviction that he was localised, so to speak, in Jerusalem gave a confidence to his people which was signally justified by the unexpected deliverance of Jerusalem from the hands of Sennacherib in the time of Hezekiah and Isaiah (700 B.C.). But it also engendered in them a false security, and prophets condemn their blind and unjustifiable reliance upon the presence of the temple, as though it were a talisman (Jer. vii. 4; xxvi. 12; cf. Mic.

iii. 11).   It is even said that one day the Ark itself should
become obsolete and be forgotten (Jer. iii. 16); contrast
the late story that Jeremiah himself hid the Ark to preserve
it (2 Macc. ii. 4ff.).

The essence of the highest prophetic teaching is that
Yahweh's word is near at hand to everyone (Deut. xxx.
11–14; cf. the Covenant in Jer. xxxi. 33f.); and that even
when Israel is carried off into exile Yahweh can hear her
cry (Jer. xxix. 12–14; cf. 1 Kings viii. 46ff.).   On the other
hand, the priest Ezekiel lays emphasis upon Yahweh's
presence in Jerusalem; for although Yahweh leaves it at
the beginning of the Exile he again returns to it (xi. 23f.;
xliii. 1ff.; cf. Zech. i. 16; ii. 10).   This is the dominant
note in the religion: Jerusalem is Yahweh's throne (Jer.
iii. 17; cf. Isa. xxiv. 23), the centre of the world (Ezek.
xxxviii. 12), and its religious capital (Isa. ii. 2–4); and from
this conviction springs the unbounded religious enthusiasm
for Zion and its temple.

The religious beliefs of Israel were not worked out consistently.   The worshipper requires an accessible god, yet is
not God far removed from men?   Was Yahweh both in
the sky and in the temple on earth?   Had Yahweh a
visible representative—the Ark, or the king?   When men
of old sought to express superhuman attributes they
frequently resorted to animal symbolism—e.g. the bull as a
symbol of strength.   On the other hand, when their language
was anthropic, they often felt its inadequacy keenly.   How
were men to think of an Unseen Power?   The more a man
got to know of himself and his kind, the less could he regard
the world of men as a fit abode for God; he therefore sought
for Him, not in the midst of daily life, but in the desert,
the glade, on the mountain top, or in the sky.   There were
two diverging trends of thought, one starting from a conviction of the nearness of God, the other from the consciousness of the gulf between the human and the divine spheres.
The stronger the conviction that Yahweh was *here*, the less
did a man trouble about possible catastrophic cosmic
changes (Isa. lxv. 17; lxvi. 22).   The very real existence of
his own God silenced all doubt and stopped all speculation.

Indeed, the tremendous reality of *this* world with *Israel's* God in it, not only made the Israelite localise all hopes for future fertility, wealth, and happiness *here*, but it also encouraged an excessive "this-world-ness" which could be harmful.

At the same time, apart from the question whether Yahweh was here or yonder, there were two ways of thinking about the future. A man might think of the future of his group, its fortunes here on earth; or he might ponder over his personal existence after death: would it be *here* with the group—one naturally recalls the world-wide ancestral cults—or with the god of the group, and where was this god? It is not always clear whether the Israelite thought of Yahweh's holy abode as being in the sky (Mic. i. 2f.; Hab. ii. 20), or on earth, or in both places (Ps. xx. 2 and 6). Certainly the holy Jerusalem on earth supplied the later imagery for the heavenly Zion (esp. in Revelation), but the earthly building had first to acquire its supernatural value as the effective abode of the god.

According to one old belief, earthly things had a heavenly pattern or origin (cf. the tabernacle, Exod. xxv. 9 and the temple, 1 Chron. xxviii. 19); but still more primitive was the anthropic conception of the unseen realm. In the same way, although the ethical attributes of Yahweh became, so to say, the pattern to be imitated by Israel, it had first been necessary for human minds to purge earlier conceptions of Yahweh of their grosser elements. Thought moved to and fro between the seen and the unseen, between the "human" and the "spiritual" spheres; and our own ready contrast between the "natural" and the "super-natural" did not necessarily exist for men who felt what we can only call the "naturalness of the supernatural," and who saw the Unseen in the Seen (cf. p. 188).

When we speak of God as being in the sky or heaven, we must remember that our distinction between a Heaven for the good and a Hell for the wicked is a secondary growth in the development of religious thought. To men of old the world of spirits interpenetrated with the world of the Seen. Even if there was a cleavage between the denizens of the

sky above and those of earth beneath, the spirits—whether
angels or evil demons—whose abode was *there*, might be
effectively *here*.   Heaven, or rather, the sky, was not men's
abode, nor was the earth the natural abode of "supernatural" beings (Gen. vi. 2).   In the Old Testament, as
also in Babylonian mythology, few "went to heaven":
Enoch, who "walked with God" (Gen. v. 21ff.; the LXX
and Targum felt obliged to paraphrase), and Elijah (2 Kings
ii. 11).   The dead went down to an underground Sheol, a
dark and dreary place; and while the Israelite in Sheol was
away from Yahweh, the Babylonian counterpart had its
own deities.   The dead could not commune with Yahweh,
or enjoy his presence, they were forgotten (Isa. xxxviii. 18;
Ps. vi. 5; lxxxviii. 4f.; cxv. 17); though Sheol itself was
not necessarily inaccessible to Yahweh (Amos ix. 2; Job
xiv. 13; Ps. cxxxix. 8; Prov. xv. 11).   Hence, although
Sheol was not precisely "Hell," to be there was to be out
of contact with Yahweh.   The relationship with Yahweh
was what mattered.   It is, however, very difficult to grasp
what was really thought.   The dead are "no more" (Gen.
xlii. 13, 36).   Jacob, plunged in grief, will go down into
Sheol (xxxvii. 35); but, later, in his happier days, he looks
forward to sleeping with his "fathers" (xlvii. 30), even as
Abraham goes to his "fathers" (xv. 15) or, like Moses and
Aaron, to his "people" (xxv. 8; cf. Deut. xxxii. 50).
Precisely what these popular phrases meant can hardly be
said; it is at least difficult to suppose that to be with one's
"fathers" or "people" was the same as to be in a dreary
Sheol.   After all, the belief in Sheol scarcely seems to be a
primitive one, since it implies acquaintance with city-life
(gates and bars, Isa. xxxviii. 10; Job xvii. 16).

   In much later times Sadducees and Pharisees notoriously
differed touching the resurrection of the dead (cf. Acts
xxiii. 8f.), but no one will suppose that the former, the
priestly party, who denied it, were atheists.   The later
writer of Ecclesiastes is disillusioned and sceptical (e.g.
iii. 21); but his hopeless attitude is corrected by the Book of
Wisdom, cf. the notable sentiment that the souls of the
righteous are in God's hand, they may seem to have died,

but they are in peace (iii. 1 f.).   A man's future rested with
God and depended upon his conduct during life.   Men were
in God's hands.   But there was no *proof* of immortality.
What convinced one man—e.g. the analogy of the death
and revival of vegetation (cf. also 1 Cor. xv. 37 ff.)—carried
no weight with another.   There might be hope for the
stump of a tree (Isa. vi. 13; xi. 1; Dan. iv. 15), but did it
follow that there is hope for man (Job. xiv. 7 ff.)?   "Who
dies if his country lives?" it has been said, but what shall
one say of the patriots whose countries have completely
perished?   Men have struggled in so many ways to express—
if not to "rationalise"—their intuitions of an existence after
death, that when we approach the Old Testament we are
struck by the absence of teaching about immortality, until
we recognise the profound fact that "life with God was
possible here—was indeed life."   The pious man of old
"did not think of the future, because he had in the present
all that could ever be received" (A. B. Davidson).   The
essential and fundamental belief of Israel at her best was
in the reality of her own eternal God, i.e. the relationship
between her and an ever-living Yahweh.   "Fellowship with
God constitutes an indissoluble bond which death cannot
sever" (*idem*).   This was practical faith and not a speculation; and although, if we express it thus, we are simplifying
a very complicated enquiry, the conception of a continuing
fellowship with God enables us to understand some of the
changing ideas now under consideration.

When we attempt to trace the Old Testament ideas of
life after death, we can distinguish, broadly speaking, two
great periods: the pre-exilic and the post-exilic, separated
by the individualism of the age of Jeremiah and Ezekiel
and the general conditions of their day (p. 118).   Ezekiel's
wonderful vision of the Valley of the Bones and of Israel's
resurrection from the dead concerns the people as a whole,
and not individuals (xxxvii.; cf. Hos vi. 2; xiii. 14).   If
Isa. liii—in many respects the most remarkable and the
most disputed chapter of the Old Testament—contains the
idea of individual resurrection, it is an isolated reference.
Job (xiv.; xix. 25 ff.) is full of doubts, and the hope that

God will vindicate him does not lead to the conviction of immortality. On the other hand, the sufferings of Israel in the Maccabaean period mark an epoch, and the expectation of resurrection after death is then, for the first time, unambiguously expressed (Dan. xii. 1f.; 2 Macc. vii. 9). It appears also in a group of chapters, Isa. xxiv.–xxvii. (viz. xxv. 8; xxvi. 19) which, on independent grounds, may be ascribed to the Greek age.

The language of the Psalmists is often ambiguous, and some exegetes have been tempted to give it a Christian interpretation to which it is not entitled. For example, the Prayer Book version of Ps. xvi. 9f. goes further than the Hebrew (e.g. "my flesh also shall rest in hope"). Moreover, since death is often thought of as a sleep (Dan. xii. 2), it is very tempting to interpret the Psalmists' metaphors of "waking" or of the "morning" as a reference to life after death (Ps. xvii. 15; xlix. 14; cxxxix. 18). But every passage must be taken on its merits. There is, however, no doubt that the striking words in Ps. lxxiii. 23ff. reach "the zenith of Old Testament teaching on immortality" (Oesterley):

"Nevertheless I am continually with Thee, Thou has holden my right hand. According to Thy purpose wilt Thou lead me, and afterwards wilt take me gloriously. Whom have I in heaven? And, having Thee, there is naught that I desire upon earth."

"This conviction of a personal relation to God, independent of time and change, and not any particular theory as to the character of the life after death, is the lasting contribution of the Old Testament to the doctrine of a Future Life" (Burney). On the other hand, when elsewhere the Psalmist trusts that he "will dwell in the house of Yahweh for length of days" (Ps. xxiii. 6), we have to decide—if we can—whether the writer is thinking only of physical life in an actual temple (cf. e.g. Ps. lxxxiv. 10) or of his life in a house not made with hands (cf. Yahweh's house, Num. xii. 7).

But while the growth of a belief in immortality can be recognised in the later stages of Israelite religion, the earlier stages are much more indefinite. Palestine, like

Phoenicia, was no doubt well-acquainted with the common Egyptian beliefs in another world. The presence of Egyptian officials, Egyptian monuments (e.g. at Beth-shan), and such objects as scarabs (which have been found in great numbers in course of excavation) would familiarise the Palestinians, as they did the Phoenicians, with Egyptian ideas about the dead. On an eighth-century inscription from North Syria a prince is bidden to pray that his dead father's soul may eat and drink with the god Hadad. In Palestine itself, the tombs with their food-offerings, personal ornaments and evidence of the care to preserve the bones of the dead, suggest that the dead were certainly not thought to be non-existent. In fact, the practice of necromancy (1 Sam. xxviii. 8, 11; Isa. viii. 19), the character of the mourning customs, rites of cutting (Lev. xix. 28), offerings for (or to) the dead (Deut. xxvi. 14; Ps. cvi. 28) suggest, further, that the dead were not necessarily in any sort of Sheol. The great ancestors of Israel were expected to be interested in their descendants (Isa. li. 2; lxiii. 16), their graves were well-known (Gen. xxxv. 20, etc.), and Rachel can still bewail her suffering children (Jer. xxxi. 15). When we meet with the belief at a late date that the pious dead are with the Patriarchs (4 Macc. xiii. 17), we may recognise a more or less "orthodox" belief associating the living and the powerful dead. But were there not less "orthodox" forms? Burial in the house (1 Sam. xxv. 1; 1 Kings ii. 34) kept the dead near the living, even as the burial of very young infants in the home retained, as it were, the "life" of the household within the precincts. We may suppose that burial with one's "fathers," or one's "people"—sometimes illustrated in course of excavation—served in like manner to encourage that feeling of group-solidarity which strict monotheistic Yahwism expressed as a relationship with or through Yahweh and Israel's first ancestors (see p. 118 n.).

The conception of immortality that slowly took root after the time of the great reforming prophets, and, in particular, after the individualism of Jeremiah and Ezekiel and the exalted monotheistic teaching of the "Deutero-Isaiah" (p. 179), represents a new growth, different from the earlier

cruder ideas that had once flourished and which the reformers
had expelled. "The belief," in a future life, which once
prevailed, "was killed by Ethical Monotheism" (Sprott);
that is to say, ideas once comparable, or identical with,
those associated with "heathen" deities (e.g. Osiris of
Egypt or Hadad of Syria), or which were opposed to a
purer Yahwism, were destroyed. Trust in Yahweh was a
more pregnant conviction than speculation as to a future
existence or than that "undue depreciation of this life's
moral and spiritual possibilities, which a too vivid realisation
of the future life has sometimes fostered in the Christian
Church" (idem). Convictions of an existence after death
have sometimes encouraged unworthy and unethical beliefs
and practices; and from the history of Old Testament religion
it can be seen that the development of Christian conceptions
of another life is indebted to the later ideas of Yahwism
rather than to those that had prevailed in earlier times.

Underlying the world's beliefs and practices relating to
the existence after death there is a fundamental conviction
that man must be bound up with something more permanent
than himself. This conviction can be expressed in the belief
that a man enjoys a relationship with the Living God, as
in the Psalmist's words already cited (Ps. lxxiii. 25). Such
a belief may demand the completest faith; but even when
there is this faith, the relationship between man and God
must be more particularly specified. A man may have his
name written in Yahweh's book.[1] Here the question has
arisen whether we should understand such references in the
Christian sense of eternal salvation (cf. Phil. iv. 3; Rev.
iii. 5, xiii. 8), or must assume, as is often done, that all
that is meant is to be written down merely as a living
member of the actual Israelite community. Yet when
Moses, who stood in so unique a relationship with Yahweh
(Num. xii. 7f.), intercedes on behalf of Israel, and offers
to be blotted out of Yahweh's book (Exod. xxxii. 32), it
is surely difficult to believe that only physical death there
and then was what he was supposed to be prepared for!
Similarly, if the souls of all men are bound up in Yahweh's

---

[1] Ps. lxix. 28; Mal. iii. 16; Dan. xii. 1; cf. Isa. iv. 3.

bundle and can be slung out at will (1 Sam. xxv. 29), are
we to suppose that the words refer only to physical life?
That is to say, if it was believed that the lives of Moses,
David and other men were in Yahweh's keeping, did this
mean that at their death they disappeared, automatically
as it were, or was the pious Israelite content so long as
he was convinced that his life was in some way in the care
of Yahweh? The latter is surely the more probable view.

Moreover, where ideas of group-solidarity ruled, the
Israelite would doubtless feel that he was part of Yahweh's
Israel, and living in Yahweh's "inheritance." A man also
felt that he lived on in his family: this explains his anxiety
to have children in order to preserve his name (cf. Deut.
xxv. 6f.)—children are a lasting memorial, like a city
(BS xl. 19; cf. xliv. 10–14). Steps were taken to preserve
the name of a man from being blotted out, for not to be
remembered is not to exist (Jer. xi. 19). The old inscription
from North Syria (p. 136) enjoins the son to make mention
of his father's name and associate it with that of the god
Hadad. Life could also be symbolised as a light or lamp
(1 Kings xi. 36; cf. the "coal" in 2 Sam. xiv. 7). David
could be called the "lamp of Israel" (2 Sam. xxi. 17), and
the idea lived on into Christian times, when lamps bear such
inscriptions as "Christ is my light." But there are more
concrete practices, when, as among many peoples, care is
taken to preserve some part of the body of the dead, or
when special sanctity is attached to the blood (p. 197).
Or else some visible memorial is set up (Isa. lvi. 5), e.g. a
pillar (2 Sam. xviii. 18), or a peg is fixed in the wall of the
sanctuary (Ezra ix. 8). So long as a man felt that in some
way he—or some part of him—survived death, speculation
seemed unnecessary.

Men have started from their experience of the world
around them and have sought to explain to themselves
their deeper intuitions; or they have started from the Unseen
world—the world of their thoughts—and have even found
it necessary to explain why man became mortal. At all
times and in all places men have been able to approach their
profounder problems either along the lines of such positive

empirical knowledge as they possessed, or from the more incontestable facts of such "spiritual" or "religious" experiences as had been theirs.   There are these two ways of thinking, and when it is said that life consists in keeping Yahweh's statutes (Lev. xviii. 5; cf. Ezek. xx. 11; xxxiii. 15), the fact is that "life" and "death" were not necessarily thought of physiologically: "death" was virtually what was as good as death, and "life" was full and abounding existence.   The world, then, is not the physical material universe, it is that which is "informed" by God; and man's place in that world depends upon the relationship between him and God and God's covenant with his "group."

The Israelite was no less at a loss than ourselves when he tried to follow up his thoughts on life and death.   Man was God-made; he was partly of the earth, earthy, and partly "spirit" (*rūakh*); and when God, who breathed into him the "spirit" (Gen. ii. 7), took it away, man died (cf. Job xxxiii. 4; xxxiv. 14 f.).   But there is a more distinctive idea: man is "flesh" (*bāsār*), and flesh comprised what *we* should call body and mind—for the intellectual and emotional faculties were found in the body itself (heart, liver, etc.).   Man was "an animated body and not an incarnated soul" (Wheeler Robinson), a visible unanalysed influence.   But unless he had Yahweh's *rūakh* he had no hope.   It was futile to trust in "flesh" and let one's "heart" (mind, etc.) depart from Yahweh (Jer. xvii. 5).   This made the vital difference between Israel on the one side, and Assyria on the other: "with him is an arm of flesh; but with us is Yahweh our God" (2 Chron. xxxii. 8).   Similarly, "the Egyptians are men and not God, and their horses flesh and not spirit" (Isa. xxxi. 3).   Here Yahweh's "spirit" is the divine quality or energy distinguishing his followers from others.

But continued reflection has always complicated ideas of mind, spirit, soul, and the like, and in the Old Testament the same word "spirit" is also used in less "religious" ways of the life-principle.   When the author of Num. xvi. 22, xxvii. 16 speaks of the "God of the spirits of all flesh," he surely did not believe that all men were immortal.   According to the author of Ps. civ., who has been called the "Words-worth of the ancients," both man and beast derive their "spirit" from God (*v.* 29 f.), and all Nature depends upon the Creator: God is the giver or cause of all life and growth.[1] The pessimistic Koheleth explicitly states that a man returns to his dust, and the "spirit" to God who gave it (Eccles. xii. 7): the individual is thus analysed away, and is no more immortal than the beast (iii. 19 ff.). Again, in Ps. cxlvi. 4 the *rūakh* is the principle of life, at the loss of which man returns to his earth (cf. 1 Macc. ii. 63). But here a vital distinction is made, for whereas all men must die, it is not so with him who has as his help Yahweh, the God of Jacob, Zion's God, the Maker of Heaven and Earth, the One who reigns for ever. As the author of Wisdom would have said (iii. 1 f.), such men only seem to have died. In such passages as these Yahweh's spirit is essentially a cosmic principle; it is infinitely powerful (cf. also Exod. xv. 8; Hos. xii. 15, etc.); and it may be thought of—anthropomorphically— as his breath. It may be the source of godlike or god-given energy (cf. Judges xv. 14, etc.); but it is not (as in Isa. xxxi. 3) that which makes the essential *ethical* difference between ordinary men and those who partake of the spirit of the living Yahweh.

Throughout the world's religions there are manifold efforts to distinguish human faculties (life, spirit, soul, mind, etc.), and Hebrew psychology is especially complex because the relevant Biblical passages, many of which cannot be dated, certainly range over several centuries, represent different points of view, and reflect significant changes in thought. There is much that is not of Yahwistic origin or that belongs to a "lower" type of Yahwism. There is no development along a single line, and the different lines cross and re-cross. Hence the long history of Old Testament religion can scarcely be traced with any com-pleteness. Moreover, when we reach post-exilic times we are in an age later than that which produced the lofty

---

[1] This Psalm has many striking parallels to the hymns of Ikhnaton; see e.g. the *Cambridge Ancient History*, ii. 117 ff., and Breasted, *The Dawn of Conscience* (1934), pp. 281 ff.

ethical monotheism of Isa. xl. ff. (where Israel's Yahweh is the sole cause of all things), an age, also, when outside Palestine at least, there were far-reaching attempts to understand the cosmos in a less "supernaturalistic" manner. These had a profound effect upon earlier ways of thinking, and they tended to sever God and His world, Man and Nature, Religion and ordinary everyday life, the psychical and the physical (see p. 206 f.).

In the history of religion a god is sometimes a *cause* or functionary and little else. But a god who is in a *personal* relationship with a group is much more than a cause. The earth could be the effective abode of the gods no less than the sky, and "sky" is not the same as "heaven." The world of spirits interpenetrated with the world of men; and on earth, men or objects (e.g. in Israel the Ark) could be effective representatives of the gods. In the Old Testament there is a constant effort to subordinate the worlds of the Unseen and the Seen to Yahweh and to refine the attributes of an *ethical* Yahweh. In monotheistic belief the Unseen, the spiritual world, is subordinated to Yahweh in such a way that our world is not also a world of both spirits and men, but essentially Yahweh's world. Yet old ideas of the sky-realm above the earth persisted and came to the front again, with the result that God's Kingdom was subsequently located above men's heads and not on earth among men. Thus the fundamental conception of the triangular relationship between Yahweh, the people and their land, and all the practical and realistic ideas associated with it (Ch. VII.), have to contend with the not less realistic experiences of the supersensuous and the Unseen Realm.

CHAPTER IX

The Struggle for Ethical Monotheism

ETHICAL Monotheism is the belief that there is one, and only one, God of the Universe, who as "God" infinitely transcends Man in all that constitutes a perfect personality, and that His attributes are distinctively ethical, and are to be imitated by those who would worship Him.

In itself, the recognition of a Supreme Power is neither so rare as has often been thought, nor is it confined to the religions which are reckoned as "higher," often simply because they are monotheistic. Indeed, among all sorts of peoples there is a not uncommon tendency to recognise the existence of a Supreme Being. It recurs among rudimentary folk, and it takes so many different forms that we cannot treat it as a climax, or as the last term in an evolutionary series from animism or polytheism to monotheism. For Supreme Powers appear by the side of, or even behind, inferior ones; they lose their supremacy or again recover it in some new form; and their vicissitudes are so varied that the mere appearance of "monotheistic" tendencies is in itself by no means so important as their persistence, their development, and their place in history.

As distinct from "monolatry" (the worship of one god above others), "monotheism" denies the existence of all gods but one. The first uncompromising teaching of it is found in Old Testament passages which can mostly be dated round about the sixth century B.C. (Isa. xl. ff.; cf. Deut. xxxii. 39; Jer. xvi. 19, etc.).[1] The monotheism of the Old Testament differs in quality from every other early monotheism, and paved the way for Christianity. But it is always difficult to maintain monotheism in its purity. A living religion takes in much that might seem to us to be of other than "religious" import, e.g. food-supply, success in

---

[1] On the Mosaic Age, see p. 183 n. 1.

war, tribal or national relationships (cf. pp. 120 ff.); and since men differ everywhere in temperament and training, and in daily and local interests, there is a lack of agreement among them on the essentials of religion, because there is no agreement as to what these are.

Now, Israel gradually framed the loftiest religious faith of ancient times: that Yahweh was the God of the Universe and of all human history, and that all peoples would one day unite in the worship of this God, who was Israel's own God, and who was to be sought *at*—or perhaps one should say *through* (p. 130 f.)—the sanctuary at Jerusalem. This ideal of a universal religion brought in its train many serious questions as to the number of gods, their function, their character, and so forth.

Even in Israel the conviction persisted that Yahweh was not precisely the sole God, though he was greater than all other gods. The first commandment forbids any rival to Yahweh, but does not exclude the belief that other gods exist (Deut. vi. 14). In contrast to this belief we should observe the explicit denial of their existence in Deut. iv. 35, 39, and the distinction made in iv. 19 (cf. xxix. 26) between the sun, moon and stars, which Yahweh allotted to other peoples—like the idols, they were not to be feared (Jer. x. 2, 5)—and Yahweh himself, who is Israel's own God. Some Psalmists admit that there are other gods (xxix. 1 mg.; lxxxii. 1; lxxxvi. 8; cxxxv. 5); but this is absolutely denied, e.g. in xcvi. 5.

Among Israel's neighbours many great gods were revered, and the head of the pantheon of some ruling city was sometimes even regarded as a Creator. Certain monotheising tendencies can be traced in or about 1400 B.C. in the efforts to unite in some way the gods of the sun (Shamash) and of the rain or storm (Hadad—the Baal *par excellence*).[1] In this, the "Mosaic" age, as it may broadly be called, the remarkable Indian ethical god Varuna was known in North Syria; and in Egypt the reforming king Ikhnaton (Amenhotep IV) endeavoured to spread far and wide the

[1] On a cuneiform tablet discovered at Taanach a man refers to the "Lord of the gods."

monotheistic cult of the sun-disk Aton (p. 94 f.).   Religious
and political ideas being inseparable, there were tendencies
towards a "monarchical monotheism": one realm, one
ruler and one ruling cult, and "politico-religious imperialism"
played a large part in co-ordinating and extending the one
rule and the one religion.   The king, typically regarded as
the representative of the god, or even as his son, would
extend or strengthen his own sovereignty and that of his
god.   A rival ruler and a rival god would be equally
embarrassing.   Hence, the co-ordination of peoples and that
of their religious and other interests were one and the same
task; and in these ancient monarchies, where the god and
the king were jointly supreme, and where the god was
king and the ruler was divine, the way was open which was
to lead to conceptions of an ideal king, the "Messiah" or
Anointed One, and a Messianic people.

When—in circumstances that are disputed among Biblical
scholars—Yahweh the god of Israel became the chief god of
Palestine, the earlier native religion did not disappear.   The
physical qualities attributed to Yahweh in the Old Testament
frequently recall those of the nature gods he had superseded;
though we may note the subtle difference between Yahweh
(as a storm-god), whose arrows *are* the lightning (Isa.
xxx. 30), and the more circumspect wording: "his arrow
shall go forth *as* the lightning" (Zech. ix. 14).   The bull or
calf cults at Bethel and Dan (1 Kings xii. 28) may be
connected with the god Hadad, whose sacred animal was
the bull; and in the blessing pronounced over Joseph
(Gen. xlix. 24) the "Mighty One" of Jacob should perhaps
be "the steer" of Jacob (*ăbīr* for *abbīr*), a suitable parallel
to the "stone of Israel," which may refer to the cult at
Bethel.   Indeed, the points of contact between Old Testament religion and the neighbouring religions are such that
the earliest Yahwism of the Israelites—the nature of which
is keenly discussed—and the native religion of the land must
have deeply influenced each other.

Both the native Canaanites and the immigrant Israelites
would practice the same ancient agricultural rites at the
old-time sacred places, for all new-comers must learn "the

manner of the god of the land" (2 Kings xvii. 11, 26f.).
Moreover, the old nature-deities of sun, moon, rain, etc.,
had not been without ethical qualities (p. 89).   In Egypt,
Ikhnaton's god Aton was a virtually universal deity, and
not only were nature-gods, as such, not confined to any
one land, but the symbol of the solar rays of Aton, each
holding out either a hand or the *ankh* (the sign of life),
would vividly express the universality of the god's presence
and power.   Also, nature-deities were, as such, both life-
giving and destructive: the sun parches and the rain-storm
can destroy; hence the conviction that a god could send
both good and evil would be familiar long before it was
translated into the language of Yahwism (Job ii. 10).

Semitic personal names compounded with the name of a
deity show what was thought of the gods, that they were
gracious, kind, merciful, healing, answering, etc., so that
in their functions, at any rate, the many diverse deities had
much in common.   Indeed, the mere fact that they were
often known by an appellative, as El (god), Adon (lord)
and Baal (owner) indicates that men found a certain unity
of character beneath the diversity of deities.   After the
Israelite settlement the lesser and local deities still flourished,
and sometimes retained their earlier names (so Hos. ii. 17;
Zech. xiii. 2).   Of the three common titles just mentioned,
El—the name of a distinct god in North Syria and Phoenicia
—was also a name of Yahweh (Isa. xl. 18, etc.); and for a
time at least the title Baal, once the name of Hadad, whom
Yahweh superseded, was borne by the god of Israel.   Baal-
names recur in the families of Saul and David (p. 40f.).
Conversely, in the dynasty of Omri, when Israel was allied
with the Aramaeans, whose chief god was Hadad, and the
cult of the Baal of Tyre stirred the reforming party to
introduce the dynasty of Jehu (841 B.C.), the names Athal*iah*,
Ahaz*iah* and *Jeho*shaphat point to the recognition of
Yahweh.   In ostraka from Samaria of Omri's age "Baal"
and "Yahweh" names occur together, the latter in the form
Yō or Yāū or the like.

Not until the middle of the eighth century does Hosea
denounce all Baalism (ii. 16f.; xiii. 1); and more than a

century later it is still being repeatedly condemned by Jeremiah. His contemporary Zephaniah heralds the destruction of the *name* of Baal (i. 4, LXX), although the reading *remnant*, in our Hebrew text, implies that some steps had already been taken. Chemosh, the national god of Moab, and Yahweh of Israel had much in common, even as had the local or provincial gods (Judges xi. 24); so that it was as easy for Yahweh and Baal to interchange as for men to use the ambiguous appellative *ba'al* indifferently of any deity. The first forward step in Yahwism was to sever the two names; and whereas the Tyrian party overthrew the altars of Yahweh and Elijah repaired the one on Carmel (1 Kings xviii. 30; xix. 10), Gideon, it is said, destroyed an altar of Baal at Ophrah and built another to Yahweh Shalom ("Yahweh is peace," Judges vi. 24). Now, elsewhere, there was an altar to Yahweh-Nissi (Exod. xvii. 15), and just as dragon-conflicts and other beliefs once attached to other gods were taken over into Yahwism, so there were sacred places, later connected with Yahweh, which were once connected with an El, an ambiguous name if Yahwism was to be without a rival (Gen. xvi. 13 mg.; xxi. 33). When, therefore, the old sites were explicitly associated with the name of Yahweh, the question sooner or later arose whether there were many Yahwehs, and the immortal "Shema" (Deut. vi. 4) asserts, perhaps, not that Yahweh is the *only* God who exists, but that all the different local Yahwehs are *one*. It is as though Roman Catholics found it necessary to insist that there is only one Madonna in spite of the many local Madonnas.

Where there were many sanctuaries there were generally variations of practice. An essential uniformity of cult was felt to be as necessary here as, centuries later, uniformity of text was demanded (p. 18). The Book of Deuteronomy therefore advocates a single legitimate sanctuary. If it does not name it—and some scholars think that in its earliest form this composite book had in view Shechem—the "Deuteronomic" history, which is a later compilation (p. 50), makes it clear that the one and only sanctuary, chosen by Yahweh out of all the tribes of Israel (Deut.

xii. 5), was the temple of Jerusalem (cf. 1 Kings viii. 16;
ix. 3).[1] But the suppression of the provincial shrines would
strike a blow at the popular religion of the land; and the
Rabshakeh's reference to the policy of suppression, ascribed
by him to Hezekiah (2 Kings xviii. 22),[2] is important as
indicating the feeling of the country when, as a matter of
fact, the work of centralising the cultus was systematic-
ally undertaken, e.g. in the reforms ascribed to Josiah
in 621 B.C.

A new point, however, now arises. Steps might be taken
to deal with the country priests (Deut. xviii. 6–8; 2 Kings
xxiii. 8),[3] but to organise Yahwism by centralising the cult
at Jerusalem and to elevate the character of Yahwism were
two different things. To Jeremiah and Ezekiel the religion
practised at the temple of Jerusalem was mere organised
hypocrisy, and scarcely superior to the Baalism of Hosea's
day; in other words, a central sanctuary did not necessarily
mean a lofty religion.

The character of the "high places" or "sanctuaries" (Amos
vii. 9, etc.) is well-known. Here were altar (*mizbēakh*,
lit. "place of sacrificial slaughter"), pillar (*maṣṣēbah*),
tree-trunk (*ăshērah*), idol or idols, sacrificial rites, and
festal occasions, accompanied by drunkenness (cf. Eli's
suspicions, 1 Sam. i. 13ff., with Amos ii. 8; Isa. xxviii. 7)
and licentiousness (1 Sam. ii. 22; cf. Hos. iv. 13f.). These
"high places" were condemned by reformers, partly because
they carried on the old religious usages, and partly because
they were incompatible with a centralised cult. Yet the
popular, though markedly didactic, stories encircling Bethel,

---

[1] The view (based on a peculiar interpretation of such passages
as Deut. xii. 13f.) that there was an intermediate step, viz. the
replacing of the many shrines by a central one in each tribe, is
unnecessary. Such a policy would have tended to sever and not
to unite the tribes.

[2] "But if ye say unto me, in Yahweh our God do we trust, is it
not he whose high places and altars Hezekiah put away, and he
said to Judah and to Jerusalem, Before this altar shall ye worship
in Jerusalem."

[3] 1 Sam. ii. 36 ("put me in one of the priestly offices") illustrates
the poverty-stricken condition of those who appealed to the Jerusalem
priesthood for help.

Ramah and other "high places" suggest that they were quite innocuous. These sanctuaries were the forerunners of the local synagogues of later ages (cf. Ps. lxxiv. 8); and there is archaeological evidence that, in the Christian era at least, the Jewish synagogues might have certain unorthodox or "heathenish" features (e.g. representations of the zodiac). Judaism itself survived the destruction of the temple and the Fall of Jerusalem because of the provincial holy places, and even at the present day local cults withstand all efforts to abolish them (p. 76). Consequently, it is only to be expected that the ancient "high places," Pre-Israelite though many of them were, continued to retain their original sanctity, although the character of their cults was greatly modified as time passed.

In a word, there were many sacred places in ancient Palestine (Exod. xx. 24; Deut. xii. 13), and later, there were strenuous efforts to abolish them. But Yahwism could only purify them; they could not be wholly suppressed. Nothing is more striking than the rare occurrence of Jerusalem in the popular narratives of the Old Testament and the prominence—and harmlessness—of such places as Beersheba, Hebron, Bethlehem, Bethel, the two Mizpahs, Ramah, Gilgal, etc. It would seem that Yahweh could be called Baal before a sharp distinction between Yahweh and Baal was felt to be imperative if Yahwism was to be cleansed (Hosea, Jeremiah). The name "El," on the other hand, seems to have been regarded as less dangerous. But, when the local sanctuaries occur freely in the popular literature it is not easy to decide whether the passages which tell of them represent, (a) a stage in Yahwism *before* the great reforming prophets denounced their cultus, or, more probably (b), a later stage, *after* they had been cleansed of their worst features.[1] For Judah it was important, on both political and ecclesiastical grounds, that Jerusalem should be the great central sanctuary—though the northern

---

[1] On this view the popular narratives are considerably later than is recognised by most Old Testament critics; but this is a conclusion already reached by the present writer on other grounds. See *Camb. Anc. Hist.* iii. 472 ff.

Israelites could point to Shechem and Shiloh as ancient sacred places—but the utterances of the reforming prophets hardly show that even the religion of the temple had as yet any ethical or spiritual superiority over the local shrines.

Varieties of Yahwism abounded. It is intelligible that the Ephod, orthodox so long as it was in the hands of the priests (cf. Exod. xxviii. 6ff.), might be considered idolatrous in other hands (Judges viii. 27), and that the priests who divined by means of the Urim and Thummim (Exod. xxviii. 30) might look askance at the Teraphim (2 Kings xxiii. 24; Zech. x. 2), popular though they were (Gen. xxxi. 19, 30; 1 Sam. xix. 13, 16). Even some of the warriors of Judah, the Maccabee, when fighting for the restoration of the national religion, did not scruple to wear mascots (2 Macc. xii. 40). That the Transjordanian Israelites should want their own sanctuary was only natural; but it would be a dangerous rival to the central sanctuary, and a curious story explains that it was merely commemorative (Joshua xxii. 26f.). Certain pillars are represented as perfectly innocuous—Bethel (Gen. xxviii. 18, etc.), Gilead (xxxi. 45, 51f.), Sinai (Exod. xxiv. 4), Egypt (Isa. xix. 19): but they could easily have been the instruments of the type of cult that the prophets condemned. It is further explained that the "high places" were tolerated until the temple of Solomon was built: Gibeon was the great high place, the Tent of Meeting was there (1 Kings iii. 4; 2 Chron. i. 3; cf. 1 Chron. xvi. 39f.); but thenceforth they were illegitimate (1 Kings xiv. 21–24; 2 Kings xxiii. 5–8). Elsewhere it is said that if people still visited them, it was Yahweh whom they worshipped (2 Chron. xxxiii. 17). Also in Samaria, after 721 B.C., the new-comers combined the worship of Yahweh with that of their own gods (2 Kings xvii. 29ff., 41), even as the invading Israelites in their day had combined the worship of their own god with the native cults (Judges iii. 6f.). A distinction must be drawn between religious ideals and the actual religious conditions.

Yahwism included, when it could not supersede, much that was alien: e.g. the ancient and famous goddesses Anath and Astarte, the Queen of Heaven, the favourite deity of

the women even in Jeremiah's day (xliv. 17f.).[1]   In the
Jewish colony at Elephantine was a stone temple, at least
one hundred years old, with a well-developed cultus.   It
had five gates, and at least five deities were recognised,
Yahu (Yahweh), "god of heaven," standing at the head.
Closely associated with him are two deities, Anath-bethel
and an apparently subordinate female deity.[2]   Bethel is
actually named in Jer. xlviii. 13 as the deity of Israel,
corresponding to Chemosh of Moab, and is well-known as a
divine name elsewhere.   "Bethel" is thus a rival of Yahweh;
and it is noteworthy that while Anath, the old goddess of
war, is united with Bethel and subordinated to Yahu,
another deity at Elephantine is called Anath-yahu, a name
which associates her with Yahu himself.   Yet this Judaean
colony was in touch with Jerusalem and Samaria, its cultus
was Israelite, and the names of its members are frequently
of a familiar type (Uriah, Benaiah, Hananiah, etc.), though
it was as indifferent to the law of a single central sanctuary
as the Transjordanian Israelites had endeavoured to be.[3]

In view of such evidence for varieties of Yahwism it is
easy to understand why on critical examination of the Old
Testament it would seem, for example, that in Israel earlier
ancestral cults were sublimated and made orthodox by the
incorporation of the "cult legends" into the story of
Yahweh's dealings with the patriarchs, and that the great
festivals, though of Canaanite origin, were regularised and
connected with the story of the Exodus (Exod. xii.; Lev.
xxiii.; Num. xxviiif.).   The reformed Yahwism sought to
shake itself free from its earlier Canaanite or Palestinian
associations, and the Biblical history as a whole prefers to

---

[1] Although in the Old Testament Yahweh stands alone without
any female consort, the language of devotion, though placing him
above sex, ascribes to him female and male characteristics (Deut.
xxxii. 18; Isa. xlvi. 3 f.).

[2] Cf. Ezek. xxiii. 4 (where Yahweh takes Oholah and Oholibah),
and the two wives of Abraham, Sarah and Hagar.

[3] In the time of Ptolemy Philopator (181–145 B.C.) and Cleopatra
it was the desire to co-ordinate Judaism in Egypt that led the
Egyptian Jews to build a temple at Leontopolis corresponding to
that at Jerusalem (Josephus, *Ant.* xiii. 3, 1).

look back, not to ancestors who were settled in Palestine from of old, but to a people born outside the old heathen land (see p. 59).

If the victory of monotheism owed most to the centralisation and co-ordination of Yahwism at Jerusalem, it was the prophets that made this monotheism ethical. Now, if one god is to be supreme, the part played by the lesser or local gods in the practical life of people must be taken into consideration. There had been functional or departmental gods (of sun, rain, agriculture, etc.); and the gods of tribal or other groups had been an integral part of the group's active life (cf. pp. 120 ff.). Moreover, some local sanctuaries had had no little reputation (2 Kings i. 2; Deut. xxxiii. 19). None the less, Yahweh did come to be regarded as the sole cause of all material benefits, financial success included (Deut. viii. 11–18; ix. 4; xxviii. 12). The first great step towards this is to be seen when Hosea (middle of the eighth century) insists—apparently as a new doctrine—that the gifts of nature come through Yahweh, and not through the local Baals (ii.; iv.; ix. 2 f.).

It has already been pointed out that even the later prophets saw little to choose between the cult of the Baals and the Yahwism of the temple religion. How the temple could satisfy the practical needs of life is set forth in various passages. Was there drought or famine? It was because the temple had not been rebuilt (Hag. i. 10 f.); the priests were negligent and evil (Mal. ii. f.); or men had not come to keep the Feast of Tabernacles (Zech. xiv. 17)—the occasion, even in later times, of a water-pouring ceremony to ensure rain for the coming year. It is Yahweh and not the gods of the idolaters who sends the rains (Jer. xiv. 22; Zech. x. 1 f.), and rains are a sign that Yahweh is in the midst of his people (Joel ii. 23–27). Restore the full cultus and pay the tithes, and all will be well; for in the sacrificial offerings Israel and Yahweh are brought together (Mal. iii. 8–11; Judith xi. 12 f.). These passages represent the thought of the age of Jeremiah and later, and it is easy to realise that the earlier religion in Jerusalem and elsewhere, under Yahweh or under other gods, would be in even closer touch with the "magico-religious" beliefs and customs familiar to students of Comparative Religion. Thus one of the reasons of the immense importance of Jerusalem was its sacrificial ritual in honour of a powerful and benevolent Yahweh.

Yahweh was the cause of both misfortunes and benefits (Job ii. 10; see p. 120 f.). If a people was defeated, polytheism could cut the knots by saying that its gods were weaker than those of the conqueror (2 Kings xviii. 33; 2 Chron. xxviii. 23; cf. Isa. x. 10 f.). But the Israelite could say that Yahweh was using Israel's foe as his tool. Yet the weapon must not boast; and, in like manner, Israel must not claim the credit for her own successes (Judges vii. 2; Deut. viii. 17; ix. 4), or forget Yahweh who could use Judah and Ephraim as his bow and arrow (Zech. ix. 13). Further, Israel's sufferings might be regarded as a divine punishment, the cause of which might be self-evident: Israel could accept chastisement and let herself be chastened.[1] It is easy to understand how anxious men were to ensure the help of a god in any difficulty and also to ascertain the cause of any failure (see p. 107): this anxiety takes the most varied forms in the world's religions, and Yahwism is unique for its endeavour to find a monotheistic answer to its questions.

By bringing Yahweh into the heart of history Israel might seem to complicate the problem of monotheism; yet by preserving her faith in her relationship with him she enlarged her conception of his place in the Universe and of the way in which he was to be worshipped. The Exile, so far from proving that Yahweh was weak or negligible (Zeph. i. 12), proved that his was a righteousness and holiness that extended beyond the present catastrophe and outside his own people. A self-conscious Israel came to feel both the justice of her sufferings and the certainty of her subsequent restoration. It was this fundamental conviction of a Supreme and Righteous Power and of its significance for *her* that lies at the bottom of Israel's efforts to think out her position in the world and that distinguishes her from other peoples.

---

[1] Jer. ii. 30; xxxi. 18; contrast her obstinacy, Amos iv. 6–11; Lev. xxvi. 23.

The same Hebrew word (*rā'āh*) covers both misfortune and moral evil.   Yahweh sends misfortunes and catastrophes (cf. 1 Kings xvii. 20; Job ii. 10); but is he the cause of evil? In Hebrew usage "the spirit (*rūakh*) of Yahweh" is beneficent; but evil comes through "the spirit of Elohim" or "from with Yahweh" (1 Sam. xvi. 14).   When David offended Yahweh by his census-taking it was said that Yahweh had urged him to do so, though the later version ascribes his temptation to a *Sātān* or adversary (2 Sam. xxiv. 1; 1 Chron. xxi. 1)—Yahweh does not cause men to sin (BS xv. 11ff.).   If David sinned, the strictly monotheistic view was that only Yahweh could be the cause; the Chronicler's version is a step towards the dualism which came in under Persian influence.   But dualism and polytheism alike cut the knots; and the more characteristic belief is that Yahweh lays stumbling-blocks (cf. Jer. vi. 21; Ezek. iii. 20), or hardens men's hearts (Exod. iv. 21; vii. 3; Isa. vi. 10).   No secondary causes are recognised: whatever men do is ultimately due to God; and since whatever exists is evidently tolerated, permitted or created by God, the great writers of Israel are confident that all that is evil and contrary to their conceptions of Yahweh cannot last in this world of his.   Yahweh is long-suffering, ready to forgive, and—as is laid down by Ezekiel (Ch. xviii.)—at any time a man can turn over from an evil course to a good one; but there is a limit to Yahweh's patience.

There is divergence of statement: if Pharaoh is disobedient it is Yahweh who hardened his heart (Exod. xi. 9 and x. 1), and Yahweh lets Israel go after the stubbornness of her heart, for which, in another passage, she herself is held responsible (Ps. lxxxi. 12 and Jer. vii. 24; cf. Isa. lxiii. 17); similarly Gog comes up of his own will, but is also brought by Yahweh (Ezek. xxxviii. 16).   The writers touch only lightly upon the deeper mysteries of the human heart.   A Jeremiah might wonder whether he had been delivering Yahweh's message; he might feel that Yahweh had "beguiled" him, and that he let himself be beguiled (Jer. xx. 7).   Continued disobedience to a higher will might, it was felt, irretrievably destroy a people (Isa. vi. 9ff.); and even a profounder spiritual experience might "result in a deadening of the moral and religious sensibilities" (Skinner). Nowhere more clearly than in the old Oriental religions is there bad religion as well as good; and religion so intensifies the inmost springs of action that Yahweh's attitude to men seems to be conditioned by their attitude to him (cf. 1 Sam. ii. 30; Ps. xviii. 24ff.).

Religion has to explain, or explain away, the evil done in its name, and monotheistic Yahwism was no exception. If men had sacrificed their children, it was something that had never entered Yahweh's head (Jer. xix. 5; cf. Topheth, vii. 31; and the Molech cult, xxxii. 35), or else it was of the nature of a punishment (Ezek. xx. 25). For the calf-cult which Hosea denounces, one writer blames the first king of the schismatic north (1 Kings xii. 28ff.); but another holds Aaron responsible, though there is some ambiguous wording.[1] The prevalence of serpent-cults has been widely illustrated by excavation, and Hezekiah is said to have destroyed the Brazen Serpent which stood in the temple (2 Kings xviii. 4). Its origin is attributed to Moses, but the popular story of its origin is careful to indicate that it was never meant to be an idolatrous object (Num. xxi. 4-9). Biblical history admits that Yahwism underwent several changes (e.g. the reforms in 2 Kings xxiii; Ezek. xliv.). The Deuteronomic Law, also, represents a new and decisive step: men are no longer to do as they had done (xii. 8); and the monarchy, too, is regarded as marking a new advance (Judges xvii. 6; xxi. 25). There come times when a choice has to be made (Joshua xxiv. 21 f.), or when Yahweh and his people solemnly enter into a new relationship (Deut. xxvi. 17 f.).[2] Thus the history of Yahwism was certainly a complex one, and the difficulty of tracing the stages, especially in the pre-exilic age, will be appreciated by every student of the Old Testament.

[1] Exod. xxxii. 35, who made the calf, Aaron or the people? He did not actually make it, it "came out" of the molten metal (v. 24).

[2] The leading note of Deuteronomy (or rather, of the nucleus of it) so unmistakably points to a time when a new purged Israel is contemplated, that it must belong to an age and a situation not less significant than that to which the old Biblical tradition assigned it.

Contact with other peoples and their religions naturally affected the growth of Yahwism. Intercourse with Philistia and other lands taught Israel their ways (Isa. ii. 6); alliance with Tyre or with Damascus (e.g. under the Omri dynasty) meant friendly feelings for their gods. The presence of Tyrian traders who did not observe the Sabbath (Neh. xiii. 16) is an illustration of the consequences of relations with men of another religion. On the other hand, Jewish traders and exiles would spread their own religion; and since, in ancient belief, it was the gods who sent men to war and who sought to spread their cult, a victorious Israel would hope for gifts of homage to Zion. Persian, Greek and Roman conquerors might demand certain specific acts of recognition (e.g. prayer and sacrifice on their behalf, Ezra vi. 10; 1 Macc. vii. 33), and Jews were advised by Jeremiah to pray for the welfare of the lands in which they were settled (Jer. xxix. 7). But Oriental conquerors were apt to be more fanatical; and forceful proselytism (as in the Maccabaean age) and the destruction of the enemy (Edom, 1 Kings xi. 15 f.) illustrate an intolerance which had a religious rather than a merely political background (cf. pp. 104, 185 f.).

Yahweh, who was behind world-history, would reward those peoples who surrendered to Babylon (Jer. xxvii. 11), he would restore the fortunes of Moab and Elam (xlviii. 47; xlix. 39), and would succour the weakness of Edom (xlix. 11). The fate of peoples depended also upon their attitude to Israel—whether they would be blessed or cursed (Gen. xii. 3; Num. xxiv. 9). The god of Israel might manifest his sovereignty by destroying other peoples (cf. also Isa. xliii. 3). On the other hand, these might be blessed through Israel (Gen. xii. 3; xviii. 18; cf. BS xliv. 21), or, as other passages state, they might treat Yahweh's blessing of Israel as a pattern for all blessings.[1] The ideal Israel was unmistakably the people whom Yahweh had blessed (Isa. lxi. 9); and peoples would be led to the worship of her god Yahweh and to entreat his favour (Zech. ii. 11; viii. 20 f.). So, the (original) Book of Zechariah closes with the words:

[1] Gen. xxii. 18; cf. xlviii. 20; Ruth iv. 11 f.; contrast Jer. xxix. 22.

"we will go with you, for we have heard that Elohim is with you" (viii. 23): the wider term "Elohim" is used, and not the more nationalistic Yahweh.   As in the similar passage, "in thee only is Elohim" (Isa. xlv. 14), Israel's Yahweh is the world's god, and in some real sense is manifested in his people.

Israel's consciousness of a mission to other peoples is seen at its best in the Second Isaiah (xlix. 6, etc.).   It takes more concrete form when she is the "priestly" people, mediating between God and the world (Isa. lxi. 6; cf. Exod. xix. 6). Her sanctuary thus gains enhanced significance: its beauty and wealth will be famous; it will be the centre of nations who have found that their gods are mere vanities (cf. Jer. xvi. 19 f.), who go there for arbitration (Isa. ii. 3 f.), and who bring thither their wealth (Isa. lx.).   Through the fame of Zion, the dispersed Jews, and the increasing number of proselytes, the name of Yahweh spreads east and west. A striking passage (Mal. i. 11, probably fifth century B.C.) speaks as though Yahweh already received widespread offerings among the Gentiles, though it more naturally refers to the cults among the Jews scattered around in Babylon, Sardis (Sepharad, Obad. v. 20), and Elephantine or Syene (so Isa. xlix. 12).   But Yahweh would let himself be found by them that sought him not, and manifest himself to a people that did not call on his name (Isa. lxv. 1). Could Yahweh therefore be known under other names?   No doubt a Jew could see in the fine ethical religion of Ahura-Mazda something akin to Yahwism.   And if the ruling gods of Persia and Israel had much in common, at Elephantine Israel's Yahu and the local Egyptian Khnum, a great creator god, certainly seem to have resembled each other. In the Greek age the writer of the Letter of Aristeas tells how the god of the Jews could be identified with Zeus. Thus it seemed possible for Yahwism—or perhaps a nominal Yahwism—to spread, on the ground that all god-fearing men were really worshipping the same God.   Perhaps this idea lies behind the hope of another late writer, that one day Yahweh would be king over all the earth, "Yahweh shall be one and his name one" (Zech. xiv. 9).

As a self-conscious part of a great empire, whether Persian or Greek, the Israelite might feel that his national god was being approached by different people under different names. But although Hellenizing Jews might admit the identity of Yahweh and Zeus, the religious imperialism of Antiochus Epiphanes and the erection of the image of Zeus Olympius in the temple (Dec., 167 B.C.), deliberately subordinated Yahweh to Zeus. This fired the Jews to revolt. The fierce struggles of the Maccabees preserved Yahwism and purified it anew; but, their victory once gained, a narrow and intolerant spirit marred their subsequent actions, and, in the long run, the victory may be said to have been a greater benefit to the history of religion in general than to the Jewish State (p. 207).

The internationalism and universalism that seemed to spread Yahwism also threatened its stability as a *national* religion. If Yahweh, Zeus, and other leading deities were essentially the same, the Jew might feel that his special religious privileges were being whittled away. But it was not a question merely of *name*. Isaiah had denounced those who draw near to Yahweh with their mouth and honour him with their lips but whose heart was remote (Isa. xxix. 13, the A.V. is preferable to the R.V.). Amos (ix. 7) had already said that Yahweh was behind the movements of Philistines and Aramaeans as well as of Israel. Not the *name* Yahweh, but its *content* was what mattered, and Israel, clinging sometimes almost fanatically to her exclusive national privileges, did not realise that in seeking to save her body she ran the risk of losing her soul.

It is noteworthy that both the Targum (the later Aramaic paraphrase) and the Septuagint miss the point of a fine passage which proclaims that the triad Israel, Egypt and Assyria shall receive an equal blessing (Isa. xix. 24 f.); and that the Targum spoils another powerful scene where Yahweh reigning on Mount Zion, holds his coronation feast for Gentiles as well as Jews (xxv. 6). It is the old problem over again—the group and its god, and the constituents of that group (cf. p. 121 f.). If Israel would be a missionary people, how much of Yahwism was the proselyte to accept?

Might not his Yahwism be purely nominal and external? Or would there be a *jihād*, when all idolators should be put to the sword (Isa. lxv. 13ff.; lx. 12)? Was Israel to be among the nations as a lion among the sheep (Mic. v. 7f.; *v.* 6 is very obscure)? Would not a militant and not always ethical religion with its centre at Jerusalem arouse the jealousy and enmity of the peoples? The ideal of a one and only Yahweh was not a simple one if different peoples were to be united in religion; and we may prefer to pass over some striking pictures of a self-centred and vain-glorious Israel, and recall her permanent conquests in the realm of ethical idealism. Her finest victories came "not by might, nor by power" (Zech. iv. 6).

It is to Israel's everlasting honour that circumstances had only to bring together comparable gods—Yahweh and Shamash, or Marduk, or Ahura-Mazda, or Zeus—for her to insist that her Yahweh was unlike all other gods. In seeking to express this "emotional monotheism" of hers and to realise it in practical life, she played out the drama of her history. In trying to formulate a practical and ethical monotheism she gave the world the conception of a Messiah. But since it was here that, as the centuries passed, the old religion and a new sect went different ways, it is necessary to try and understand that this bifurcation and the separation of Judaism and Christianity had its roots in earlier problems of the nature of Yahweh.

Looking back, we see that even after Yahweh had been introduced definitely into Palestine and had superseded the earlier gods of the land, the fight for ethical monotheism was slow, painful, and not without set-backs. Not only has a thorough-going monotheism to face the problem of uniting peoples of different shades of religious and other thought, but deeper reflection upon the Divine Nature and Divine Government of the world brings problems of another sort. Thus, Job feels the difference between what God seems to be in His external dealings with men, and what God really is (xvi. 20f.; xvii. 3): "one God holds him guilty, another knows his innocence, and he appeals to the one against the other" (Davidson). There was the one actively interfering in the affairs of men, and the other, the God who, Job knew, verily existed. Yet there were not two Gods! How was Hebrew thought to do justice to religious experience and maintain its practical theism along with its conviction of God's real independence of the ways of men? It was a *practical* problem before it passed into the realm of philosophy and metaphysics.

We may observe, first, how in the late post-exilic age the Jew preserved the supremacy of Yahweh. "Worship him, all ye gods," writes the Hebrew Psalmist (xcvii. 7); but in the Septuagint the "gods" become angels or messengers. Corresponding to the group or national gods of old there now are tutelary "angels" (BS xvii. 17; and the LXX of Deut. xxxii. 8 for "children of Israel"). At an earlier stage other nations who had other gods could be contrasted with Israel who had Yahweh for herself (cf. Deut. iv. 19). But in Maccabaean times even Israel comes to have her own guardian; and it is he who protects Israel, and not Yahweh (as in Isa. lxiii. 1–6; contrast the "angel" in *v.* 9). God is now supreme, and the angel (*mal'āk*) who is his deputy for Israel bears the significant name Michael, "who is like El?" (Dan. x. 13, 20f.; xi. 1; xii. 1). The tutelary "angels" contend with one another; and upon the results of their conflicts depend the fates of their respective nations (Dan. *loc. cit.*). Yahweh can punish at one and the same time this heavenly host and the corresponding earthly rulers (Isa. xxiv. 21ff.). Accordingly, we have in this late age the conception of guardian or representative *angels*, and contending *angels*, whereas under polytheism (as seen best in Babylonia), countries or their kings once had representative or guardian deities, and the wars on earth had their counterpart in conflicts between the corresponding powers in the heavens. The old religion has gone, but the characteristic angelology of the late post-exilic age preserves the last traces of it.

Next, to replace the purely national god Yahweh by a tutelary guardian Michael was only one way of preserving the supremacy and majesty of Yahweh the God of the Universe. Earlier types of thought had been strongly

M

anthropic, but the extraordinarily anthropomorphic scene on Mount Sinai in Exod. xxiv. 9–11 is counterbalanced elsewhere by the insistence that the people, at least, saw no manner of form (Deut. iv. 12, 15). Yahweh has his agencies: his Name, his Face or Presence (p. 126), his Spirit (Isa. xlviii. 16; lxiii. 11f.), his Word, or his Glory. Jewish monotheism had constantly to fight against the tendency to regard these as independent or distinct entities, like the "Wisdom" of the later books (p. 204f.). Of special importance is Yahweh's "angel" (*mal'āk*), conceived not as a distinct messenger (p. 129), but as one that was effectively Yahweh. This *mal'āk* speaks as Yahweh, acts for him, or proves to be Yahweh (Num. xxii. 22ff. and 31; Gen. xvi. 7ff. and *v*. 11; xxxi. 11, 13). From the Hebrew and Greek text in some passages we can see that later editors or readers found it difficult to deal "theologically" with what was evidently a complete manifestation of Yahweh but not precisely Yahweh himself (Gen. xviii. f.; Judges vi.; xiii.). A difference can be seen between passages where the *mal'āk* is evidently human and those where he is more remote and calls from the sky (Gen. xxii. 11, 15). It is a heavenly *mal'āk* who intercedes for Israel (Zech. i. 19ff.; cf. iii. 6f.); but Yahweh's *mal'āk* might be a prophet (Hag. i. 13), a priest (Mal. ii. 7), or a more mysterious figure, the forerunner of Yahweh (Mal. iii. 1; cf. iv. 5?). Both the *mal'āk* and the "interpreter" or "ambassador" (*mēlīṣ*) could be purely human (cf. Isa. xliii. 27 mg.; 2 Chron. xxxii. 31 mg.), or—like the "holy" intercessors—of the supernatural order (Job v. 1; xxxiii. 23). This is the important fact: it was equally possible in ancient belief to recognise the existence of supernatural beings—not necessarily "holy" in an ethical sense—who performed earthly service, or to think of men of flesh and blood as so endowed with supernormal or divine powers as to be almost supernatural beings.

In the Ancient Near East the divine kingship was a well-established institution; and the Amarna Letters show that it had been familiar in Palestine (p. 90f.). The Pharaoh was in effect the god manifest. He was identified with Re, the great god of the land; but though he was the "son" of

a god he was thoroughly human. "Egypt," says an
inscription of Merneptah (*c.* 1225 B.C.), "is the only daughter
of Re whose son sits on the throne." Re was once king of
Egypt and, through the relationship between the Pharaoh,
Re and the other gods, the human king could regard Re as
his father and the lesser deities as his brothers and sisters.
Belief in divine kingship takes different forms and is so
deeply rooted, wherever political and religious ideas are
one, that we cannot be surprised to find traces of it in
Israel.

In Israel Yahweh is king and Jerusalem is his throne
(Jer. iii. 17; xvii. 12; Ezek. xliii. 7). The human king is
"Yahweh's Anointed" (*māshīākh*) or "Messiah." He is
formally adopted as Yahweh's "son" and first-born (2 Sam.
vii. 14; Ps. ii. 7; lxxxix. 26f.). The Davidic kings rule as
deputies of Yahweh, and one can speak of "the throne of
David" (Jer. xxii. 30; xxxiii. 17), or of the king as sitting
on Yahweh's throne (1 Chron. xxviii. 5; xxix. 23; 2 Chron.
ix. 8; cf. xiii. 8).[1] Any tendency to treat the king as divine
would be contrary to the stricter monotheistic Yahwism;
and in the popular didactic narratives the king is "as"
Yahweh's *mal'āk* possessing superior insight (1 Sam. xxix. 9;
2 Sam. xiv. 17; xix. 27). The "house of David" is "as
God, as Yahweh's *mal'āk*" (Zech. xii. 8), even as Moses is
to "God-ward" in relation to the people, or "as God" in
relation to his mouthpiece, Aaron the prophet (Exod. xviii.
19; iv. 16; vii. 1). To curse the king was as heinous an
offence as to curse God (Exod. xxii. 28; 1 Kings xxi. 10),
and stories tell, perhaps for a purpose, how David himself
would not injure his enemy Saul because he was Yahweh's
Anointed (1 Sam. xxiv. 6; xxvi. 9; cf. 2 Sam. i. 16).

The royal palace and temple were as one, and the kings
were buried in the sacred area (Ezek. xliii. 7f.). From
David's care for the Ark (2 Sam. vii.) to Josiah's far-reaching
reforms (2 Kings xxiii.) they take a leading part in the cult.

---

[1] It is very noteworthy that the earlier version of 2 Chron. ix. 8,
viz. 1 Kings x. 9, speaks of David on "the throne of Israel," a less
theocratic conception. Chronicles is more in harmony with old
Oriental usage.

The king or "prince" has both a crown and a priestly mitre or turban (Ezek. xxi. 26), and the future ruler (*addīr*), like the priests, still has access to Yahweh (Jer. xxx. 21). But a change came in, and certain anti-monarchical and pro-priestly tendencies can be recognised in the later parts of the Old Testament. Ezekiel's programme restricts the rights of future rulers, although the "prince" (*nāsī*), as he is styled (cf. 1 Kings xi. 34, of Rehoboam), must still provide for the sacrifices (xlv. 17). One late story condemns the king for encroaching upon the rights of the Aaronite priests (2 Chron. xxvi. 18); and Zech. vi. points to some rivalry between the royal and the priestly heads and subsequent harmony or compromise. The high-priests of the post-exilic period sometimes seem to have inherited almost regal powers. In fact, the political development of the Jewish State under the Hasmonaean high-priesthood and the conception of a priest-king "after the manner of Melchi-zedek" in what is a late Psalm (Ps. cx.) indicate the persistence to a very late date of that combination of religious and political authority that characterises the priestly kingship and the earlier divine kingship.

King and kingdom could be so identified—as e.g. in the dirge over Tyre (Ezek. xxviii.)—that the former can be spoken of as the people's "lamp" (2 Sam. xxi. 17), or as their *rūakh*, their breath or spirit (Lam. iv. 20). The latter idea has many parallels in the Amarna Letters and elsewhere, and the conception of the life-giving breath of the divine sovereign is the forerunner of the Israelite conception of Yahweh's *rūakh* (Ezek. xxxvii. 14, etc.; pp. 90, 139). Outside Israel, at least, the conduct of the divine king could be held to have an influence upon the land and people second only to that exerted by the god. Of this idea, too, there are traces in Israel, and when we recall the importance of the temple-ritual (p. 151) and the king's part in the cult, it is noteworthy that the "prince" envisaged by Ezekiel (xlv. 16ff.) must provide for the festivals of Passover and Tabernacles, and a special atone-ment for the temple in the first and seventh months, i.e. the opening months of the year according to the two current modes of reckoning. Here, his part, on what were specially fateful occasions, certainly seems to go back to the time when there was a "divine kingship" in Israel similar to that found elsewhere.

A new king, and especially a new dynasty, would often mean a new era in the land's history. An ideal king will be anticipated—the successor of Ahaz (Isa. ix. 2–7), Zedekiah (Jer. xxiii. 6 ?), or his successor (Ezek. xxi. 27). The hopes aroused by the advent of the Davidic Zerubbabel can be read in the prophecies of Zechariah and Haggai; and they enable us to imagine what other prophets might have said of the Davidic Nehemiah later, when the royal dynasty was being overshadowed by the priesthood, and even the governor's presence in the temple might be resented (Neh. vi. 6, 11). Besides the writings with the familiar expectation of an ideal scion of David, a sapling from the stock of Jesse (Isa. xi.; Zech. iii. 8; vi. 12), a native of Bethlehem of Judah (Mic. v. 2), there are others which find no place for Yahweh's Anointed, and the future depends rather upon the priesthood (Malachi and Joel). In one case (Jer. xxxiii. 17–21), by a compromise which recalls that between Zerubbabel and Joshua (Zech. vi.), room is found for both Davidic and Levitical heads.

In their hopes for the future, it is not—at least at first—for some wholly new order, but for a better one, that the prophets look. Freedom from evil is not expected, but there will be ideally perfect justice (Isa. xi. 4f.; xxxii. 1ff.). A Golden Age is heralded (Isa. xi. 6ff.), the sketches of which are now sober and now extravagant; and there are dreams of agricultural prosperity such as could be shared by Palestinian or Canaanite natives, and would hardly have arisen, in the first instance, among Israelite or other nomads from the desert. A time of peace is often looked for (Hos. ii. 18; Isa. ii. 4); but the vision of a world-wide peace under the aegis of Zion's lowly and pious king does not exclude the expectation of sanguinary scenes when the Jews, with Yahweh's help, will defeat their enemies (Zech. ix. 9ff.; cf. Mic. v. 8f.). But it is Yahweh who introduces the Messiah or the Messianic age: it may be Zerubbabel (Hag.

ii. 21 ff.), or it may be the deliverance of Jerusalem from the heathen and the inauguration of universal monotheism (Zech. xiv.).

Yahweh himself is the saviour; but he must use a human medium to manifest his power. This is important, for the "Messiah" or Anointed One is not always the real or ideal king, but also, sometimes, the people (Hab. iii. 13; Ps. xxviii. 8, etc.). Yahweh manifests himself in either. In some passages "the glory of Israel is his glory, he and Israel are not two, but glorified Israel reflects his glory" (Davidson; cf. Isa. xliv. 23; xlv. 14 f.; xlix. 3).[1] The ideal Messiah-king partakes of Yahweh's attributes (Isa. ix. 6 f.; cf. x. 21; xxviii. 29, etc.). In him is Yahweh's *rūakh* which "clothes" men (Isa. xi. 2; cf. Judges vi. 34; 1 Chron. xii. 18), and Yahweh's strength and the majesty of Yahweh's name are the source of his power. Just as the prophet is Yahweh's mouthpiece, so the Anointed One is his agent: Yahweh and his agent form, as it were, a moral unity. "To Isaiah the Messiah is a semi-divine personage, the radiant source of supernatural powers which regenerate nature and human society." "His reign is the pledge of his people's welfare and victory through Yahweh's gracious presence with them through him" (Skinner). But the Messianic figure is not a god, nor has he power of himself. Popular narratives insist that there is a gulf between man and Yahweh (e.g. the Tower of Babel, Gen. xi.; cf. the forbidden tree in Eden, iii. 5), and there are allusions to the downfall of monarchs of Tyre (Ezek. xxviii.) and of Babylon (Isa. xiv.) for their "ambitious aim against the throne and monarchy of God" (Milton), which indicate how extraordinarily realistic could be the conceptions of the divinity of the deputies of the gods.

To the same world of thought as the Messiah belongs also the mysterious "Servant of Yahweh," who appears in a series of passages culminating in Isa. liii. Difficulty of interpretation is caused (*a*) by the way in which the figure seems to pass from an individual to an ideal, or real, or elect

---

[1] On this connection between Yahweh, the people and their representative, of, above on the "group," its representative and its god (p. 117).

Israelite body and back again. This reminds one of the varying ways in which the title Messiah or Anointed One is applied to the king, or to Israel, or to the patriarchs (Ps. cv. 15), and of the successive application of the words "Son of Man" to Ezekiel (ii. 1, etc.), to an ideal Israel (Dan. vii. 13), or to a future deliverer (Enoch xlvi. 2 ff.). Further (b), as often happens in prophetic literature, the writer gathers up past, present and future in one, and history and vision are blended. And (c), the language seems to swing between the description of a unique human individual, or group, and a spiritual vision for which human language is inadequate. In any case, the fact that in this figure (presumably of the sixth century B.C.) Christian exegesis inevitably found the closest association with the "Christ" of several centuries later, proves that Israelite thought was struggling with certain profound conceptions which, *as it would seem*,[1] left no recognisable traces upon the immediate course of history and religion.

The Yahwism of the Old Testament stands between (1) the *later* developments in Daniel and the apocryphal and other literature which form the prelude to the rise of Christianity, and (2) the *earlier* cruder and more "mythological" beliefs and practices which have either disappeared or have been sublimated. There is nothing extravagant in the view that in the older religion there was a divine kingship, with the king as the representative of Yahweh, and that grisly human sacrifices to Molech were made *for* or *to* the king. The "Messianic" idea had a long history behind it; and the old religion, before it was reformed by the prophets, contained much that recalls the beliefs and practices of "barbaric" peoples.

More to the present purpose, however, are certain general considerations. In both Egypt and Babylonia men could speak of "God," meaning thereby the particular deity which the context suited. It was never a mere word, and in a living religion it must have a definite meaning and application. Certain men were evidently adequate representatives of current ideas of gods and the divine;

---

[1] See however, pp. 193, 201.

but the ideas were often crude and rudimentary, and the supernatural beings though "holy" or "sacred" were not necessarily of high ethical worth.   In trying to frame and purify her conceptions of a one and only Yahweh, Israel clung to anthropic imagery, though striving to maintain both the essential difference between him and man and his essential presence in all his manifestations.   Problems concerning the Godhead were implicit from an early date, and it is not Israel's fault that "ethical monotheism" has not yet been attained.   A chauvinistic monotheism directed from an earthly Zion could neither have conquered nor won the peoples, and Israel's religious writers were the first to recognise that a universal monotheism must start from the monotheism of individuals if it is to be truly ethical. Israel is not to be blamed because her highest ideals were not translated into actual life: rather is it to her honour that she hewed out paths from which other peoples, with her history before them, cannot depart without risking a worse fate.   This achievement was due to her prophets.

CHAPTER X

The Prophets

HEBREW prophecy is an inexhaustible subject. Here is unsurpassed language of beauty, vigour, emotion and worship. Here are passages so powerful for consolation and encouragement, for warning, threat, or discernment of the future, that on countless occasions they have answered the mood of the West as surely as they did the not dissimilar occasions which first called them forth. For every age Hebrew prophecy has seemed to have some, though not always the same meaning; and it is its meaning for to-day which is the goal of those who seek to reinterpret the Bible to modern needs. The modern effort to treat prophecy historically is due in large measure to the modern attitude to the changes of history, and to the (perhaps subconscious) feeling that the greater impulses that lie behind the ancient prophetic movements, including the movement that ushered in Christianity, *must* have some meaning for the profounder issues of to-day. The prophets of the Old Testament and the New come before us as great creative figures who helped to make universal history, and the better we understand them, the clearer is our outlook on both the past and the future.

The supposition that Prophecy is merely or mainly Prediction is misleading and makes for Superstition, the worst enemy of Religion. But it is a common opinion; and the Book of Daniel has often been more highly esteemed than the far more significant writings of the prophets, strictly so called, simply because it seemed to depict a future as yet unrealised. There is, of course, the closest association between the two Testaments: they turn upon two great periods in Palestinian history, and, on any view, the Hebrew prophets point both backward and forward. They point backward, since, on the traditional view, whether Jewish or Christian, the Hebrew prophets are, as it were, the exponents of the Mosaic Law, to the fundamental principles of which they recall Israel. They point forward; but whereas for Christianity the New Testament supersedes the Pentateuch, this latter is to the Jew, of course, the foundation of his Judaism. Our retrospect of the pre-Christian period depends upon our ideas of the place held therein by the Pentateuch and of its relation to the religious movements that arose after the period covered by the Old Testament; and the Biblical critic is impressed by the difference between the Pentateuch, as a whole, and the prophets, whom he is forced to regard as earlier than the Mosaic Law in its present form (p. 48). The Pentateuch, on this view, did not become authoritative, in fact, did not receive its present form, before the age of Ezra.[1] None the less, the prophets still point backward, not to a forgotten Mosaism which they revived, but to an older and cruder religion which they transformed (p. 186 f.).

The prophets of Israel were of all sorts and conditions: members of an established class by the side of the priests, men attached to the court, wandering bodies ("sons of the prophets"), or isolated individuals (Isa. iii. 2 f.; 1 Kings xxii. 6). Some were diviners who expected a gift or fee (1 Sam. ix. 7; 1 Kings xiv. 3; 2 Kings v. 15); it was their living (Amos vii. 12), and they might impose upon the trust or credulity of their clients (Mic. iii. 5, 11). Some were inspired by dreams and visions; and wine and music were among their means of inducing an appropriate psychical state (Isa. xxviii. 7; 2 Kings iii. 15). Their ecstatic behaviour when they "played the prophet" (Saul, 1 Sam. xix. 24; cf. 1 Kings xviii. 28 f.) justified the taunt that the prophet was a madman (2 Kings ix. 11; Hos. ix. 7; Jer. xxix. 26). The prophet has "second sight" (cf. 2 Kings v. 26); he has a double "self" (Isa. xxi. 6–9). He is often intensely introspective; and the behaviour and prophecies of a Jeremiah and an Ezekiel indicate that they could not have been average types of Israelite mentality.

Even though, at their best, the prophets were not what

[1] On the date, see p. 194 n.

we might call perfectly normal individuals, we must recognise the self-possession of an Isaiah and the slow conviction of a Jeremiah (xxviii.; xxxii. 8; xlii. 7). The prophets are not mere vehicles, or rather, they range from the man who feels himself to be the mouthpiece of Yahweh (cf. the relation between Moses and Aaron, Exod. vii. 1), to the man capable of self-control and discipline such as meets us in the writings of Jeremiah. Abnormal behaviour (cf. the trance, Num. xxiv. 3f.) has always been impressive to Eastern observers; but it is a higher type of prophecy when the prophet's utterances are part of his personality, part of his usual thinking (see p. 188f.). Yet the prophet is not his own master. There comes upon him an overwhelming "strong hand" (Isa. viii. 11); he cannot withstand Yahweh's purpose. What Yahweh says, that must he speak (1 Kings xxii. 14)—as illustrations of this we have only to recall the stories of Balaam and Balak (cf. Num. xxii. 18), Jonah's flight, and the disobedient prophet of Judah (1 Kings xiii.; see *vv.* 21f., 26). When Yahweh chooses his prophet, he gives him the strength he needs (Jer. i. 4–10, 17; xv. 20; Ezek. ii. 6; iii. 8), or sends him a helper (Exod. iv. 10ff.); and the story of Jeremiah shows that once a man has put his hand to the prophet's plough he cannot draw back (Jer. xx. 9).

The prophet finds food for thought everywhere: in the growth of the stump (Isa. vi. 13), the almond tree (Jer. i. 11f.), the potter and the clay (Jer. xviii. 1ff.), the metal worker (Jer. vi. 27–30; Ezek. xxii. 17–22), the rusty pot (Ezek. xxiv. 6ff.). In the prophecies of Hosea personal experiences—a tragic married life—and the apostasy or "whoredom" of Israel are intermingled; but it would be difficult perhaps, even on psycho-analytical grounds, to make much of the fact that the clear-headed Jeremiah was a bachelor (xvi. 2), and the strangely ecstatic Ezekiel married (xxiv. 15ff.). The prophets stand in the council of Yahweh (Jer. xxiii. 18, 22; cf. Ps. xxv. 14 mg.); but a line is firmly drawn between Moses and other prophets (Num. xii. 6ff.). By reason of their function a heavy responsibility lies upon them (Ezek. iii. 17–21; xxxiii. 1–9):

they are powerful intercessors (cf. also 1 Sam. xii. 23)—
though the situation may be hopeless (Jer. vii. 16)—and
their iniquities have the more fateful consequences for their
land (e.g. Lam. iv. 13).

There were diviners, seers, prophets of all sorts: there
were prophets of Baal (1 Kings xviii. 19), men and women
who would consult the dead (Isa. viii. 19; 1 Sam. xxviii. 11,
etc.); and among the accredited prophets of Yahweh there
were often sharp differences of opinion. Consequently the
problem of distinguishing "true" and "false" prophets
would come to the fore, especially in times of crisis. There
were prophets who were accused of relying upon false
dreams and visions; what they speak comes "of their own
heart" (cf. Jeroboam, 1 Kings xii. 33), and not from Yahweh
(Jer. xxiii. 16, 28, 32). Some speak in the name of other
gods (Deut. xviii. 20); but even those who claim to speak
in Yahweh's name may be false (Jer. xiv. 14; xxiii. 21;
Ezek. xiii. 7). Some cocker up rulers and people (1 Kings
xxii. 12 f.); they support the priests and the people who
"love to have it so" (Jer. v. 31; cf. Mic. ii. 11); they steal
one another's words (Jer. xxiii. 30); they say "peace,"
when there is no peace, and heal the hurt of the people
lightly, making nothing of the imminent peril (Jer. vi. 14;
viii. 11; xiv. 13). So, the "burden" of Yahweh becomes a
real burden (xxiii. 33–40). The conduct of some is evil
(Jer. xxiii. 11, 14; xxix. 23); and their indifference to
morality may find an explanation in the prevalence of
inveterate sensuous rites (Hos. iv.). Even "false" prophets
could give signs—so could Pharaoh's magicians (Deut.
xiii. 2; cf. Exod. vii. 11 f.); but their message leads to
apostasy from Yahweh. The fulfilment of prophecy is the
mark of the "true" prophet (Deut. xviii. 21 f.; Jer. xxviii. 9,
16 f.; cf. 1 Sam. ix. 6); but though men may look for speedy
fulfilment (Isa. v. 19; Jer. xvii. 15), the vision may tarry
(Hab. ii. 3), and both the promises and the threats are
conditional. Freedom of choice is emphasised (Jer. xviii;
Ezek. xviii.; xxxiii.; Isa. lv. 6 f.), and at any time any
individual, or a people (like the men of Nineveh, Jonah
iii. 10), may change for the better—or for the worse (Ezek.

xviii. 24 ff.)—and Yahweh will then change his purpose (Jer. xviii. 7 ff.).

One point in particular deserves notice: apart from the occasions when their outlook upon the immediate future was justified (e.g. Micaiah, 1 Kings xxii.), the necessity of distinguishing between true and false prophecy comes to the front when the men who are denouncing the "false prophets" stand for conceptions of Yahweh which actually purified Israelite religion, and directed it along lines which proved permanently effective. Further, the condemnation of divination and false prophecy in Deuteronomy (xiii. 1 ff.; xviii. 9 ff.) is especially significant, since the book as a whole reflects the teaching of the reforming prophets: their work was done, and it only remained to build up the new people of Yahweh on its foundations (see p. 185 f.).

Divination, prophecy, and the like, play a great part in the larger concerns of life (1 Sam. xiv. 36 f.; xxviii. 6, are typical). The prophets come before us, urging ruthless warfare (e.g. against Amalek, 1 Sam. xv.; cf. 1 Kings xx. 42; 2 Kings xiii. 19), exulting over the downfall of Babylon (Isa. xiii.), Nineveh (Nah. ii. f.) and Edom (Isa. lxiii. 1–6), glorifying an ever-victorious Israel whom no curse could harm (Num. xxiii. 18–24), or stirring Jeroboam II to restore the fortunes of the Northern Kingdom (2 Kings xiv. 25). They condemn foreign alliances, for these weaken religious solidarity and betray lack of faith in Yahweh. They despise the policy of reliance upon Egypt or Assyria (Jer. ii. 18; Hos. vii. 11); or, like Isaiah and Jeremiah, they take up a definite political attitude towards the Great Powers—though on religious grounds. Denouncing their nation for its sin and apostasy, they are whole-heartedly encouraging in its darkest hour. They live—or at least the greatest of them live—in the midst of sweeping historical movements; and they are great, not only because of their deep insight into the profounder factors that make history, but because their survey of events is not confined to their own country.

Prophecy is not "history written beforehand." The mention of Cyrus in the Second Isaiah is exceptional (Isa.

xliv. 28; xlv. 1), and that of Josiah in 1 Kings xiii. 2 is no doubt part of a prophecy *post eventum*. The prophets are concerned only with what is intelligible to their age; and though they prophesied "into the future," the traditional belief that Isa. xl.–lxvi. belong to the time of the Isaiah of Hezekiah's reign, or that the Messianic prophecies had in view the events of many centuries later, misses the real importance of the Bible for Universal History. The great prophets undoubtedly helped to guide the course of history; but, on the whole, they were conscious of the *principles* of God's dealings with men rather than of the form that men's dealings with one another would take (cf. p. 109 and note).

Between history-making prophecy and the actual writing of history there is no impassable gulf. There were prophets who could make and unmake kings (notably Samuel), prophets of whose religious and other activities stories were preserved (e.g. Isaiah, 2 Kings xix.f.; Jeremiah, Ch. xl.ff.). There were prophets to whom the author of Chronicles ascribes didactic histories, and even the so-called "Historical Books" themselves (Joshua–2 Kings) came to be called the "Former Prophets" (p. 24). Prophetical writings were sometimes duplicated (Isa. ii. 2ff. and Mic. iv. 1ff.), readjusted (Egypt, Ezek. xxix. 17ff.), supplemented (Moab, Isa. xvi. 13f.), or expanded (Moab, Jer. xlviii.; Edom, Jer. xlix., cf. Obadiah). Prophecies relating to Jerusalem (Jer. vi. 22–24) and Edom (xlix. 19–21) were taken over and applied to Babylon (l. 41–43 and 44–46); and those referring originally to the Scythians seem to have been adjusted to a subsequent foreign invasion (Jer. iv. 5–vi. 30).

Similar occasions might, and often did, call forth similar utterances or writings. This is obviously true, of course, of the appeal for reform, of denunciation of evils, and the call for repentance. But there are several important "repetitions" in the national history: the ravaging of Judah by Sennacherib in Isaiah's day and by the Babylonians a century later in the time of Jeremiah; the fall of Samaria in 721 B.C. and that of Jerusalem in 586 B.C.; the exile of the Northern Israelites at the former date and that of the

Judaeans at the latter.   The fate of the Holy City became a
type for similar disasters, even in writings of the Christian
period; and the actual return from Exile in the time of
Zerubbabel lies behind the prophecies of an actual or hoped
for return of the Jews of the Diaspora.   Thus, the Fall of
Jerusalem, the Exile and the Return formed a sort of
"pattern"; and the interpretation of prophecy is frequently
complicated by our difficulty of distinguishing between
symbolic and highly idealistic descriptions of events present
or impending and very realistic pictures or visions of the
future.   If to this we add the frequent lack of logical
arrangement of ideas, the accumulation of miscellaneous
passages united merely by some catchword or sentiment,
and the frequent impossibility of dating passages in writings
which are indubitably composite, the intricacy of the study
of the prophets will be apparent.

Centuries later there were prophets among Christians and
Jews.   Josephus the historian, a Pharisee, and of a priestly
family, was an accomplished prophet.   A second Jeremiah
in his conviction that Israel had been forsaken by her God
for her sins, he was persuaded that God had raised up
Vespasian to be lord of all men (*War*, iii. 8).   John Hyrcanus,
too, had the gift of prophecy (*ibid.*, i. 2, 8).   Outside Israel
there were other prophets besides Balaam (the Philistines,
Isa. ii. 6; the Phoenicians, 1 Kings xviii.), and an eleventh-
century story of the visit of the Egyptian envoy Wen-Amon
to the court of the prince of Byblos, tells how a noble youth
became ecstatic, and prophesied as the prince sacrificed
to his god.   It is unnecessary to give examples from further
afield.   The prophet, *in the widest sense of the term*, is no
isolated phenomenon; the distinctiveness of Israel lies in
the fact that prophecy is directed towards the religious,
social and national history of Israel and to the relations
between her and her god Yahweh.   In an ancient land, a
land in closest touch with its neighbours, prophecy becomes
part of the framework of the history of Israel, in that it
was through a "prophet" that Yahweh brought Israel
out of Egypt (Hos. xii. 13), and Moses himself is the head
of a succession of prophets, though without an equal among

his successors (Deut. xviii. 15 ff.; xxxiv. 10). So runs the canonical tradition.

After the time of Moses, however, several centuries pass before we reach the beginning of the line of "written" prophets. There were prophets before them: the guilds ("sons of the prophets") who are mentioned in stories of the time of Saul and of Elijah and Elisha were naturally not confined to those stirring periods. The terrible Aramaean invasions that preceded the rise of Jeroboam II (e.g. 2 Kings xiii. 4f., 7; xiv. 26f.) and the circumstances of Israel's recovery would, on all analogy, give rise to prophecies of warning, consolation and encouragement, the nature of which we can easily imagine. But it is not until the middle and latter half of the eighth century that four "written" prophets make an almost contemporary appearance.

Amos, who disclaims all relationship with the accredited prophets (vii. 14f.), tells of the approaching fall of the Northern kingdom. He strikes the authentic note of Hebrew prophecy. Yahweh has universal power, his interest is not confined to Israel alone (ix. 7), and if Israel claims special privileges, she will be judged by a higher standard (iii. 2). Like all her neighbours she must suffer for her transgressions (i. 3–ii. 4), for Yahweh demands right conduct rather than religious rites (v. 21–24); he is the universal God of righteousness. Insistence upon Divine Righteousness characterises Amos; and if he ignores the calf-cult and other evils denounced a little later by Hosea, it is because, for him, first things come first, and he is more concerned with principles.

Hosea, the prophet of the decline of the Northern Kingdom, is a man of quite another type. He fights against a false Yahwism, which is really Baalism; it is Yahweh, he declares, and not the Baals whom Israel must approach for the things of life, and he breaks up the older physical ideas of the relationship between Israel and God. He emphasises the love and compassion of Yahweh; it unites him and his people, and the people among themselves. Yahweh's righteousness—as taught by Amos—condemns all those who have fallen short, whereas Hosea thinks of Yahweh's

loyalty to a faithless "spouse" and his grief over a back-
sliding people, a grief not caused by Israel's breaches of the
law of righteousness, but by her gross ingratitude. Hosea
emphasises the *personal* relationship between Yahweh and
Israel, and Amos the *principle* of Divine Righteousness.
The two supplement each other. "All's love yet all's law":
either by itself is incomplete; and these two great complementary conceptions stand at the head of Old Testament
prophecy.

Micah, the prophet of the poor, manifests that democratic
tendency which regards Yahwism as the religion of the
people as a whole, and condemns the leaders as the cause
of the land's ruin. Like the rest of the prophets the book
presents difficult critical problems, and Chapter vi. (*vv.* 1–8),
which contains one of the most inspiring utterances on the
true religion of Yahweh, is generally agreed to be by a later
hand.

In contrast to Micah and his Judaean peasantry is the
court-prophet Isaiah, who by common consent is the
grandest of all the prophets, and whose language is Hebrew
of the Golden Period. Yahweh, "the Holy One of Israel,"
dwells, or rather reigns, unseen in Zion, preserving its
inviolability and filling the whole earth with his glory.
He is confronted by a people weak, faithless, men of unclean
lips, doomed to perish for their blindness. But in quiet
and steadfast reliance upon Yahweh there is safety and
continuance for the faithful (vii. 9; cf. 2 Chron. xx. 20);
and Isaiah is "the prophet of faith."

After a long interval another group of more or less contemporary prophets appears. To Nahum the impending
fall of Nineveh (612 B.C.) demonstrates the judgment of an
ethical Yahweh upon a cruel oppressor. Habakkuk, on
the other hand, the "father of speculation"—as he has
been styled—finds it difficult to reconcile with Yahweh's
character his use of a cruel and boastful agent. If a famous
passage means that the righteous will remain unshaken
(ii. 4; cf. the faith of Ps. lxxiii. 17), quiet and firm confidence
is also the climax of the "Pentecostal" hymn (Ch. iii.).
Here, Yahweh's might shown in the past for Israel sustains

N

men amid their present distress; and Burkitt's paraphrase
of the concluding verses is worth quoting: "however bad
the year may be, we will hold our Harvest Festival all the
same." Zephaniah, perhaps of royal descent, tells of
approaching doom: *Dies irae, dies illa* (i. 15), and he contrasts
men's insolent indifference to Yahweh (i. 12) and Yahweh's
consistent righteousness (iii. 5). Ultimately, however,
Yahweh will be supreme, and this prophet—or a later
writer—looks forward to a universal Yahwism and a single
language (iii. 9).

As for Jeremiah, in the book that bears his name we
learn more of the psychology of religious genius than any-
where else in the Bible. He is "the father of true prayer"
(Wellhausen); he is "the father of Hebrew psalmody," for
in him prophet and psalmist are combined. In his "Confessions" (xi. 18 ff.; xii. 1-6; xv. 10-18; xx. 7-18) we meet
with one of the loneliest, the most sensitive, yet the most
courageous of men. If he saw the downfall of his people
(ix. 11; x. 22; xxiv. 8-10), there was no self-seeking in
him, no anxiety to see *his* word proved right (xvii. 16).
If he had spoken Yahweh's word boldly, had he been
deceived, had he deceived himself (xx. 7)? Yet, if he
restrained himself, it was as burning fire in his bones, and
he could not be still (xx. 9). Standing, as he felt he did, in
Yahweh's council, he could none the less realise how his
"vileness" (or "cheapness") could prevent him from being
a true mouthpiece of his God (xv. 19).

The prophetical writings of Hosea and Jeremiah have
much in common. Each is the prophet of a dying nation,
and in a concluding enigmatic utterance of Jeremiah to
his scribe Baruch (Ch. xlv.) we have words which, if our
interpretation be correct, link together the Old Testament
and the New, just as we irresistibly associate the teachings
of the prophets Jeremiah and the Second Isaiah with the
spirit of Christianity. For Baruch has come to see that
Israel is doomed: Yahweh's own creation will perish. "What
I have built up, that I pull down; what I have planted,
that I pluck up." Throughout it was the same Yahweh, who
would be what he would be (Exod. iii. 14 mg.), who could

make and could destroy (cf. Isa. liv. 16; Job. x. 8ff.). Yet events were to prove that a new Israel would arise, indeed, that the foundations had already been laid. In this respect the fate of the land and people differed from the catastrophes at that last fall of Jerusalem, when the destruction of the Jewish State and the growth of Christianity meant the end of the visible Israel, as such, and the birth of a new Israel after the spirit. It is precisely then that an unknown but genuinely Jewish patriot is plunged into despair at the sad end of his people; in his grief, he can find no comfort, until at last it flashes across him that his sorrow could not be greater than the grief of Israel's God: "lovest thou that people better than he that made them?" (2 Esdras v. 33; viii. 47).

This was the consolation that monotheistic Yahwism could find, and it was a true and noble one. Later (see p. 214), we shall contrast the fate of Israel in the first century A.D. with its earlier reconstruction in and about the sixth century B.C.; for the more clearly we can see the points of contact between those two creative periods, the more emphatically can we realise the part that the prophets played in history. Here, however, in the earlier period, we are at an age of death and rebirth; and for the history of religious thought it is profoundly interesting to meet in Jeremiah and in his words to Baruch the first expression of the conviction that, "the Creator, just because He is the Creator, must be filled with love for His creation" (Peake).

Jeremiah, the "father of Pharisaism," and his later contemporary Ezekiel, the "father of Sadduceeism," form a pair. They have much in common (e.g. the doctrine of individual responsibility). But they have different views of Israel's past, and Jeremiah sees a declension (Jer. ii. 2f., 22; cf. Isa. v. 1–7), whereas in the eyes of Ezekiel Israel was stubborn from the first (Ezek. xvi.; xx. 7ff.; xxiii. 3; cf. Ps. cvi.). Ezekiel is a priest-prophet, a theologian, the "father of Judaism." Less sensitive, less lyrical than Jeremiah, he is remarkable for his visions, his imagery, and his ecstasy. There is in his prophecies a certain native crudeness, harshness and sensuousness; they take one to the temple sacrifices,

the smell of blood and the blare of temple music, rather than
to the "still small voice" (1 Kings xix. 12). But he sees,
as no other prophet saw, the majesty and holiness of Yahweh
confronting the grossness of Israel, and yet can hope for his
people. For Yahweh desires the death of no man (xviii. 30f.);
he can give man a new heart (xi. 19; xviii. 31), and man
can turn from his evil course and mend his ways. Israel's
sufferings were a just punishment; but because it was
Israel's God who was inflicting it, He could not cast off His
people for ever. Yet there must first be drastic changes.
Of the ultimate reconciliation Ezekiel has no doubt, and
Yahweh, he knows, will once more dwell in the midst of
his people (xlviii. 35). He has a striking philosophy of
history; and while Jeremiah appeals more to the simple
religious mind, Ezekiel manifests a power of thought and
reflexion, one of the many indications of the intellectual
and literary variety of the age.

Some decades later a series of anonymous chapters or
writers represent new conditions. Certain parts of Isa.
i.–xxxv. are of exilic or later origin (so in particular,
Ch. xxiv.–xxvii.); but the historical background of the
whole of Isa. xl.–lxvi. is later than the Fall of Jerusalem
in 586. The "Great Unknown," as Ewald called him, opens
with words of comfort for a distressed and exiled Israel
who has worked off the punishment for her sins, and who
will now return to Zion. The uniqueness of Yahweh, the
futility of idols, and the downfall of Babylon are the leading
themes in Chapters xl.–xlviii. Next (Ch. xlix.–lv.), we
hear more of Zion and of the new situation in the now
redeemed city. The conception of the "Servant of Yahweh"
and his Mission make the Deutero-Isaiah the high-water
mark of Israelite religion. Finally, quite another group
of chapters deals with Zion's internal religious conditions,
the temple, its future glory, and the denunciation of false
worship (lvi.–lxvi.). This transition to other subjects must
be carefully noted.

The consolatory note distinguishes the Second or Deutero-
Isaiah from the prophets of earlier history. Yahweh's care
for a despondent and troubled Israel is described in language

of unequalled beauty, for the writer has all the tenderness of Hosea (xlix. 14f.). Israel's sins are blotted out, and Yahweh has returned to his people. Though the language which describes him is anthropic, Yahweh himself is regarded as incomparable: there is none before or after him, he is alone (xliii. 10; xlvi. 9). Other gods are as nothing: image-worship is ridiculous. The God of the Cosmos is sole creator, above and before the creation of heaven and earth; he is God of a world which he formed that it might be inhabited (xlv. 18). His thoughts transcend man's (lv. 8f.); but his worship is to be universal, and all peoples shall look to him, the Redeemer of the whole earth. He is raising up one to help his people Israel—no Israelite, but the Persian, Cyrus. Other passages describe the future of Israel, her destiny to be Yahweh's witness, and to manifest to the world his character (xliii. 10). But instead of the alien, Cyrus, there now appears an Israelite figure, the Servant of Yahweh. This mysterious and ever-discussed figure is not Messianic, and it is disputed whether it represented an ideal or spiritual Israel, or an individual, and how far it belonged to the present or to the future. The Servant has a mission to Israel, for Israel, and beyond Israel; and the people now crushed and worn have a future before them. In magnifying the majesty of Yahweh, of Israel's God, Israel herself gains a new glory and a new destiny.

But when we pass to Isa. lvi.–lxvi. there is a change of atmosphere as unmistakable as the difference between the pre-exilic Isaiah and the exilic and later "Isaiah." The changes are such as to justify the subdivision of Isaiah (Ch. xl.–lxvi.) into a "Deutero-Isaiah" (Ch. xl.–lv.) and a "Trito-Isaiah" (Ch. lvi.–lxvi.). There is a less hopeful note, a less "spiritual," and a more "materialistic" treatment. Laxity, idolatry, degeneration, self-righteousness and dis-illusionment are so marked that we have clearly passed from a state of expectancy to one of disappointment and the sense of a need of a new intervention of Yahweh.

Now, the historical background to Isa. xl.–lxvi. can be recognised if we consider the Fall of Jerusalem (586 B.C.), the Exile, the overthrow of Babylon by Cyrus, the permission

to return granted to the exiles by Cyrus, the return of
Sheshbazzar and Zerubbabel, the hopes raised by the
appearance of the latter, and then, after a perplexing
blank in the history, the unhappy situation in Judah and
Jerusalem in the days of Nehemiah and Ezra. What
actually happened is extremely obscure, but the contrast
between the hopes of the Deutero-Isaiah and of the prophets
Haggai and Zechariah, and the rivalries, indifference and
religious declension in the days of Nehemiah, the governor,
and Ezra, the scribe, provide the best available clue to the
transition from the early part of Isa. xl.–lxvi. to the later
chapters.

There is no doubt that after the fall of the kingdom of
Judah, the burning of the temple by the Babylonians, and
the Exile, there was a restoration, a reorganisation: in
many respects the age of the Exile, or, more broadly, the
sixth century B.C., was one of far-reaching changes in
history and religion (pp. 98, 192). The "critical" problems
are excessively difficult; but a close study of the Deutero-
Isaiah reveals the conceptions of a new Israel, another
exodus (e.g. xlviii. 20), a new creation, and a reunion of
Yahweh and his people. In contrast to the indifference of
Zephaniah's day (i. 12), and the doubt and pessimism of
Ezekiel's contemporaries, Israel has rediscovered her God;
there is a restatement of monotheism, and it is impossible
to resist the belief that the secret of the successful reorganisation of Israel and the long post-exilic history that followed
was not so much the fact that Judaean exiles were allowed
to return as the outburst of a new religious enthusiasm which
put new life into Yahwism.

The history, it must be emphasised, is problematical.
Yet vital developments of thought can be traced. Condemnation is followed by consolation, and earlier prophecies
of threat and overthrow (cf. Jer. xxviii. 8) give place to new
visions of hope. Yahweh was a devouring flame and
jealous God (Deut. iv. 24): he was jealous because Israel
served other gods, jealous because his uniqueness was
disregarded. But this *jealousy* (*ḳin'ah*) because of Israel,
becomes *zeal* for Israel. He had been angry, and had given

Israel to be punished; now he has slaked his wrath (Ezek.
v. 13). He had given her to the foe, but now he, her
"Creator," has redeemed her (Isa. xlii. 24f.; xliii. 1ff.).
The enemy had gone too far (Zech. i. 14–16; viii. 2), and he
who once left his temple at Jerusalem will now return to
it with mercies (Ezek. xi. 23; Zech. i. 16). He rises up
like a warrior (Isa. xlii. 13), amazed that there is no one to
intervene (lix. 16); and his wrath now is against Israel's
foes (e.g. Edom, Ezek. xxxvi. 5). Israel's apostasy had
reflected upon her god, and so she must be punished; but
her sufferings reflected in another way upon him, and so
she must be restored and avenged (Ezek. xxxvi.f.). The
"Day of Yahweh," which according to the earlier reforming
prophets would be one, not of victory, but of judgment
upon Israel (Amos v. 18ff.; Isa. ii. 12ff.), becomes one of
judgment upon Israel's foes. Israel had sinned but has now
"worked out" her sentence (Isa. xl. 2); and her penitence
and change of heart have moved Yahweh to pity (Jer.
xxix. 10ff.; see Deut. xxx. 1ff., and 1 Kings viii. 46ff.).

Throughout, Yahweh was invariably "righteous" (cf.
Zeph. iii. 5). At first the failure of Israel to maintain
"righteousness" drew forth the repeated denunciations of
the prophets; but in the end Yahweh manifested *his*
righteousness by restoring Israel and by overthrowing
Israel's enemies. Israel by her penitence and change of
heart had merited this: her righteousness entitled her to
her rights. In overthrowing Babylon—by the hands of
Cyrus—Yahweh declared that Israel was now in the right
and has claims upon him (Jer. li. 10); she could no longer
complain that her "due" (*mishpāṭ*, Isa. xl. 27) was ignored.
The change in the meaning of Yahweh's "righteousness"
is one of the most significant developments in the religious
thought of Israel; it is the result of decisive historical
developments, and it enabled Israel to maintain the consistency of Yahweh's purpose in spite of the varying fortunes
of her neighbours and herself (see. p. 113).

Another significant change has to be noticed. The
prophets denounce contemporary religious practices: the
worship of other gods, adherence to other cults, human

sacrifice, licentious practices, eating the flesh with the blood, magic, sorcery, and the consulting of the dead. They attack both what is hostile or contrary to Yahwism and certain aspects of Yahwism contrary to their own conceptions of what Yahweh requires of men. Not only the calf cult and the Brazen Serpent (see. p. 154), but also aught that savoured of externalism fell under the ban of the Reformers. Circumcision, they affirm, should be inward and not of the flesh (Jer. iv. 4); and true fasting is more than outward rites (Isa. lviii. 5 ff.). Narrow localisation of Yahweh at the temple of Jerusalem is deprecated: Yahweh is not to be tied down to a specific place, symbol, or rite. Characteristic of the earlier prophets is their attitude to the sacrificial ritual.[1] Even if, as some maintain, they were not opposed to all ritual as such, but only to its worst features, others are certainly justified in pointing out that to the prophets ritual was of secondary value. It had not the vital importance that institutional religion attached to it.

But, as we pass down the ages we find not only evidence for the persistence of an impure Yahwism and of crude practices in the writings of Jeremiah and Ezekiel, and to a certain extent in the Trito-Isaiah (lvii. 3–10; lxv. 2–5), but also stress laid upon the externals of religion—the Sabbath (Isa. lvi. 2; lviii. 13), circumcision (see p. 199), and the temple (p. 195). There is a transition from the religious idealism of the few outstanding individuals to a Yahwism which, it must be recognised, has been purified of its worst features. Moses, the "prophet," must now have by his side the priest Aaron[2]; and the priestly religion, as we meet with it in the post-exilic period, though not without its ethical features, is also not without some of the faults which the prophets opposed. A new prominence of the temple and priesthood is one of the most striking features of the centuries between the return from Exile

---

[1] See Amos v. 21 ff.; Hos. vi. 6; Isa. i. 11 ff.; Mic. vi. 6–8; Jer. vi. 20; vii. 21.

[2] In the older narratives of the Exodus, Aaron, as has been wittily observed, often "appears only to disappear"; but in the latter he is more prominent than Moses (p. 196).

and the rise of Christianity: the individualistic and democratic spirit of the prophets could only be preserved when
enclosed, if not almost hidden, within the shell of formalism
(pp. 195 ff.).   Popular religion encouraged a perfect trust
in Yahweh, one that could ask for a "sign"—How shall
I know . . .? (Judges vi. 17, 36–40; 2 Kings xviii. 20, etc.);
but in the Book of Deuteronomy, which is an endeavour to
regularize religion, Yahweh must not be put to the test
(Deut. vi. 16).   Israel might be Yahweh's priests (Isa.
lxi. 6); but for practical purposes a "kingdom of priests"
(Exod. xix. 6) would be unworkable, and not less so a
people composed of "prophets" (Num. xi. 29).

The older religion has undergone decisive changes.   Hosea
had ethicised the idea of a physical relationship between
Yahweh and Israel, and marital imagery, once dangerous
(p. 103), can now be used innocently (Isa. liv. 5f.; lxii. 4f.).
The temple-cult still preserves traces of what was once the
magico-religious idea of sacrifice (p. 151).   If we are struck
by a falling-away, by the "descent" in post-exilic Yahwism
from the highest religious ideals of the prophets, we at
least witness a change which has its analogies elsewhere:
indeed, was there not a similar "descent" after the "Mosaic"
age?[1]   None the less, it is with mixed feelings that we pass
from the universalism of the Deutero-Isaiah to the grim and
rather horrible scene of the avenging Yahweh with which
the Trito-Isaiah closes (lxvi. 22–24), and contrast Malachi's
attack upon the harsh treatment of *Israelite* wives (ii. 14)
and the drastic treatment of the *foreign* wives whom
Israelites had married (Ezra x. 2; Neh. xiii. 27).[2]

The sixth century witnessed sweeping events in history
and thought.   The prophets had considered Israel's position
hopeless: the leopard cannot change its spots (Jer. xiii. 23);
one cannot sow among thorns, ploughing must precede

---

[1] Deut. xxxii. 15 ff.   Although scholars differ as to the content
of the religion of Israel in the "Mosaic" age, there were some
important religious movements then (p. 94 f.), and subsequent declension or deterioration or counter-reformation is only to be expected.

[2] Contrast also the picture of the "Servant" of Yahweh with the
elevation of Yahweh's "servants" over their opponents in Isa.
lxv. 13 f.

sowing (Jer. iv. 3). They insisted upon the independence of Yahweh: there is no natural bond between him and Israel, she has no claims upon him. So Yahweh has become as a stranger to her (Jer. xiv. 9f.), and she is as one over whom his name had not been called (Isa. lxiii. 19). For Yahweh is the God of all men, and especially of the widow, of the orphan, and of those most likely to suffer under the old social order. The prophets virtually introduce a new conception: it is no longer the group's god, but the god and a new group, not *Israel's* Yahweh, but *Yahweh's* Israel: it is as though Yahweh started afresh, replacing an old association, such as that to which Amos refers (iii. 2, "you only have I known"), by a new Israel. We meet with the same crisis again, later, at the rise of Christianity (p. 210).

How did the change come about? There were men who felt themselves to be the only representatives of true Yahwism—the spirit of the words of Elijah, "I only I am left" (1 Kings xix. 10)—men who thought that the continuity of Israel could be preserved only by a "Remnant." It is a familiar idea that a small band may be the sole repositories of a tradition, the link between some earlier stage and the future. Jeremiah, above all, seems to have thought that he himself was the spiritual "kernel" of Israel, and that "the whole cause of Yahweh in the world hung on his individual life" (Skinner). And if one man could think thus about himself, what shall we say of the enigmatic reference to the atoning value of the suffering "Servant of Yahweh" (Isa. liii. 4–6)? The passages that relate to this mysterious figure strongly suggest that behind the Deutero-Isaiah with its majestic conceptions of Yahweh, Israel and the future of Israel, there lies some reforming movement of profound spiritual power which gave new life to a dying land. Conjectural though this view is, it is not far-fetched to believe that the conception of the Suffering Servant, which so closely associates itself with the new Jewish sect that became the Christian Church, at a time when the Jewish State perished, originated in a period of not less historical importance, a period, in fact, that also saw the passing of Israel through death to a new life. But the

Biblical history of Israel does not admit any such spiritual regeneration: Judaeans go into exile, Judaeans return, the Second Temple is built, and, after a strange gap in the narratives, the Law of Moses is ultimately reintroduced by Ezra (pp. 31, 193f.).

It is instructive, at this point, to contrast the restatement of Yahwism in the Deutero-Isaiah—Israel's rediscovery of her Yahweh—with Deuteronomy. This book is the prelude to the "Earlier Prophets" (Joshua–Kings), and certain portions of it, at least, are of the sixth century, if not later. It is an attempt, on the basis of the teaching of the reforming prophets, to reorganise a people who are entering a polluted land, to eradicate from them all idolatry and to strengthen their solidarity. Along with the loftiest conceptions of Yahweh, who chose, loved and redeemed Israel, and whom Israel in return must love and serve joyfully, there is in Deuteronomy a high social morality, a noble humanism. Kindness to man and beast, good manners, and generosity to the poor and helpless are enjoined. There is a certain "rationalism": the Sabbath is to be kept as a day of rest (remember that you too once were slaves, v. 15; contrast the reason in Exod. xx. 11); and common humanity is the motive for the payment of the triennial tithes (xiv. 28f.), the leaving of the gleanings (xxiv. 19f.), and other rules which might have been justified by religious—or "superstitious"—reasons (e.g. xiv. 21; xxii. 5). There is to be one religion and one central sanctuary; there is little ritual, and the kingship is far from prominent. Offences are not matters for sacrificial atonement; the people as a whole share the responsibility for wrong-doing and must root it out—"burn it out" is the expressive phrase. For there is a book (xxx. 10; cf. xvii. 18f.); and if Israel keeps Yahweh's law, she shall have prosperity and success, but disobedience brings distress and ruin (cf. xxviii.). Idolatry must be ruthlessly put down, and all non-Israelites and false Israelites—who endanger Israel's right relations with Yahweh, and therefore her well-being—must be made harmless. Deuteronomy is narrowly and fanatically exclusive, its kindness is for Israel only (similarly Lev. xix. 17f.)—the

enemy is to be hated (cf. Deut. xxiii. 3 ff.; Ezra ix. 12)—
and its answer to the question, "and who is my neighbour?"
would have found no place for the alien.

Instead of the ideal of an individual covenant between
Yahweh and every man, Deuteronomy would establish a group
or communal relationship (cf. p. 118). It is the beginning
of "book religion." It left its mark thenceforth; and in
formalising religion helped to prepare the way for Judaism.
Its religion is not the monarchical type of religion where
the people as a whole have less share in the national religion,
nor is it the priestly religion of the post-exilic type. It
seems to come in between the two—as a brave democratic
effort to establish a people of Yahweh. One cannot too
highly value the ethics of Deuteronomy, while deploring its
narrowness; one must appreciate the part it has played in
inculcating generosity, while regretting its fanaticism. It
sought to raise up Yahwism on a basis with which Jeremiah,
at all events, would hardly sympathise—though whether he
actually condemned it (Jer. viii. 8) is disputed. The book
is another illustration of the different lines of thought that
went to shape the course of Israelite history. If, as seems
probable, an earlier form of it was intended for the north
(for Samaria rather than for Judah, see p. 146), in its present
form it is thoroughly Judaean in its insistence upon the
single sanctuary at Jerusalem; and while, in the book itself,
priestly interests are inconspicuous, Jerusalem and its
priesthood ultimately took over the "Deuteronomic"
history and incorporated it within their own (p. 50).

The reforming prophets gradually came to hold a secondary
place in a religion which laid the major emphasis upon Moses
and the Pentateuch. But although the laws and "Law"
itself were in due course attributed to Moses, there
were legal usages among the Jews of Elephantine
which have no Mosaic derivation; and the old Code of
Hammurabi and other early codes testify to the existence
of laws outside the Pentateuch, some of which were doubtless
in operation in Palestine (p. 88). Even the conception of
Justice and Righteousness would not be unknown where
the sun-god, the god of Justice, was honoured; and—as

excavation has proved—the existence of the corresponding Egyptian goddess of Truth (Ma'at) was not unfamiliar in Palestine.   The old ethical deity Varuna, guardian of Arta (social and cosmic order) and predecessor of the Zoroastrian ethical god Ahura-Mazda, was honoured to the north of Syria (p. 94 f.).   Moreover, the Semitic term for "righteous-ness" is itself an old one, and personal names associate it with such gods as Yahweh (in the name Jehozadak), El, Ramman (i.e. Hadad) and Chemosh.   In a word, the general conceptions of right and justice are old, as also is the idea that there is some sort of order in nature (Isa. i. 3, the ox; Jer. viii. 7, the stork, etc.).   Hence there is no reason to suppose that the Law (or direction, *tōrah*) to which the prophets recall the people is necessarily that which is now preserved in the Pentateuch.

The ideas of both Righteous and Holy (*ḳādōsh*) were old, and were not confined to Israel.   But they were words of too general a meaning, and the work of Israel—or rather of the reforming prophets—lay in determining more pre-cisely what they connoted.   What is to "know" the god (Jer. ix. 24; xxii. 16; xxxi. 33f.)?   Why is the *ḳĕdēshah* (see Gen. xxxviii. 21 [mg.], 24) not "holy"?   Indeed, what was a man to understand by the divine name "Yahweh" itself, which unlike some divine names (e.g. Baal) carried no obvious meaning with it?   The prophets' task was to purify the meaning of these terms along the lines of ethical monotheism, so that in their history, their manner of life and their cultus, the people of Israel were to show that they were Yahweh's "witnesses" (Isa. xliii. 10; xliv. 8). The prophets are conscious of the divine demand for higher ideals than those that inform the current religious and social life (cf. later, Matt. v. 20); and it is precisely the most pregnant of terms which they take and charge with a fuller meaning, replacing the old shell by a new one, reshaping the old clay into another vessel (Jer. xviii. 4).

The ideas of Righteousness and Holiness easily diverge, and the major emphasis is then laid solely upon Social Conduct or upon Ritual respectively.   We may contrast the more ethical note in Zechariah (v. 1–4; viii. 16f.) with the stress which his contemporary Haggai lays upon the temple. A broad divergence between the religious idealism of the prophets and the ritualism of the priests can be traced, but need not be exaggerated. Yet it is there. Priestly insistence upon ceremonial "sanctification" before taking part in any sacred ceremony, because those who participate must be "holy," contrasts with the prophets' insistence upon ethical integrity, because Yahweh dwells only with the spiritually pure (Isa. vi. 5; lvii. 15; lxvi. 2; Jer. xv. 19). Inward religion is better than a thing that is taught: it rests upon a personal covenant (Jer. xxxi. 33f.), and the prophets would build up social or national religion on the basis of the religion of the individual. What severs man from Yahweh is not his ritual state, but his conduct (Isa. lix. 2); and the true "fast" is not a mere ceremony (lviii. 6, 7f.). The right relationship between a man and God, vital for individual and national welfare, is secured by ethical Righteousness rather than by ritual Holiness. In imitating the divine attributes men are brought into an effective fellowship with the divine power, and all it means; but ceremonies which tended to externalise this relationship —to render it visible—also tended to lay false emphasis upon unusual or abnormal psychical states.

To put it otherwise, the prophets are teaching that the ethical gulf between God and Man is far more significant than the gulf between normal, right and natural life and the realm of the supernatural or supersensuous. The category of the divine, and all that men associate with God, belong to a world, not our world of space-time, but still a "natural" world. Any supposition that this belief necessarily made God less exalted is as erroneous as the not uncommon view that the prophets were essentially social reformers, and nothing more. Their demands for a better order of social, national and political life were based upon and grew out of their theism, their sense of the tremendous Reality of their God. For them, Yahweh's Righteousness was the highest law, and men must establish higher ideals of Righteousness among Yahweh's people. The prophets were not mystics—there is for them no *unio mystica*—they were intensely realist and rationalist. Yahweh was *within* all that was real and rational; and it was his "word," rather than any "spirit (*rūakh*)" of ecstasy, that moved them. Prophecy at its highest was not a psychological phenomenon with psychological criteria: it was the sanity of the prophets and not their manticism that made them such tremendous factors in human history.

That the prophets were exceptional, if not extreme men, must be granted; but they exercised lasting influence, not because of their "otherness," but because they were rare specimens of the usual run of men. Their vision was clearer, their hearing keener. Their relation with Yahweh was one, they felt, that was not confined to them. Their own deepest experiences had a universal significance. Their most intimate consciousness of Yahweh left them with the conviction that Yahweh was equally the God of all his people—and that people was Israel. Their whole world of thought was bounded by God, who was First and Last and Ever-present (Isa. xli. 4). Their reflections upon the beginning and end of things led at once to God, the Creator of heaven and earth, who was to be ultimately the Creator of a new heaven and earth (lxv. 17). Yet they felt keenly the gulf between the world of daily life and "God's world," which their deeper consciousness apprehended; and the gulf between *this* world and that inner world—the latter being the more real to them—could only be bridged by God's intervention or interposition: He takes the first step. Thus the prophets laid the foundation of a religious philosophy that would bring the supersenuous and the world of Space and Time within the same focus.

What they found God to be, *that* they felt, He had always been; and they saw a spiritual unity in history to which in due course the opening chapters of Genesis give expression. All wrong-doing, they felt, was a falling-away; and this sense of lapse was carried back into past history—in the story of the Fall. When they looked forward, everything seemed imminent; the Day of the Lord was always near, hastening to come. History seemed to be rapidly approaching a climax, and the future is almost complete before it has

begun.   There is a certain timelessness; all history is present
to the prophet at once, and his private personal history
is part of universal history.

The prophets are men with very human passions; but,
however universal in their outlook, they are, in the end,
Israelites. They combine the experience of the absolute
"otherness" of God with that of an intimacy, a kinship,
which associated Yahweh and Israel, and pointed to a
happy finale—at least for Israel.   Instead of subordinating
their conceptions of God to current religious thought, they
work from God downwards, and, starting from their consciousness of a Yahweh who is both far and near (Jer.
xxiii. 23), they construct their world of thought from a
blend of their higher and lower experiences.

There were men who forgot the gulf between them and
their god, like the kings of Tyre and of Babylon (Ezek.
xxviii. 2; Isa. xiv. 13f.); and the reality of that gulf is
emphasised in the story of the Tower of Babel (Gen. xi. 6),
and in such passages as Gen. iii. 5, 22, Isa. ii. 17.   There
were men who seemed "madmen," there were others like
Jeremiah who were covered with scorn and obloquy by
their contemporaries.   The description of the mysterious
Servant in Isa. liii. seems to represent a scandalous, wretched
and despised creature—stricken with leprosy (*v.* 4)?—yet,
one who had penetrated further into the *arcana Dei* than
most men.   In fact, a dispassionate survey in the light of
Comparative Religion of the multifarious world-wide beliefs
in the supernatural and the supersensuous leads to the
conclusion that the great teachers of Israel owe their greatness
to their endeavours to purify men's ideas of those profounder
realities of which our notions of *this* world of Space and Time
represent only one part, being, as they are, due to one part
only of the complete human consciousness.   And their
convictions of all that lay outside *this* world were subordinated to their consciousness of the overpowering reality
of their God.

In a land of remarkable extremes of religious and mystical
experience, Israel's teachers sought to combine the two
hemispheres of human experience.   In their conceptions of

a one and only God whose attributes were ethical, they set up certain standards of conduct and certain regulative principles of thought which have had an incalculable influence in history.   That this subsequent influence was part of Yahweh's purpose from the beginning would have been Israel's verdict.   One might almost say that Yahweh was "immanent" in the people of his choice, and that Israel was an intermediary between him and the world. There were certain fundamental ideas which were not unfamiliar outside Israel; but in the course of a few centuries Israel gave them the form that made them of universal value.

But Israel itself is, as it were, an "idea"; it was taken over by the Jews who laid the foundations of Christianity, it has been held by non-Jewish Christians ever since—the men of the new Israel.   As we go back and trace the stormy history of Palestine, we can see that the actual *people* that constituted "Israel" underwent many far-reaching changes (cf. pp. 97, 101), and an "Israel of God"—an "Israel of the spirit"—was always more significant than any Israel "after the flesh."   Thus the very "idea" of Israel and her God, originating in the East, and carried over into the West, is essentially independent of land and race; and the progressive development of the fundamental idea, by whomsoever it may be furthered, will mark the further development of Religion itself (cf. p. 223f).

As, in the middle of the first millennium B.C., Israel's more powerful neighbours declined and fell, she took a path that separated her more and more from other peoples.   She gained a new life which carried her down intact through the Persian, Greek and Roman ages.   This long and triumphant career of Israel is part of the drama of universal history: it became a tragedy when she was called upon to take a further step, and failed.   But for us to sit in judgment over her and to say that she was untrue to the spirit of her great prophets is to set up a standard by which Christianity, too, might haply some day be judged.

CHAPTER XI

The Post-exilic Age

MANY of the Biblical passages and ideas referred to in the preceding chapters were written after the capture of Jerusalem by the Chaldaeans or Babylonians and the fall of the Judaean monarchy (586 B.C.). The exilic and post-exilic ages to which they belong once seemed relatively uninteresting, but by common consent they are now regarded as of supreme significance for the rise of Christianity. Unfortunately, of the inner history of Palestine after 586 little is known, except at certain isolated points.[1] The Exile is, however, an important landmark, not merely by reason of the break in the history of Judah, when Judaeans were carried off by the Babylonians, and their descendants permitted by Cyrus to return, but also because in and about the sixth century B.C. there were other considerable changes of population in Palestine (pp. 97, 118).

The middle of the first millennium B.C. was marked by some extremely vital movements over a very large area. In Jeremiah, Ezekiel, and especially in the Second Isaiah we reach the zenith of Old Testament religion. More or less contemporary with them is the rise of Zoroastrianism, Jainism and Buddhism (India), Taoism and Confucianism (China), while in the Greek world it is enough to recall the Mysteries, Orphism, and the beginnings of Greek speculative thought. Accordingly, in and about the sixth century B.C. we have a remarkable epoch in the history of religion; new lines of thought were inaugurated, and the post-exilic age, when Palestine came under the influence, first of Persia, then of the Greeks, and finally of Rome, seems to be severed from the earlier and more "Oriental" ages of contact with

[1] Of the history of Samaria after the downfall of the North Israelite kingdom in 721, still less is preserved in the Old Testament.

Babylonia, Assyria and Egypt by the great prophets just mentioned.

Palestine, after 539 B.C., was part of the Persian Empire, and the Jews enjoyed and took advantage of the favour of the Persians, whose supreme deity, Ahura-Mazda, was, like their own Yahweh, an ethical god.   On the other hand, the more exclusive Jews naturally fought to maintain the distinctiveness of their Yahweh (cf. p. 157 f.), especially when Artaxerxes II endeavoured to spread the cults of the divine intermediary Mithra, and of Anaitis, a goddess of the Ishtar-Astarte type.   The Persian age was one of considerable intellectual activity, and we cannot fail to be struck by the varieties of Jewish theism which we encounter in the centuries between the Exile and the Christian era. This richness is due partly, not merely to the fact that a number of Jews (i.e. Judaeans) returned from exile in 538— many remained behind and flourished in their new homes— but to the passionate monotheism of the prophets.[1]   Their doctrine of the absolute supremacy and *reality* of Yahweh, and of his unfailing interest in Israel, and the religious individualism associated with Jeremiah and Ezekiel, and also with Deuteronomy (xxx. 11–14), must, in the nature of the case, have left their mark on others besides these Judaeans.

But in the books of Ezra and Nehemiah—practically our only source for the history of the period—interest is confined to the exiles who returned, each to his own city (Ezra ii. 1). Encouraged by Cyrus (539–38 B.C.), they came to rebuild the ruined temple at Jerusalem, and, after a set-back, succeeded in doing so under the Davidic Zerubbabel and the priest Jeshua in the reign of Darius (520–16).   Finally, after a blank in the history, we read of the return and drastic reforms of Ezra, in the seventh year of Artaxerxes (458,

---

[1] Moreover, just as we do not seem to have the literature that would help us to connect our (contemporary) knowledge of the "Amarna Age" in Palestine with the Yahwism which the prophets condemn, so too the literature illustrating the monarchical and pre-exilic age appears to be too restricted in its scope to permit us adequately to trace all the connections between the pre-exilic and the post-exilic ages.

Ezra vii. 8), and of Nehemiah, thirteen years later (445, Neh. ii. 1).[1] In Nehemiah's time the monarchical and Messianic enthusiasm of the prophecies of Zechariah and Haggai at the rise of Zerubbabel has entirely disappeared. A Persian official is the civil head of the Jews, and when Nehemiah's enemies suspect him of aiming at a restoration of the monarchy they threaten to report him to the Persian king (Neh. vi. 6ff.). The scenes are laid in a very restricted region around Jerusalem, and both Nehemiah and Ezra represent an exclusive Yahwism which rejected the advances of Samaritans, and others, interested in the rebuilding of the temple and the restoration of the cultus (Neh. ii. 20; cf. Ezra iv. 2ff.). The exclusiveness of these Judaeans—cf. the dismissal of foreign wives (Ezra ix. f)—and the maintenance of a Yahwism that would have no religious intercourse with outsiders, constitute one of the most characteristic features of the post-exilic age. But it is only one.

A vivid picture is presented of the conditions that confronted Nehemiah and Ezra, and the necessity for thorough reorganisation. It is now many years since Jerusalem fell in 586, and it is clear that the Pentateuch—Mosaism—is coming to have a place that it had not held before (Neh. viii. ff.). It does, in fact, henceforth become the foundation-stone of Judaism, but whether this "Mosaism" was of the "Mosaic" age is quite another question. On the traditional view we have the renewal or re-establishment of what was essentially of about the "Amarna Age" (p. 94); whereas, on the modern "critical" view, the Pentateuch reached its present form about now, and combines contemporary and much older elements (p. 49f.).

Now, if the Pentateuch were essentially very old, it evidently still met the needs of the fifth century, in spite of the profound historical and religious changes since it was written. With its many archaic and crude elements, some

---

[1] There are, however, good reasons for the view that the secular governor Nehemiah prepared the way for the distinctively religious reforms of Ezra. Hence many scholars give Nehemiah the priority, some suggesting that Ezra returned in the reign of the *second* Artaxerxes, the seventh year of whose reign would be 397.

of them contrary to the spirit of the great prophets, it will
represent a Yahwism that never reached their heights or
that could not remain there. If, too, the cultus of the
tabernacle, as depicted in Exodus, Leviticus and Numbers,
actually existed long before, it now forms the precedent for
the post-exilic priestly religion; whereas if the latter be
really a blend of usages new and old, thrown back by a
"legal fiction" to the Mosaic age, the Book of Jubilees
affords an excellent analogy (p. 37). The traditional and
the modern critical views of the Old Testament imply
radically different conceptions of the general character of
Old Testament religion and of its history: the extreme
importance of this difference for the philosophy of history
and religion does not concern us here and now, but it is not
to be overlooked. However, both views agree that the
books Ezra–Nehemiah are of the utmost value for the
subsequent history of Judaism (p. 31f.), and that the
Pentateuch contains different types of religion, the priestly
type being thoroughly archaic and primitive in important
particulars.

The post-exilic priestly religion centres on the intense
reality of God, and the presence of His Majesty and Holiness
among His people. Yahweh is a personal God, One whom
it is dangerous to approach heedlessly. Uncircumcised
aliens may not go in and out of his abode as they did in
the days of the first temple (Ezek. xliv. 7; cf. 1 Kings
xiv. 28; 2 Kings xi.). The holy place and the holy things
are only for the holy. Holiness is dangerous and contagious.[1]
Hence we read of the tabernacle that it was dangerous for
laymen to come in contact with its holy objects (Num.
iii. 38; xvii. 13), and the Levites form a guard around it
(i. 49–53). But even the Levites themselves must not
touch the contents of the tabernacle (iv. 15ff.; cf. iii. 10):
this privilege is reserved for the priests. Finally, even
Aaron himself must not go in and out the Holy of Holies
at his pleasure (Lev. xvi. 2). Holy food is reserved for the
ritually holy class (cf. Lev. vi. 16f.), and a ritual error by
the "sons" of Aaron is punished supernaturally (x. 1ff.).

---

[1] Cf. Ezek. xliv. 19; xlvi. 20, and the mystic cult in Isa. lxv. 5.

There is a three-fold division into laity, Levites, and the Priestly Levites or Aaronites; whereas in Deuteronomy the Levites and the priests are one and the same. But Ezekiel elevated the faithful Zadokites of Jerusalem over the other Levites, whom he degraded for their irreligion (Ezek. xl. 46; xliv. 6ff.; xlviii. 11); and this distinction, which is described as a novelty, appears as a "Mosaic" institution established in the Wilderness when Yahweh choose for his service both the priestly and the other Levites (Num. iii.; p. 47). The latter are indeed in an inferior position, but it is none the less an honourable one. In point of fact, the priesthood must have had a very complicated history: in the Pentateuchal narratives Moses overshadows Aaron, who afterwards becomes the head of the priests; and of the Levitical names Mushi, Gershon and Eleazar (1 Chron. vi. 47, 43, 50), the first is simply "the Mosaite," and the others correspond to Gershom and Eliezer the two sons of Moses (cf. p. 182 n.).

The welfare of the people does not depend upon the prophets as watchmen (cf. p. 117); the priests are responsible for the due performance of an elaborate sacrificial cultus, the practical significance of which was still recognised (p. 151). The High Priest himself is the Jewish head of the community; like the king of old he is anointed (Lev. iv. 3; Num. xxxv. 25), and in his outward glory he is the heir of the kingship (BS l. 1–21). His death marks the end of an epoch (Num. xxxv. 28). Every year, on the tenth of the seventh month, occurs the Day of Atonement, a specially solemn ceremony of purification and expiation, and cleansing of the holy place and of the people. It ensures Yahweh's gracious presence, and it involves the older physical idea that "sin" could actually taint a place (cf. Lev. xvi. 16) and that it could be washed or wiped away. In the priestly religion there is a deep sense of uncleanness and sin; and sin includes both ethical and ritual offences, offences known and recognised, and also those that are unintentional or unwitting.[1] Although ethical ideas were by no means absent from the Priestly Law, the same series of laws enjoins the Israelite

---

[1] Cf. Job and his sons, i. 5; Ps. xix. 12; xc. 8.

to love his neighbour as himself, and to refrain from certain "heathenish" ways of dressing his hair and cutting his flesh (Lev. xix. 18, 27 f.). Ritual cleanness was not everything (cf. BS xxxiv. 19, 25; xxxv. 1–11), and Yahweh might be besought to pardon those *laymen* who were not ritually purified.[1] Still, ethical offences, forbidden in the "Ethical Decalogue" (Exod. xx.; Deut. v.), were put on a level with touching a dead body (Lev. xi. 39; Num. xix. 12), being in child-bed (Lev. xii.), "breaking the Sabbath" (the incident in Num. xv. 32 ff. is typical), and the "leprosy" of men and buildings (Lev. xiv., note *v.* 53).

Primitive ideas of sanctity or holiness had certainly become somewhat ethicised, but there was a lack of proportion. Ideas concerning blood were primitive. Blood was the cleansing instrument ordained by Yahweh: it was the life itself (Lev. xvii. 11; cf. *v.* 14). On no account must men partake of it; and this prohibition is instructive, because among some peoples the sanctity or potency of blood was a motive for drinking it. Even in Israel it was necessary to repudiate the notion that Yahweh could feed on the blood and flesh of sacrificial victims (Ps. l. 13; cf. Deut. xxxii. 38). But this vehicle of life belonged to Yahweh; and sacrificial blood was a means of "un-sinning" men, of removing the barrier between him and them, and of obtaining his forgiveness and the relief it brought. Deuteronomy, which is distinctly more "ethical" and "humanist" and less "ritualistic" than the priestly religion, ordains that the blood of animals slain for food must be poured out upon the ground (xii. 15 f., 20 ff.), whereas the Priestly Law is more in accord with primitive thought as to its potency and treats it with greater reverence. The Priestly Law deliberately gives binding force to what Deuteronomy relaxed. It is also in keeping with the "rationalism" and "antisupernaturalism" of Deuteronomy that Yahweh's beneficent presence and all his gifts depend upon men's conduct and not upon priestly rites (cf. p. 185 f.). It is the more noticeable, therefore, that in due course the priestly system gained the upper hand.

[1] 2 Chron. xxx. 18 ff.; but contrast the priests in *v.* 3 and xxix. 34

The Priestly Law (P) not only retains magico-religious ideas of sacrifice; but, instead of regarding sin and forgiveness as a matter between a man and his god (p. 111 f.), lays stress upon the ritual condition of the offender. The supernatural aspect is far more conspicuous than the ethical; and in its failure to distinguish different sorts of sin and defilement, and in the immense importance it attaches to blood rites, P departs from the spirit of the prophets.

The efficacy of sacrifice—even though the blood be the "life"—is taken for granted rather than explained. We can understand the impressiveness of human sacrifice, especially of the first-born; but such sacrifices were—it would seem—put down by the prophets, though they persisted elsewhere, viz. among the Carthaginians (see p. 99). There is always a tendency to replace the human victim by an animal substitute.[1] But the lamb or ox that is led to the slaughter cannot arouse the same emotions as a human being, and the extravagance of the post-exilic sacrificial system certainly seems to require some reasonable explanation. It has been pointed out (by A. B. Davidson) that in the Second Isaiah the great redemptive conceptions usually connected with priest and sacrifice are connected with the Servant of Yahweh; "a step of immeasurable magnitude" is taken, "of translating the sacrificial idea out of the region of animal life, and throwing it into the sphere of human and personal life, and of conscious voluntary self-sacrifice." Unfortunately, scholars are not agreed as to the right interpretation of the conception of the "Servant of Yahweh," and what religious movements lay behind it: it is however possible that they gave new force and meaning to older sacrificial ideas.[2]

[1] The sanctity of the Levites is once explained on the theory that Yahweh chose them as sacrificial substitutes for the first-born males (Num. iii. 11–13, 41 ff.; cf. xviii. 15).

[2] It is difficult to explain animal sacrifice in general unless the animal had become a conventional victim, and was primarily a recognised surrogate for a human victim (cf. the story of Abraham and Isaac, Gen. xxii. 12 ff.). Originally, as Robertson Smith argued, the difference between animal and human life was not appreciated and both men and animals might be of the same kin (as in totemic groups).

At all events, the priestly religion kept alive archaic conceptions of blood and sacrifice, combining a crude insistence upon blood-rites, more in harmony with earlier stages of religious development, and a sacrificial terminology which Christianity sought to spiritualise. The priestly system localised Yahweh, confined him to one place, and specified the ritual by which to approach him. In this respect it may be said to have made for unity and solidarity. Sabbath and circumcision were its sacraments; and the chief feasts and festivals were worked into a common "history." It was the religion of a community, whether of an Israel disciplined in the desert (as in the Pentateuch), or away in exile, or at home in a land held by a foreign power (cf. Neh. ix. 36f.). In fact, Israel hardly feels at home amid the aliens. There is a sense of timidity: Israelites are as "sojourners" (1 Chron. xxix. 15f.); and the "sojourner" (gēr), who, in the Deuteronomy law was to be kindly treated by Israelites on humanitarian grounds, is now almost a proselyte, a member, as it were, of the Church of Israel (Num. xv. 15f.). Moreover, the older freshness of religious experience has gone—contrast the theophany in Exod. iii. (E) with the more "literary" narrative in Ch. vi. (P).

None the less, the priestly religion had a practical value; it kept its members together, and endeavoured to preserve in institutional form the ethical teaching of the prophets. But our Pentateuch is a strange combination of popular narrative, which always appeals to us, and a certain formalism, impressive, though often stylistically dull— cf. the two accounts of Creation, Gen. i. (P) and ii. 4ff.(J). Each of its different constituents by itself would have been inadequate, and the whole strikes one as a compromise: strictly illogical, but practical and effective. How and when the Pentateuch was compiled we do not know. It made the "Mosaic" Law pre-eminent; it taught by precept and example—for much of the popular narrative is didactic and disciplinary—and it set forth what Yahweh had done, and—by implication (cf. Hab. iii.)—could still do. The Pentateuch was an inspiration as a *whole* and not in its parts; it evoked an unquenchable enthusiasm, and in the second century B.C. men were ready to die for it.

The Pentateuch was more ambitious than Deuteronomy, more universal in its scope: its scheme of history (Gen. i.-xi.) had in view all mankind. It is noteworthy that it was accepted by the Samaritans, who built their rival temple on Mount Gerizim (probably in the fourth century B.C.); but relations between them and the Jews varied, although like the Jews they would claim Jacob as their father (John iv. 12). It is no less noteworthy that although the literary structure of the Book of Joshua unites it most closely with Deuteronomy—hence scholars often speak of the *Hexateuch*—the line has been drawn so that the Jewish Torah ends, not with the gathering of Israel at the Samaritan sanctuary of Shechem (Joshua xxiv.), but, more neutrally, with the death of Moses (Deut. xxxiv.).

Among the heirs of the old Israel were men of different parties. The Jews often gained high positions among the Gentiles, and their religious exclusivism often made them unpopular (cf. Esther iii. 8). Their antipathy to foreigners is rebuked in the story of Ruth, the Moabite ancestress of the Davidic dynasty, and in that of Jonah and his annoyance when Yahweh had compassion upon Nineveh. If the people of Samaria were of singularly mixed origin (2 Kings xvii.; Ezra iv. 9f.), the men of Judah had a considerable admixture of Edomite blood (1 Chron. ii.). In the colony at Elephantine (fifth century B.C.), Jews, Persians, Egyptians and others freely intermingle, and the Jew Tobit claims as kinsman the cosmopolitan and astute vizier Ahikar (p. 86). As appears more clearly in the Greek age, a strong party of Jews strongly objected to the religious policy of their more "narrow" brethren (1 Macc. i. 12–15); but it was the latter and the concentration of religion at Jerusalem that preserved Judaism, and made the subsequent history of the Jews differ from that of the Samaritans.

The Torah was by no means the possession of the Jerusalem priests alone. Outside Jerusalem were important centres of religious influence. Once there were sanctuaries (Amos vii. 9), later there were synagogues; and the

Chronicler's version of the history of the monarchy shows an interest in the northern tribes who feared Yahweh (cf. 2 Chron. xv. 9; xxx. 25; xxxiv. 9). Some of the Psalms seem to have been written or preserved in northern centres, and it is precisely in the Psalms as a whole that personal religion found its finest expression. The date and historical circumstances of many of them cannot be determined; numerous parallels to their phraseology can be found outside Israel (in Babylonian literature). There are Psalms that read like those of *the* individual—the pre-exilic king; but after the teaching of Jeremiah and Ezekiel the personal religion of the individual—in his own right, and not as the member of a State or a Church—grew in strength and such Psalms may still be post-exilic. The Psalms tell of the uniqueness of Yahweh, his rule over the world, and his choice of Israel. They associate his deeds in the past with prayers for his intervention now. Some breathe a love of the Torah (Ps. xix.; cxix.), they sing of the glory of Zion and the longed-for pilgrimage to Yahweh's seat (Ps. xlii.). The "I" of the Psalms is Israel (cf. cxviii. 10; cxxix. 1), or the Israelite, the individual and those who are with him in body or in spirit. Hence the Psalms have always lent themselves equally to corporate and to individual use. They are often extremely difficult for the Hebrew student; and of the wonderful praise of the immanence and transcendence of Yahweh in Ps. cxxxix. one can only agree (with Cheyne) that "the debased Hebrew of the original is not worthy of the noble thought."

The world of Palestine in the post-exilic period was a new one compared with that of earlier days. In and about the sixth century there were both the loftiest of ideas and the strangest of cults (Ezek. viii. 12; Isa. lxv. 4ff., 11; lxvi. 3ff.). The intense monotheism of the Second Isaiah and its sweeping claims on behalf of Yahweh may account for the later (priestly) emphasis upon Yahweh's holiness and the danger of uncleanness and sin, and also for the Psalmists' consciousness of Yahweh's presence and help. But from the heights of the Second Isaiah it is a long descent to the fiercely anthropic Yahweh of Isa. lxiii. 1–6, and to the

doubt which could ask whether there is a God (Ps. x. 4;
xiv.), and is it not futile to serve Him (Mal. ii. 17; iii. 14f.)?
In passing from the days of the Second Isaiah to those of
the New Testament we pass through all the extremes of
faith and scepticism.

God exists—but what manner of God is He? The Book
of Job is a protest against an easy optimism, the sublime
confidence of the prophets, and simple trust in His goodwill
towards men. God is unjust. He slays alike the perfect
and the wicked (ix. 21f.): Job would have agreed with
Ezekiel's contemporaries that "the way of Yahweh is not
equal" (Ezek. xviii. 25, 29). Job suffered in body and
estate; but he was unconscious of any sin. The dualism
of Zoroastrianism conveniently attributed good and evil to
different rival Powers; in Babylonian polytheism there were
rites for men who suffered for some unknown reason; and
P had sacrifices for unknown sins. But Job compels our
admiration for his fine ethical principles (Ch. xxxi.; cf. xxix.)
and for his unflinching monotheism; and in the end he
finds consolation in the conviction that behind this world
of space-time is a God who is neither so arbitrary nor unjust
as He might seem to be. The prosaic Epilogue (xlii. 7–17)
is a concession to the popular desire for a happy finale, but
it obscures the grandeur of the book.

The knowledge of God's majesty answers all doubts. To
the true monotheist it is enough that the God who made
man must know him (Ps. cxxxix. 13ff.), and in his child-
like trust he renounces "great matters" (Ps. cxxxi.; cf. BS
xviii. 6f.). The Oriental may be sceptical (cf. Prov. xxx.
2–4), but he is not speculative, and Job's position is to be
noticed. What he had picked up "by hearsay" (xlii. 5) he
now *knows*; and in his vivid consciousness of God's power
in the Universe he abases himself. He had deliberately
distinguished between man and the tree-stump which has
chances of recovery (xiv. 7ff.), whereas, to others, the facts
of the death and rebirth of nature have often seemed to
confirm man's intuition that his death is not the end of
him (p. 134). Job has severed, as it were, the external
world of nature from the human world. Man is a worm

(xxv. 6). "What is man?" he cries (vii. 17), and he does
not share the confident piety of the Psalmist (viii. 5),
whom he parodies, or the faith of the priestly religion.
There is, indeed, a Divine Wisdom; but it belongs only to
God (Ch. xxviii., excluding *v.* 28): a sentiment very different
from that of other Biblical writers on "wisdom." Job's
intellectual standpoint is his own.

Oriental "wisdom" is, in itself, very ancient (p. 85),
and as international as the quatrains of Omar Khayyam.
The Biblical and other "Wisdom" writings are, however,
now in post-exilic form and reflect the intellectual life of
that age, of those who live in towns and are not under the
priestly régime.   In some respects this literature carries on
prophetic ideas.   Mercy and truth atone for iniquity (Prov.
xvi. 6); justice is better than sacrifice (xxi. 3); and the right
spirit in sacrifice is essential (BS xxxiv. 18; xxxv. 4).   Love
covers sins (Prov. x. 12); forgive and you will be forgiven
(BS xxviii. 2ff.; cf. Prov. xxv. 21f.).   If you rejoice over a
fallen enemy Yahweh may cease to be angry with him
(Prov. xxiv. 17f.; cf. Zech. i. 15f.).   The wicked flee when
none pursueth (Prov. xxviii. 1; cf. Lev. xxvi. 36).   The sage
is no religious enthusiast, but looks at things from the human
side (e.g. adultery, Prov. vi. 32).   Wrong-doing is not
merely wickedness; it is stupidity and folly: contrast Ps.
li. 4, "against thee, thee only, have I sinned."   He condemns
drunkenness (xxiii. 29–35), inculcates chastity; and regards
the marriage obligation as a divine law (ii. 17; BS xxiii. 22).
A well-peopled land is better than a thinly populated one
(Prov. xiv. 28).   The righteousness that exalts a nation
(Prov. xiv. 34) is not that of the prophets; and the righteousness that delivers in the day of death is specifically beneficence
and almsgiving (xi. 4; cf. x. 2; BS iii. 30; xxix. 12f.; xxxv. 2).
There is appeal to self-regard (Prov. i. 10–19).   Kindness
pays (Prov. xi. 17; xix. 17; the poor have a mighty redeemer
(xxiii. 11, *gō'ēl*): and by the poor are meant the needy, and
not the "poor" ones of the Psalms (Ps. x. 2; xii. 5; xviii. 27,
etc.; cf. Isa. xxvi. 6; Zeph. iii. 12) who are, properly speaking,
the afflicted and oppressed pious.   Wealth has advantages
and poverty disadvantages (Prov. x. 15): poverty is better

than baseness (xxviii. 6), but it is best to avoid the extremes
of poverty and wealth (xxx. 8f.). If you are ill, offer a
sacrifice, pray unto God and consult a physician (BS xxxviii.
9–14). The sages enjoin honesty, good manners at the
table (BS xxxi. 12ff.; xli. 19), and prudence in all things;
and the alphabetic acrostic in praise of the prudent house-
wife (Prov. xxxi. 10–31) admirably illustrates the responsible
and independent position that women could enjoy. The
general outlook is optimistic. There is retribution in this
world, and one of the ten happy things of life is to witness
the fall of your enemies (BS xxv. 7). It is left for Koheleth
to preach pessimism and disillusionment, the avoidance of
extremes (Eccles. vii. 15–17), and the futility of a world
where there is one fate for all, good or bad, men or beasts.

The "Wisdom" literature is international. Yahweh is,
so to say, denationalised, and there is little or nothing—at
least in Proverbs—that is especially "Israelite." And just
as Yahweh is, from the Israelite point of view, king of all
(cf. Ps. xlvii. 9; cii. 22), or—like Zeus—god of heaven, or
sky-god (e.g. Ezra i. 2; v. 11, etc.), so Wisdom (*khokmah*)
is all-embracing. This "Wisdom" is a new conception.
It (strictly, *she*) is a power—like "the word of Yahweh"—
a moral faculty, the possession of practical knowledge, and
its effects. It is the art of right living in its highest sense:
it is the principle by which God would have men live in
order to gain the fullness of life. The highest wisdom is
divine. Wisdom invites men to her company; but it
requires discipline to gain her (BS iv. 17; vi. 24f.); she
lays her yoke on men (li. 26), but she richly rewards them.
She is the divine world-plan which is accessible to man
(Job xxviii. 28; contrast *vv.* 1–27). It is "the fear of
Yahweh" that is wisdom (Prov. ix. 10; xv. 33); this is its
root, its beginning, its crown and its fullness (BS i. 6, 14,
18, 20).

Wisdom is sometimes conceived half mythologically. It—
or she—is pre-existent, and dates from the beginning of
Creation (Prov. viii. 22ff.; BS i. 4; ii. 49). "In wisdom"
Yahweh made all his works (cf. Ps. civ. 24); and this attribute
becomes an emanation, a mirror of God's power and an

image of His goodness (Book of Wisdom, vii. 25 ff.). "Wisdom" is hardly a distinct personality; there is no mystical union with her.   She is not an intermediary between God and Man—like "Yahweh's angel"—but in or through her men can live the best of lives on earth.   This Wisdom, which in Proverbs is in no sense national, becomes distinctively Israelite with the keen patriot Ben Sira (Ch. xxiv.; cf. xliv. 1–l. 24).   Here Wisdom is the Torah; and Wisdom lodges with Israel and is established in Zion.   On the other hand, in the "apocalyptic" Book of Enoch (Ch. xlii.) Wisdom finds no dwelling-place among the children of men (cf. John i. 11); she returns to her place among the angels, but will come again in the Messianic age.   That the Israelite Ben Sira should have made the comprehensive conception of Wisdom (as it appears in Proverbs) more particular by identifying it with the Torah of Israel, is not surprising. A couple of centuries later St. Paul (Col. i. 15 ff.) will attribute to a pre-existent Christ the functions and characteristics which had been ascribed to Wisdom (esp. Prov. viii.); and Christ, the personal intermediary between God and Man, will take the place of the Torah.

In all this variety of thought we find ourselves linked up with the world in which Christianity arose rather than with the old world of the pre-exilic age, although we have always to remember that the latter left survivals just outside Jewry (p. 99 f.).   Characteristic of this new world is its dualism.   There is a fearless and objective scrutiny into the ways of God, in order to reconcile monotheism—for the existence of a Supreme Being is almost always taken for granted—with fresh and deeper experiences due, in large measure, to contact with Persians, Greeks, and peoples more of the West than of the East.   Men of religious feeling are testing their ideas of Man and the Universe.   A difference is felt between this world and a world yonder.   Heaven is for Yahweh and the earth is for men, though the difference is differently felt (cf. Ps. cxv. 16 and Eccles. v. 2).   Yahweh is being confronted with Satan, as is the Zoroastrian Ahura-Mazda with his foe Ahriman (Angra Mainyu).   Light is opposed by Darkness—though strict monotheism affirmed that Yahweh made both (Isa. xlv. 7); and Truth or the Right is opposed by the Lie. Instead of treating the individual, with his conflicting experiences of the super-sensuous and of the world of space-time, as an undivided entity, there is a tendency to make a distinction (1) between Body and Spirit (which is not necessarily immortal, cf. p. 140), and later, between Body and Soul (Book of Wisdom); (2) between the Good and the Evil Impulse in man; and (3) between Man and Nature (pp. 123, 141). In the thought-world of the prophets God and all that He connotes is within the "natural"—it is an ethicising and spiritualising of a widespread primitive way of thinking—whereas the priestly religion definitely severs the "natural" from the "super-natural," and the later writers of apocalyptic literature are apt to indulge in a supernaturalism that is exaggerated and rather crude.

It is difficult if not impossible to place the development of post-exilic thought in a strictly historical framework; although it seems increasingly clear that more and more of the Old Testament in its present form is of that period. Some scholars are convinced that they can recognise the effect of the conquests of Alexander the Great (336–23 B.C.) upon the writers or revisers of certain prophetical passages. But there is no really clear date until the Maccabaean age. The Hellenising party of the Jews had no sympathy with a narrow Jewish nationalism, or with men who shared the anti-foreign sentiments of Isa. ii. 6f., or Zeph. i. 8. Hence we may suppose that they were not affronted when Antiochus IV Epiphanes, as the "god manifest," attempted to consolidate his kingdom and secure his position by making the kingship a rallying-point and by spreading Hellenistic culture everywhere (cf. 1 Macc. i. 11–15). The Jews were, as often, divided among themselves, and in 167 B.C. the Seleucid king went so far as to dedicate Yahweh's temple at Jerusalem to Zeus Olympius, a veritable "Baal of the Heavens" (see p. 41 n.). The persecution and martyrdom of those who bravely defied him were the seed of a new growth in the Jewish Church (? cf. Ps. xliv. 22). The desperate fight of the Maccabees for Yahweh and for the

Torah culminated in the cleansing of the temple and a fresh dedication of it to Yahweh: 25th December, 164 B.C. is one of the outstanding dates in the history of Yahwism.[1]

The Book of Daniel illustrates the situation; it was one when men must uphold their faith against all odds. It combines a splendidly disinterested confidence in the God of the Jews (iii. 17 f., with which cf. Job xiii. 15) and a scheme of history culminating in the establishment of His kingdom. More explicitly than ever before it expresses the belief in a general resurrection of the dead when the righteous and the wicked shall receive appropriate rewards and penalties (xii. 2 f.).

Judaism was saved—by its martyrs, and for a time (142–63 B.C.) a new Israel held up its head. The Jews entered upon a fresh period of expansion, enjoying the dangerous patronage of Rome and, later, profiting from the intervention, not of Persia, but of her successor, Parthia. A priestly ruling house—"after the order of Melchizedek" (Ps. cx.)—became increasingly monarchical. Fierce sectarian feuds weakened the State. Forcibly "Judaizing" the Idumaeans (the former Edomites), the Jews took the step which ultimately placed on the throne the Idumaean Herod, who ruled and ruined their State; and by similarly "Judaizing" the mixed people of Galilee, they founded another centre of Judaism from which were to spring events that gave the death-blow to their religious organisation. It is we who, on looking back upon the internal situation of the Maccabaean age, and after, can recognise that the scene was being set for the New Testament.

We have left behind us the age of the Second Isaiah and other great creative prophets; their living energy is a thing of the past, and "apocalyptic" literature (Daniel, Enoch, etc., p. 28 f.) has now lost hope of this world and dreams of supernatural cataclysms. In its own way it consoled men— as did the Psalms in another—though it led men to think more of the few who would be saved than of the "Remnant" who were to save others (cf. p. 184). Some looked for a Saviour—like the Persian Saoshyant—or a Messiah, or for the kingship of Yahweh. But to those to whom the Torah

---

[1] Cf. above, on the history of the Canon, p. 32 f.

was everything there was no need of a Messiah! Once more it is obvious to *us* that the world of thought of these Jews cannot be severed from that of the first Jewish Christians and that changes were imminent.

The Jews had now become an important factor in the Roman Empire. Their monotheistic teaching, their lofty ethical idealism, their imposing traditions and, above all, the temple at Jerusalem gave them a unique status in the ancient world. But viewed as a whole, Judaism with its many varieties of thought, ranging from the priestly religion to the Book of Wisdom and Philo, presented an unarticulated and disorganised mass. One might have imagined that only through the Torah and the organised sacrificial system centred in Jerusalem could Judaism hope to preserve its individuality; but the priesthood was mixed up with current political conflicts and was divided against itself. Moreover, the ideas which made Judaism a coherent system, as it seemed, were too radically those of a bygone age, and, though impressive in their ethical aspects, they were housed in a diseased and effete body. The parting of the ways was at hand.

CHAPTER XII

The Old Israel and The New

STRICTLY speaking we have reached the end of the Old Testament, but a few concluding remarks have to be made. The New Testament not only stands at the beginning of a new age, it is also the last chapter of the old, and the rise of Christianity is the last act of a stirring drama. The early Christians were conscious of their complete continuity with the past; they also felt that they were on the threshold of a new order, one that might have its scene in heaven or upon a new earth. We can look back upon the course of history and religion in Palestine, and can perceive both the inner connection between the pre-Christian and the Christian centuries, and the distinctiveness of the new tendencies which were to give a new direction to human life and thought. It was a fresh creative age.

Jesus of Nazareth comes before us, a Jew of the Jews, a prophet (cf. Mark vi. 15), penetrating, iconoclastic, with demands for a higher righteousness, and with that universalism and supra-nationalism that distinguish the greatest of his predecessors. He was much more than they; but only when we approach him in the light of the history of thought in the Old Testament do we realise how the earlier religion, as reformed by the prophets, was now being shaped afresh. It does not fall within the scope of this book to dwell upon the fundamental connection between Christianity and Yahwism, or to survey the many ideas which it derived from Hebraic thought in general and the Old Testament writings in particular. We need only refer to the Servant of the Lord, the expected Messiah, the Kingdom of God, the New Covenant, and the renewed and stronger emphasis upon the worth of the individual in the eyes of his Heavenly Father.

But it is important to notice that the new religion did not simply evolve or grow out of the current situation. It went back, as it were, and took up creative ideas of the past. Israel's traditional claims were swept aside: it is not that the old Israel now found new conceptions of her God, but that a new choice has to be made by those who would be members of the New Kingdom. Yahweh was the God of Israel and of every Israelite: once again, instead of *Israel's* Yahweh, *Yahweh's* Israel was being formed anew (cf. p. 184). If the new "Israel of God" was soon to be a Church, its members united by their religious and social ideals, even the post-exilic "Israel after the flesh" had been a Church rather than a political organism. The actual historical, physical unity of the Israelite tribes had given place to a Judaea that claimed to be the true Israel, and the bond that united the men of post-exilic Israel was the Torah. And now the Torah had to give place.

There were many varieties of thought in the post-exilic age (p. 200 f.), and the Old Testament was of no narrowly Israelite or Hebraic origin. Palestine had never been completely out of touch with other lands or peoples, and Biblical religion cannot be isolated from the religions of the neighbouring lands. It is a special and unique development in the universal history of religion which can be traced in and behind the Bible, and the rise of Christianity is part of an Oriental revival or reaction as the eastward flow of Hellenism (under Alexander the Great) began to subside.

Many tendencies had gone to prepare the way for Christianity; but, in spite of the varieties of thought that could be claimed to be Jewish, this new religion had to break away from the parent stem. The more probable it seems that some reinvigorating and creative movement lay behind the earlier conception of the "Servant of Yahweh" in the exilic age (p. 184), the more instructive are the points of resemblance and difference between (1) the age (sixth century B.C.) that came in between the monarchical period and post-exilic religion and (2) the later age (first century A.D.) when a new movement gave birth to a new religion. Jewish monotheism had never been a simple doctrine (see Ch. IX). One has only to think of its angelology and the Angel of Yahweh, of the conception of Wisdom, of the part played by the Messianic king or the high priest as intermediary, and above all, of the Torah as the bridge between the Jew and his God. But now a new system of thought was growing up around Jesus Christ, the Messiah, the final High Priest, the Divine Wisdom or Logos. The Torah was being "fulfilled," and its function superseded. In place of Israel, the first-born of Yahweh, there is a new community, claiming the old privileges. The gulf between *this* world and God's kingdom, which is characteristic of post-exilic thought (p. 205 f.), is bridged; the "Christians" revive the prophets' experience of the reality of God's work among men, and there is a new intimacy between the Father and His children. In other respects, too, the new religion reverts to or revives "primitive" ideas, which it sought to spiritualise: the common meal, the marital relation between Christ and the Church, the efficacy of blood and the human victim.

We can see that the stage had been prepared throughout (e.g. the Hebraic conception of "Wisdom" and the Johannine "Logos"): but there has been an interposition in the person of Jesus Christ. There was no mere synthesis of existing ideas, but a movement "from outside," as it were, which took only what it needed and moulded it to a new purpose. Current Jewish anticipations were not realised. In the past the prophets had warned Israel against pinning her faith on the "Day of Yahweh" (Amos v. 18); even Cyrus, the "Servant of Yahweh" (Isa. xlv.), had not fulfilled men's hopes. So, when there appeared the "Anointed of Yahweh" men had thought that the kingdom of God should immediately appear; and, with the brilliant age of the Hasmonaean priest-kings behind them, they looked for a revival of Israelite power and freedom from foreign rule.[1] There came, instead, the tragedy—the Fall of Jerusalem in A.D. 70.

In the exilic age Israel took a forward step, and the regeneration of Yahwism is in striking contrast to the efforts in Egypt and Babylonia to revive old times. But whereas in Israel an old religion was then reshaped and

[1] Cf. Luke i. 52; xix. 11; xxiv. 21; Matt. xx. 20 ff.

reinvigorated, now there sprang up out of an old religion a new one which speedily outgrew its parent. Surely the tragic end of the Jewish State was the more bitter by reason of the determined progress of the new sect! The teaching of Jesus would seem too anti-national, too universal; and it cannot be surprising that institutional Judaism rejected it: it superseded the Torah and set up a new approach to God. Moreover, whereas Judaism looked back on its past and pointed to the completeness and finality of its own system, the new religion looked forward, and was rapidly proving that it could stand by itself and expand.

Yet, when we consider the history of Israel and realise what she had achieved, we cannot shut our eyes to the tragic nature of the last act in the drama. Perhaps no one can really understand the background to the fall of the Jewish State and the rise of Christianity who has not read the *Jewish War* of Josephus, and has tried to enter into the miserable and degrading story of the last days of the old "City of Righteousness" (Isa. i. 26). Making all allowances for the exaggerations and foibles of the pro-Roman propagandist, we cannot be blind to the fact that the centre of Judaism was hopelessly corrupt, and that the very fervency of its religion—or its fanaticism—as described by Josephus, only made the situation worse. It is a depressing story that he has to tell, and it is useless to-day to speculate whether the history of Judaism might conceivably have been different. The Jewish State came to an end—but it was not the end of a people who were to discover that through their Torah they could live their lives without a mother-city, a temple and a sacrificial system.

In and behind the Bible there are events and conflicts of real history. There are extremes of triumph and failure; minds creative, if not too individualistic, and minds conservative, systematising and deadening; prophets and priests, fanatical and inspiring; profound depths of religion and crudities of magic; simple piety, quietism and bloody religious strife. We see, as it were, something of the career of a genius, very human, but a genius none the less, a people

who lived and thought dangerously.   And it is just because
modern research is making the Bible and Biblical history
so completely a part of human history, removing it from
the sphere of the falsely "supernatural" into the realm of
the natural, the actual and the real, that Biblical study,
the study of some tremendous events in the growth of Man,
becomes increasingly significant.

All lovers of the Bible, whether higher critics or funda-
mentalists, find in it their religious values.   If it tells of
God and Man, and what God has done in the past, we
must read it as a whole—to the close of the final tragedy.
Nor can we isolate from the general history of Mankind
those few centuries over which its contents extend.   The
greatest truths which men find in the Bible are always
true, and will re-express themselves in the future as they
have done already in the past.   Modern criticism has no
doubt often destroyed the garb of history in which some of
these truths have been clothed; but they themselves remain,
and the larger history of Man which research is labouring
to recover, not only does not make them less true or less
impressive, but also discovers new ones.

The old Biblical writers had their philosophy of history.
They felt that there was a purpose in all things.   They
knew why other nations fell—and the best of them knew also
their own danger.   They were convinced of the uniqueness
of their own people, but also of the conditions of the relationship between them and God.   They are unique for their
effort to solve the problem of undeserved suffering and
unmerited misfortune, and for their retention of a fundamental faith in the reality of God, His righteous rule in the
Universe, and the moral law ruling in peoples and individuals.

The downfall of the Jews brought a new and terrible
problem.   The Christians were forward-looking, whereas the
Jews had to bear the full misery of this catastrophe to the
Holy City.   Did any look back to that earlier catastrophe
when, however, in spite of the Fall of Jerusalem (586 B.C.),
events were to prove that both Israel and the city itself
had a future before them?   Be that as it may, there was
one writer (2 Esdras, or the Ezra Apocalypse) who, "thirty

years after the downfall of the city" (iii. 1, i.e. after A.D. 70),
used the earlier disaster as a background for his reflections
upon the sufferings of his own day (see p. 177). This
Apocalypse is of extreme interest for the many points of
contact between it and the thought of the New Testament,
but it is the tragedy of his own Israel and not the hopes of
the new one that concerns the writer. Why does Israel
suffer? The only answer to his question the seer can find
is along the lines of the best Old Testament thought.
Sadly may he grieve over the fate of his people, but he
cannot love the creature more than the Creator does:
"lovest thou that people better than he that made them?"
(v. 33; viii. 47). At an age when the evangelist of the
young religion declares that "God is love" (1 John iv. 8),
and when the death of its Founder, the Only begotten Son
of the Father, was a sign that God's love was universal
(John iii. 16), the Israelite seer can find in God's love for
His people a consolation. It is a consolation of universal
import, for both the old religion and the new had its martyrs.

At no time can men look into the future and read what
shall be; but the principles of Divine Righteousness that
rule in the old and new Israel throughout are of eternal
validity. St. Paul looks ahead and sees certain possibilities
(Rom. x. f.), and we of to-day have our own hopes and fears
of the further course of history and religion. The youthful
West is slowly discovering for itself and restating the real
historical value of the Bible, and although its contents might
seem to belong to ancient history, the process of reinter-
preting them unites the past, the present and the future.
The real history of the religion which we trace in the Bible
began long before the first of its contents was written; and
its history will continue so long as men continue to study
and to reinterpret the Bible. Nations may rise and fall,
civilisations may grow up and vanish, but "Slowly the
Bible of the Race is Writ."

The Old Israel and the New—this, it may be suggested,
is the keynote of the reinterpretation of the Bible, and
although this book is concerned only with the Old Testament,

it is possible to indicate briefly upon what lines a reinterpretation would run.   We may summarise it under three
heads: (i) the historical development; (ii) the nature of the
religious development; and (iii) general conclusions arising
therefrom.

(i) Although the knowledge of the ancient world which
we are gaining is still very incomplete, it is enough to form
the framework within which to place the Old Testament.
The Old Testament itself, it is true, contains a history, but
it must be critically examined before we can co-ordinate
Biblical history and world history.   In undertaking this
task we can admire the insight and skill of the authors of
Gen. i.–xi., without feeling ourselves called upon to justify
the historical knowledge of a bygone age.   And although
it is possible that the tradition of veritable intensive
inundations in Babylonia (viz. at Kish and Ur), before
3000 B.C., explains the introduction of the story of a world-
wide Deluge blotting out antediluvian man, we may appreciate the acute use of historical tradition rather than the
historical value of the story itself.

Again, in the "patriarchal" period, it is sounder method
to perceive that there was some recollection of events than
to attempt a premature combination of the contemporary
"external" evidence and the written "internal" evidence
of the Old Testament.   There is a wide gulf between the
Biblical narratives themselves and the historical facts which
they are presumed to reflect.   On the other hand, when we
come down to the age of the divided monarchy and the
Assyrian invasions of the Westlands, the combination and
co-ordination can, on the whole, be made satisfactorily and
effectively.   But, in general, we are frequently led to
conclude that some of the outstanding names (e.g. Abraham,
Jacob, Moses and Joshua) are older than the narratives in
which they now appear, and that of such events as the
Descent into Egypt, the Oppression, the Exodus and the
Conquest, the extant traditions are by no means ancient.

In the endeavour to place the Old Testament, viewed
critically, within the framework of world history, we do
not ask at what point in the Old Testament authentic

history begins, but at what point in this framework we can begin to use the Old Testament. We have often to sacrifice "history" in the narrower sense of the term, and remember that even thoroughly unhistorical narratives and views of the past may be important testimony to what was believed. Beliefs and convictions may throw more light upon the course of history than the events to which they refer: not the bare events themselves, but their meaning it is that makes history. Indeed, it is perhaps the most characteristic feature of the Old Testament history that the account of its growth, which scholars are recovering— e.g. the Deuteronomic history, the prominence of the Priestly Writer—proves to be more valuable than the authenticity of this or the other narrative. The Old Testament becomes much more interesting *for us* when we pass from the record of happenings to the processes which produced it, the leading ideas which moved the writers, and the significant history-making developments to which they bear witness.

Hence we have gained a rather different history of the past, one that satisfies our questioning better than the old inherited view. We pass from what the ancient writers believed to be true to what we feel that we can accept as true. But when we speak of the "Truth" of the Bible we should ask ourselves, what are the contents or aspects of it which we consider "true" or whose "truth" we are anxious to maintain? Conformity with the "facts" of contemporary history, or the results of archaeology, or the study of the physical geography, may give us "truth"; but there are profounder needs that have to be satisfied when we speak of the "Truth" of the Bible.

Yet the first aim of the Old Testament student is to understand as completely as possible "what actually happened," and there are still many difficult questions that await an answer. There is one, in particular, of fundamental importance to which brief reference must be made. The "Amarna Age" is extremely well documented, but there is no natural agreement between the contemporary material and the Biblical account of the Mosaic and premonarchical ages.[1]　Next, not only is it difficult to agree precisely how the Israelite Yahweh replaced the earlier gods of Palestine, but the Yahwism which the reforming prophets condemned is cruder than that religious spirit which characterises the Old Testament as a whole, and which we may call the "canonical" religion.　And finally, we have the "priestly" religion of the post-exilic but not of the pre-exilic period; we have the "hymn-book" of the second temple, but not of the first; and the general character of the post-exilic age presupposes earlier conditions upon which our sources often throw little, if any, light.　Of the true sequel of the Amarna Age and the true prelude to the post-exilic age little remains; and when we turn to the Biblical records upon which we are to rely for our picture of the earlier periods we find that they are in large measure distinctly didactic, and written under the influence of recognisable but one-sided aims (see pp. 53 ff.).

Now, the ordinary reader is perfectly justified when—unless he looks beneath the surface—he feels that one and the same profoundly religious spirit pervades practically the whole of the Old Testament and unites it with the New Testament.　But no less justified are those scholars who have pointed out that behind the "canonical" religion there are abundant traces of a religion, vigorous and passionate, but much more in harmony with the magical and barbaric features of other ancient religions.　Both are right, and it is not difficult to reconcile them.　It may suffice to quote some striking words of the late Bishop Gore on the "victory of the true prophets."[2]　He writes: "It is the chief spiritual advantage that we gain from the modern critical estimate of the Old Testament that it has restored to the prophets their proper primacy."　The modern student "will recognise that the spirit of the prophets was finally so far victorious in Israel that it remodelled the whole intellectual heritage of the people, purging and inspiring with deep truth their folk-lore, their legends, their historical tradition or written records, their 'wisdom,' their poetry and especially their

[1] See pp. 94 ff., 227.
[2] *The New Commentary*, pp. 2, 8.

culture—making this last a real treasure house of spiritual meaning."

This is an impressive opinion. It means that the permanent elements of Yahwism which we value are to be associated with the great reforming prophets and their successors, that they come after a Yahwism which, whatever admirable features it contained, was in need of reform, and that they belong to a relatively late rather than to a relatively early part of Israel's history. It should be observed that the *religious* criterion is crucial. The effects of the prophetic spirit are widely pervasive in the Old Testament, and leave their mark upon the large body of didactic literature; but behind the Old Testament are all the signs of an earlier and more rudimentary type of Yahwism. Already in the history of Old Testament criticism it was the profound difference between the spirit of the prophets and the spirit of the Pentateuch as a whole which made scholars feel that the former should precede the latter (p. 48); and it is precisely the deep spirituality of the prophets which—in the opinion of the present writer— forces the view that it was only through their influence that even the earlier historical narratives received their present religious colouring. And on this view they are evidently later than is usually held by most Old Testament critics (see p. 148, n.).

(ii) In passing from the historical development of Israel to the question of the nature of the religious development we start from the ordinary view of the ordinary reader who finds a spiritual unity in the Bible as a whole in spite of the gulf between the two Testaments. But there are at least three epochal changes to be examined: (a) the actual introduction of Yahweh and Yahwism into a land of ancient culture, (b) the prophetic reforms, and (c) the rise of Christianity. As regards the first of these (a), although some may seek to trace a development from the Pre-Mosaic or patriarchal religion (in Genesis) to the Post-Mosaic, the general tendency is to attempt some reconstruction based upon details in Genesis and in the "external" evidence and so offer a picture of the Pre-Mosaic stage. But from what has been said, it is obvious that widely different opinions prevail both as to the Yahwism of the Mosaic age and still more so as to Pre-Mosaic religion.

On the other hand, the external and contemporary evidence yields many important facts. For example, the evidence for the religious reform of Amenhotep IV in Egypt and for the ethical gods Varuna and Mitra in North Syria cannot be left out in any discussion of the nature of Revelation and Inspiration (p. 101 n.). Nor can we ignore the monotheising tendencies at that, the "Mosaic" age (pp. 94, 143 f.). But although the evidence is impressive, more vital is the difference between the actual progressive development of religion in Palestine and the fate of the various reforms and tendencies elsewhere. The facts of religious experience are undeniably impressive, but more crucial are the "contents" of the experience and the consequent effects for the history of lands, peoples or individuals.

(b) Of the development of religion in the age of the prophets we are, of course, better informed. But something like six centuries—estimates will differ—sever the age of Moses from that of Amos and Hosea, and the climax of the prophetic movement comes about a couple of centuries later, in the "Second Isaiah." There is a highly instructive contrast between the "Deuteronomic" effort to make a new Israel (p. 185 f.), and the lofty teaching of the "Great Unknown" seer (p. 178); and in the teaching of this writer (or body of writers), representing Israel's rediscovery of her God, the religion reaches a new height. The social-political crises, the religious individualism, the Fall of Jerusalem, and above all the fresh monotheistic enthusiasm combine to form a series of sweeping events that must guide our interpretation of the history of religion. Here is the watershed between two great stages, the later and better-known of which leads on to the rise of Christianity.

The age round about the sixth century B.C. was a "live" one, when wide-spread and exceedingly important changes in world history and religion inaugurated conditions of thought which have prevailed ever since (p. 192). Israel's greatest minds were not unconscious of the part that their religion was to play; but upon what narrow lines have the historians traced the course of an epoch-making age! No one, passing from the books of Kings (and Chronicles) to those of Ezra and Nehemiah, would realise what lay behind the Fall of Jerusalem, the Exile and the subsequent Return. Israel possessed no adequate account of the really fateful steps in her history. If the reforming prophets had made one new Israel, it was another new Israel that came into existence in the post-exilic age and forgot the break in her past, and the movements to which she owed her continuity with the past. In her anxiety to maintain unity and continuity she lost sight of the life-giving processes to which she owed not only her survival but her progressive development.[1]

So, the conviction grew in the post-exilic age that the Mosaism—of the far-off "Amarna Age"!—was simply re-established, and that the Pentateuch was in all essentials that of those distant centuries. But precisely what happened, how much was old, and how much new, is one of the most important of Biblical problems for our knowledge of a remarkable rebirth or reconstruction. The age of Moses and the introduction of Yahwism are naturally also of great importance; but a more practicable enquiry is that into the changes during the middle of the first millennium B.C. See the Chronological Summary, p. 229 f.

(c) The reorganisation led up to the third great epochal change. But of the birth of Christianity all that need be said here is that we must emphasise the impossibility of drawing a rigid line between the Old Testament and the New, as though in our examination of the course of life and thought among the Jews of Palestine we can find some date B.C. or A.D. where a division between the two can be made.

The Bible testifies to unique religious developments, the nature of which cannot be studied too exhaustively. Their consequences for the West, for Christendom, have been such

---

[1] For the study of religious development it is to be observed that the idealised history of her past, which so inspired post-exilic Israel, stood in the way, later, when the finest monotheism the world had seen must give way to a new movement which proved to answer new needs.

that it is no exaggeration to regard them as of incalculable significance for the course of human history and religion. Even our theories of development or evolution in the physical universe are really of secondary importance compared with those progressive changes in man's efforts to think out his thoughts of himself, his world and his God. For they are the changes which helped to make Western thought what it became, and so to create the mental environment of the scientist, the jurist, the philosopher, as well as of the theologian.

Looking back, we see specific developments as regards conceptions of God, intermediaries, the individual, and his destiny. New situations brought new requirements; old questions called for fresh answers. Social, political and economic changes were factors in the developments; and, notably round about 700–400 B.C., there were decisive changes in thought comparable in their strength to those through which this age seems now to be passing.

Throughout, Palestine and Israel were not isolated, and at the greater epochs their history was part of a larger canvas. The history and religion of the Bible are part of a vaster history and religion, and the Old Testament is no narrowly Israelite production, even as the New Testament, in turn, is not indebted merely to the Old. To interpret the Bible aright we have to go outside Israel, for Israel herself was indebted directly and indirectly to much that was Pre-Israelite and Non-Israelite. There were Israelites before there was the "Israel" which we associate with the permanent value of the Old Testament, even as Yahwism had a history before the prophets gave it the form which has made the Old Testament immortal. What we value is not Israel or Yahwism, as such, but what Israel made of her inheritance when the occasions arose. Her passion, her strong nationalistic monotheism, and her ethical idealism constitute the genius of Israel. If we see a continuous and progressive working out of ideas, it is something ideological rather than strictly ethnical, even as the history of Christianity is not that of a single land or of a few spans of time.

Thus, the "New Israel" of the Christian era did not precisely grow out of an "Old Israel," and, as we look back, we can see that what was achieved at the various stages was no mere revival or rehabilitation. The secret of the progressive continuity lies deeper. Was it not "reinterpretation"? The prophets certainly reinterpreted the past, and the New Israel of Christianity likewise found a new meaning in what had gone before. A new interest in the past is not necessarily an antiquarian fancy, though the antiquarianism of Ashurbanipal (p. 97, cf. p. 85), and of Egypt and Babylonia round about the sixth century bore no fruit for the future. But to find a new meaning in the past, one that has a significance for the future—that surely should be the aim of any reinterpretation.

Obviously there are limits to our ability to recover all we would wish to know of the past. No less obvious are the limits to our power of understanding the mentality of an age that is bound up with past and obsolete conditions of life and thought. Often the dead must be left to bury the dead, and present needs must control the value we set upon the past. The most detached and objective attempt to understand the past may lead us to realise that it is our own point of view which needs reconsidering. This is especially true of the Bible, the proper understanding of which requires the appropriate *rapport* between us and it. There is, indeed, a sense in which the Bible does become its own interpreter; but in the act of so doing it is our own mode of approach, and the light in which we approach it, that—consciously or not—have undergone some development. What is vital for any reinterpretation is the discovery and reassertion of the things that evidently matter most, and so, for example, it makes a world of difference whether we look upon the prophets of old as foretelling what the future will be, or as inspiring us both to guide that future and to face what it brings. (Cf. p. 167.)

(iii) We have passed to the last of our three heads. The Bible is more than a "religious" book. In such subjects as anthropology, folk-lore and ancient history it is brought into the field of ordinary trained research, part of current learning; and, so far, the use of it is in accord with natural knowledge. Likewise students of comparative religion and of the psychology of religion handle the Bible in accordance with their special disciplines, when they concern themselves with what men have believed to be most real and true. Not truth for us to-day but for them of old comes first; although it soon appears that certain beliefs and ideas evidently proved far more effective than others. Ordinary comparison quickly brings to light their value for men, peoples and the world of thought; and in trying to understand old-time points of view we learn to purge and affirm our own.

Religious experience is no doubt a world-wide phenomenon; but especially in and about Ancient Palestine is one struck by the horror, cruelty, sensuousness and stupidity that "religion" could tolerate or encourage. Every student of the world's religions soon finds that there are *qualities* of religion—whether we are to speak of "Religion" and "Magic," or of "True" and "False" religion. From time to time there are shocking conceptions of what the gods require, and of what is legitimate, laudable or necessary, for men or nations; but these also serve to awaken men to higher conceptions of righteousness, of what is right, and of what God requires of His people. Our conceptions of religious "Truth" must take into account all that we consider religious "Error"; and it was the very reality of God—one might almost say the "naturalness" of the experiences of God—that accounts for the best as also for the worst features of super-naturalism in the old Oriental religions.

Behind us stretches a history of inconceivable immensity. We are learning of the physical Universe, the cooling of the earth, the dawn of life, the appearance of man, and his efforts to supply his needs and satisfy his quests. In Palestine, in the Bible, we begin to trace a certain progressive continuity that can be followed down to the present day. Our own history—in the narrower sense of the word—does not derive from Palestine; although it is there that we can trace the ideas that have proved so powerful. Such is the place of the Bible in history that we may say that the Book is more permanent than any one people who may make it their own.   And such is the power of the "Israel" idea that there might be a further development, historically as unsuspected as the passage nineteen centuries ago from Palestine to the West.   So, we shall be heedful how we judge the events at the rise of Christianity and the fall of the Jewish State, for not until a people has passed through its great religious crises can it venture—if even then!—to condemn the "blindness" of the Jews of that age.   In a word, the history of religion as a world force has reached the stage where the question of its future is far more vital than all the mistakes of Scribes and Pharisees upon which Christianity has been apt to dwell in the past.

At the Renaissance and Reformation the infant West began to discover a connection between its Bible and its history—what had happened long before was still a living force.   In recovering and in rewriting the past, men have tried to find the "Truth" that should satisfy their needs. Truth of Life and not Truth of Doctrine is the first aim; and in coming to realise the great permanent truths in the Bible men come to find that a Truth that has been manifested in the past is still to be manifested in the future. The "truths" of the Bible, of the book of bygone centuries, are not mere intellectual propositions; they require a new embodiment so that they may be seen to be "true" in life and action; and there is much that the Israelites of old discovered that may have to be rediscovered and restated by an age or a people that would be as true to itself as they were.

Thus, at the end, one's mind turns back to that development, not only from Jeremiah and the Second Isaiah to Jesus, but rather from Amos to Paul.   Here one is witnessing the most impressive series of changes of which we have knowledge.   The Bible is an indivisible whole, and to rest content with either the Old Testament alone, or with the New Testament alone, is to lose the real inwardness of all that which makes the Bible the most remarkable book in the world.

Chronological Summary

This summary is for working purposes only. Many of the dates are quite conjectural, and often there is considerable difference of opinion. Reference may be made to the Chronological Tables in the volumes of the *C.A.H.* (= *Cambridge Ancient History*), in the *Clarendon Bible* (by Miss E. W. Hippisley), and the lists given by S. L. Caiger, *Bible and Spade*, pp. 196–201.

Geological Periods.[1] It is noteworthy that Palestine, after becoming a meeting-place of continents, also became one of flora and fauna. One wave from the north is typical of Europe and Northern Asia, and the other from the south is "a tongue of Africa (the Ethiopian region)" penetrating northwards (see *Q.S.*[=*Quarterly Statement* of the Palestine Exploration Fund], 1935, p. 208).

Prehistoric Man. Abundant evidence (skeletons, flints, rock-drawings, etc.). Points of contact with the European, Asian and African Stone Ages.

c. 4240	Earliest Egyptian date. (The Sothic cycle instituted in 4238 or 4241 B.C.)
	Evidence adduced for great local (but not contemporary) inundations at Kish, Ur, etc. (see V. Gordon Childe, *New Light on the Most Ancient East*, 1934, p. 168).
3000–2500	*Early Bronze Period.*[2]
	Egyptian colonies or settlements (Byblus, etc.).
	Babylonian expeditions to the Mediterranean Coast.
2500–2000[3]	*Old Canaanite Bronze Age.*
	Third dynasty of Ur (*c.* 2300–2100): period of spread of Babylonian culture (Sydney Smith, *Early History of Assyria*, p. 77).
	The important FIRST DYNASTY OF BABYLON (from 2169, Fotheringham; but other authorities prefer 1955).
c. 2000	Hammurabi (p. 93).
	Approximate date of Abraham, according to Biblical chronology (p. 93).

[1] See J. L. Myres, *C.A.H.*, I, Chs. I–II.
[2] The periods adopted by archaeologists are italicised.
[3] Albright, who divides at 2600, further subdivides into Early Bronze II (2600–2300) and E.B. III (to 2000).

c. 2000 ELEVENTH EGYPTIAN DYNASTY. Egyptian list of rebels names Askalon, Jerusalem, etc. (Albright, *Journal of the Pal. Orient. Soc.*, VIII, 1928, pp. 223–256).

TWELFTH EGYPTIAN DYNASTY. Strong Egyptian influence in Palestine and Syria. The visit of Sinuhe (p. 86; see *C.A.H.*, I, 226ff.).

Archaeological evidence for the founding of various cities in the hill-country: e.g. Shechem and Tell Beit Mirsim (identified with Kirjath-Sepher).

Round about this period the culture of the Near East assumed the form it continued to maintain (p. 85; S. Smith, *Hist. Ass.*, p. 165f.).

2000–1600 *Middle Canaanite Bronze.*[1]

Rise of Hatti ("Hittite") power in Asia Minor.

c. 1800 Kassites in Babylonia and HYKSOS IN EGYPT (p. 93).[2]

Alphabetical script (between Egyptian and Phoenician) in Sinaitic Peninsula.

Computed date of Jacob's descent into Egypt, 1847 B.C.

Archaeological evidence claimed to represent sudden cessation of settlements in the Dead Sea region soon after 1830: the "historical" basis of the story of Sodom and Gomorrah (Albright, *Archaeology of Palestine and the Bible*, p. 137).

1600–1200 *Late Bronze (subdivided into L.B. I and II, at 1400 or 1350).*

1580 Expulsion of the Hyksos. The EIGHTEENTH DYNASTY of Egypt (1580–1346). Conquests of Thutmose I (1545–1514) and especially of Thutmose III (1501–1447) in Palestine (see p. 93).

Tidal, contemporary of Abraham, Amraphel (? Hammurabi), Chedorlaomer, etc. (Gen. xiv.) identified by some (following Böhl) with Dudkhalia, name of Hatti (Hittite) kings, and preferably the first, *c.* 1500.

Computed date of the Exodus, 1447, and of the fall of Jericho (Josh. vi.), *c.* 1400 (Garstang).

---

[1] Or M.B. I (2000–1800); M.B. II (1800–1600).

[2] Fall of First Bab. Dynasty is variously dated at 1806 or 1758.

1411   AMENHOTEP III (otherwise dated 1416) and
AMENHOTEP IV, IKHNATON (1380–1362). Relations
with the Hurrian State of Mitanni (North of Syria),
which was of great importance in the history
(S. Smith, p. 237 f., cf. *ibid.*, p. 71 f.). Indo-Iranian
elements with recognition of the gods Varuna,
Mitra and Indra (*ibid.*, p. 213 f.). Close intercourse throughout Egypt, the Levant (esp. Crete)
and South-west Asia. Ikhnaton's monotheistic
Aton religion. Invasions of Palestine from the
north.

The AMARNA AGE is illumined by the tablets
from Tell el-Amarna, Ras Shamra (p. 83) and the
Hatti (p. 83), and rich archaeological material;
this—approximately the "Mosaic Age"—is one
of the best known of ancient times (see further
above, pp. 93–96).

1346–121   NINETEENTH EGYPTIAN DYNASTY. Beginning
of weakening of Egyptian power in Palestine.

1314   Seti I re-establishes the authority of Egypt.

1300   Ramses II commonly identified with the
Pharaoh referred to in Exod. i. 11 (Pithom and
Ra'amses built by Israelites).

1225   Merneptah (on his famous stele, see p. 95).
Inroads by sea-peoples.

Round about 1250 archaeological evidence is
claimed for changes at Bethel, Lachish (Tell
ed-Duweir) and part of the Shĕphēlah (Albright,
Q.S., 1935, p. 105 f.); also for fresh settlements in
Edom and Moab (Glück, *Q.S.*, 1935, p. 11);
hence the view that important historical events
must have occurred in which Israel was concerned.

The Period of the Judges of Israel. For the
attempt to correlate this with the Egyptian
evidence, with the result that the alternating
periods of oppression and of rest are due to
periods of Egypt's weakness and of strength (and
hence ability to protect Palestine), see Garstang,
Joshua, Judges, pp. 344 ff. (cf. Caiger, pp. 106 ff.,
196 ff.).

1200–900   *Early Iron I.*

Rameses III (1204–1172): influence of Egypt in
Palestine still continues.

Appearance of Philistines and other sea-peoples.
Widespread Aramaean and other movements elsewhere. Period of the Trojan War (*C.A.H.*, II,
547). Hatti power in Asia Minor wiped out;
the name survives in North Syria.

c. 1100   Story of Wen-Amon (p. 173) indicates marked decline of Egyptian *political* influence. Also the Sinaitic peninsula is no longer held by Egypt. Expedition of Assyria (Tiglath-pileser I, *c.* 1115) to the Phoenician coast.

The ISRAELITE MONARCHY rises after subjugation of the Philistines (1 Samuel). Independent states of Edom and, later, of Damascus; see p. 96.

c. 1000   Approximate dates of Saul (1025), David (1010) and Solomon (974).

c. 970   Building of the temple of Jerusalem (1 Kings vi. 1); cf. pp. 79, 95. Alliances with Egypt and Tyre (1 Kings v., ix. 16).

937   The DIVIDED MONARCHIES of Judah and Israel.

930[1]   Invasion of Shishak.

900–600   *Early Iron II.*

Increasing strength of ASSYRIA IN THE WEST (p. 96f.).

895   Osorkon I of Egypt. (? The historical basis of the invasion of "Zerah," see *C.A.H.*, III, 360.)

887   Omri of Israel, founder of Samaria, and father of Ahab.

853   BATTLE OF KARKAR. Ahab, a member of the Aramaean anti-Assyrian league (see p. 96f.).

841   RISE OF JEHU, founder of a new dynasty; pays tribute to Shalmaneser III.

The period—approximately that of the Homeric poems—is illustrated archaeologically by the excavations at Samaria, in particular by the ostraka (cf. p. 145). The league with the Aramaeans and the alliance with the Phoenicians (Ahab's wife Jezebel) meant a religious syncretism, opposed by Jehu as a champion of Yahweh. It is the age of Elijah and Elisha (for the latter, see p. 52). Moab's revolt (the stele of king Mesha), is part of a general unrest in the south (*C.A.H.*, III, 366f.). The rise of Jehu, and the bitter wars that followed, make the middle of the ninth century an important landmark as regards religious, social and political history.

c. 800   Joash's victories. Stele of Bar-hadad (*C.A.H.*, III, 28f., 375f.). Adad-nirari III subdues Damascus. Time of Assyrian weakness follows.

Others date the invasion at 922 (Albright, p. 199).

c. 780–50   Period of the two powerful and contemporary kings, Uzziah (Azariah) of Judah and Jeroboam II of Israel. Power of Urartu (=Ararat, Armenia), heir to the older Mitanni power (*c.* 785–736). First of the great written prophets: Amos and Hosea. Age of Hesiod.

745   Tiglath-pileser III revives power of Assyria; begins to subdue the West. Overruns Syria and Palestine, 734; subdues Damascus and Samaria, 733; siege and fall of Damascus, 732.

727   Shalmaneser V, wars in the West: siege of Samaria (721).

722–1   Fall of SAMARIA; it revolts against Sargon (715) who introduces colonists. The Biblical history ceases; but see 2 Kings xvii.; Ezra iv. 2, 9f. General unrest among Arabian and Aramaean tribes (*C.A.H.*, III, 384).

700   Sennacherib (705–681) lays siege to Lachish (archaeological evidence found); unexpected deliverance of Jerusalem; but Judah suffers seriously. Age of Isaiah (and Micah). Siloam inscription usually dated here (2 Kings xx. 20).

681   Powerful Assyrian influence in the West, including Egypt. Esarhaddon (681–669) and Ashurbanipal (669–626). Weakening and decay of Assyria. Reign of Manasseh (*c.* 692–638). Egypt regains independence (finally, in 651). Babylon becomes stronger. Rise of Scythians and Medes.

637   Josiah; his reforms (621).

616   Assyria confronted by Babylonia and Medes.

612   Fall of Nineveh (p. 97). Babylonia under Nebuchadrezzar defeats Egypt at Carchemish (605).

605   CHALDAEAN OR NEO-BABYLONIAN EMPIRE (see p. 97f.). Marked revival of antiquarian interests in both Egypt and Babylonia.

600–300   *Early Iron III, or Middle Palestinian Age.*

597   Fall of Jerusalem: the first Exile. (Rise of Carthage, 590–80.)

586   The second Exile.

581   Fresh deportation by Nebuchadrezzar. Important ostraka from Tell ed-Duweir (Lachish); a seal of Gedaliah; archaeological evidence claimed for widespread devastation of Judah (Albright, p. 171f.).

c. 581   Age of Jeremiah, Ezekiel, etc. (see p. 175f.), and later, the age of the Deutero-Isaiah.

Internal political and sociological changes (p. 97). Contrast paucity of *Biblical* history with the full knowledge of historical and other conditions in the Near East; see pp. 180, 192. Note the dates—Zoroaster, *c.* 600 (*C.A.H.*, IV, 616); Confucius, 551–478, and his older contemporary Laò-tse; Buddha, *c.* 560–480, and his older contemporary Mahavira, the founder of Jainism.

Solon (*c.*638–538). The Ionian school of philosophers, followed by the Italian school (Pythagoras).

c. 550   Persia under Cyrus, takes the place of the Medes (pp. 98, 192).

539–332   PERSIAN EMPIRE: Cyrus in Babylon (539) succeeds to the Babylonian Empire; vain effort to subjugate Carthage. Sheshbazzar's journey to Palestine.

529   Cambyses. A Jewish temple already in Elephantine.

521   Darius. Return of Jews (in Ezra i. ante-dated to time of Cyrus).[1]

520–16   The Second Temple of Jerusalem.

500–   Persia *versus* Greece. (Marathon, 491/0; Xerxes invades Greece, 480).

464   Artaxerxes I. ? Ezra's return in his seventh year (see below).

445   Nehemiah's return in the twentieth year. Second visit twelve years later. Samaritan schism ? (Neh. xiii.).

411   Destruction by Egyptians of Jewish temple at Elephantine, the papyri from which illustrate the life and culture of a long-established Jewish colony which had enjoyed Persian favour (see p. 98).

404–338   Artaxerxes II (Mnemon), successor of Darius II Nothus (423–04).

? Ezra's return in the seventh year, i.e. 397 (p. 194 n.).

The age of Socrates (*c.* 470–399), Plato (428/7–347), Aristotle (384–22) and of Aeschylus, Sophocles and Euripides (525–406).

358–338   Artaxerxes III.

See Baynes, *Journ. of Theol. Stud.*, XXV, 155; Albright, p. 172; *C.A.H.*, III, 409.

333	ALEXANDER THE GREAT; battle of Issus. Conquers Egypt, 332; settlement of Syria, 331. ? The Samaritan schism (see p. 33). Death of Alexander, 323. Pompey takes Syria, 319; but it is seized by Antigonus, 315.
312	Oct. Seleucid era begins.
300–50 B.C.	*Recent Palestinian Period.*
283–245	Ptolemy Philadelphus II, patron of letters (*C.A.H.*, VII, 252, 297). Translation of the Pentateuch into Greek (p. 25 above).
276–239	Antigonus II of Macedon, patron of philosophy; mission of the Buddhist emperor Asoka (*C.A.H.*, VII, 204 f.). *c.* 330 Zeno and Epicurus. Egyptian–Syrian wars.
201/0	Palestine becomes Seleucid.
c. 180	Ben Sira (author of Ecclesiasticus).
175	Antiochus IV, Epiphanes (pp. 99, 206). Strong Hellenising tendencies in Jerusalem.
167	Attempted suppression of Judaism by Antiochus. Probable date of Book of Daniel, 166. Rise of the Maccabees (the house of Has[h]mon).
164	25 Dec. Re-dedication of the Temple. (On the date, see *C.A.H.*, VIII, 515.)
161	Hasmonaean embassy to Rome. (160, Parthian conquests begin.)
145	Expansion of Jewish power.
134–04	John Hyrcanus.
c. 132	Prologue to Ecclesiasticus (see p. 25).
103	Alexander Jannaeus, priest-king. Revival of the old Davidic idea.
63	Pompey enters Rome. Fall of Hasmonaean family.
50 B.C.–A.D. 300 (or 350)	*Roman Period.*
40 B.C.	Parthian invasions.
37–4 B.C.	Herod (of Idumaean origin); kingship and priesthood are separated (*C.A.H.*, X, 322 f.).
c. A.D. 33	The Crucifixion of Jesus (*C.A.H.*, X, 649).
70	FALL OF JERUSALEM.
37/8	Josephus. Lives in Rome, 70. Publication of the *Jewish War* (*c.* 75–79); the *Antiquities* (*c.* 93/4); the *Life* and *Contra Apionem* (after A.D. 100).[1]

[1] See H. St. J. Thackeray, *Loeb Library : Josephus*, I (1926), pp. vii ff.

70–135   Jamnia Period (p. 18).

100–   Fixing of Text and Canon of the Jewish Sacred Writings (p. 18 f.).

132–5   The Second Jewish Revolt.
         Persistence of old *motifs* outside Judaism (p. 99).

250–600 *Sasanian Period.*

323–336 Constantine. Recognition of Christianity.

340   Death of Eusebius of Caesarea, author of the *Onomasticon* (dictionary of Biblical place-names).

350–640 *Byzantine Period.*

640   *Arabian Period.*
         Persian conquest of Palestine and Syria (616), followed by the Arabian (636). Mohammed's flight, the Hegira (622); his death (632); fixing of the Koran (650/1), p. 19 n.

895   Oldest dated Hebrew MS. (p. 18).

1482   First Hebrew Pentateuch printed.

Bibliographical and other Notes

GENERAL WORKS. A convenient *Scripture Bibliography* of books in English, and not too technical, is published by the Society for Old Testament Study (Nisbet, 6d.), which also issues to its members an annual annotated book-list of selected works (foreign included). More comprehensive and advanced surveys of the literature up to 1925 are given in the *C.A.H.* (= *Cambridge Ancient History*), Vol. III, pp. 729–40, and for 1914–25 by R. H. Pfeiffer in the *Harvard Theological Review*, XXVIII (1934), pp. 241–325. For contemporary literature, besides the *Journal of Theological Studies* and *The Expository Times*, attention may be drawn especially to the *Theologische Literaturzeitung* and—above all—the *Zeitschrift für die Alt-testamentliche Wissenschaft*. In addition to the usual Bible Dictionaries (Hastings' *Dict. of the Bible* and Black's *Encyclopaedia Biblica*), note should be taken of the articles in *Chambers' Encyc.* and the *Encyc. Britannica*, 11th Ed. and (generally abbreviated) 14th Ed.

An admirably full and general introduction to the discipline as a whole, is given by C. A. Briggs, *The Study of Holy Scripture* (Edinburgh, 1899); and a landmark in British Biblical criticism, a classic and still valued, is W. Robertson Smith's *The Old Testament in the Jewish Church* (1st Ed., 1881; 2nd Ed., 1892). Introductory essays—historical, religious, linguistic, psychological, critical, etc.— by various members of the "Society for Old Testament Study," are collected in *The People and the Book*, edited by A. S. Peake (Oxford, 1925). J. Hempel, *Die althebräische Literatur und ihr hellenistisch-jüdisches Nachleben* (Berlin, 1930) gives a good survey. The *Clarendon Bible* (Oxford, 1926–36) covers the Old Testament period in 5 vols., with a general introductory volume on the history and religion, and is specially suitable for students and for class purposes.

HISTORY. For general information, see Oesterley and T. H. Robinson, *History of Israel*, Vol. I, to 586 B.C.; Vol. II, to A.D. 135 Oxford, 1932). A. Lods, *Israel*, Vol. I (1932)[1] writes more fully on the earlier beliefs and customs in the pre-prophetical periods; Vol. II continues with the prophets down to the beginning of Judaism. Invaluable for its full bibliographical and other notes is N. H. Baynes, *Israel amongst the Nations* (1927). Much wider in its scope is *The Cambridge Ancient History* (Cambridge, 1923–), Vol. I, to 1580 B.C.; Vol. II, to 1000 B.C.; Vol. III, Assyrian Empire; Vol. IV, Persian Empire, etc.; Vol. VI includes Persia, Egypt and Palestine; Vols. VII–XI cover the Hellenistic period, the destruction of the Jewish State and the rise of Christianity. There are separate volumes of illustrations. The *Geschichte des Altertums* (Stuttgart–Berlin, 1907–31) of Eduard Meyer gives an excellent, authoritative survey.

[1] All books in this list in English are published at London, unless otherwise stated.

As a students' handbook, H. R. Hall's *Ancient History of the Near East* (illustrated) is especially useful. Rostovtzeff gives a suggestive *aperçu* of the field in his *History of the Ancient World* (2 vols., Oxford, 1926–30). Well documented and illustrated is Olmstead's *History of Palestine and Syria to the Macedonian Conquest* (New York, 1931). Good, popular and well-illustrated is the *Universal History of the World*, by numerous specialists, edited by Hammerton, and his *Wonders of the Past* (1934) is also to be recommended for its illustrations.

RELIGION.   The outstanding works include W. Robertson Smith's epochal *Religion of the Semites* (2nd Ed. 1893, reprinted with introduction and numerous notes by S. A. Cook, 1927).   Another point of view is taken by M.–J. Lagrange who, in his *Études sur les Religions Sémitiques* (Paris, 1905), lays more stress upon the ancient cultures of the Near East.   G. B. Gray, *Sacrifice in the Old Testament, its Theory and Practice* (posthumous, Oxford, 1925), furnishes a series of very important highly technical studies.   Baudissin, *Kyrios als Gottesname im Judentum und seine Stelle in der Religionsgeschichte* (Giessen, 1929) is invaluable for its vast collections of material, for the discussions of religious phenomena in Vol. III, and for the additional notes by the Editor, Otto Eissfeldt, in Vol. IV.   Though verbose, it is indispensable for students (see analysis and estimate of the work in the *Journal of Theological Studies*, XXXII, pp. 228–50).

More suitable as an introduction are Oesterley and T. H. Robinson, *Hebrew Religion, its Origin and Development* (1930); H. P. Smith, *The Religion of Israel* (New York, 1925); note also E. O. James in *The New Commentary* (1928), pp. 659–88, a useful "comparative study" of the history.   For Old Testament theology, A. B. Davidson's *Theology of the Old Testament* (Edinburgh, 1904), has proved of great service in the preparation of the present volume; it can hardly be said to have been superseded as a whole.   W. Eichrodt's massive *Theologie des Alten Testaments* (Leipzig, 1933–), though extremely well documented, is along rather different lines.   Pedersen's *Israel, its Life and Culture* (1926), stands in a class by itself, as a brilliant effort to get back behind the Hebrew mind.   Attention may also be drawn to A. Bertholet, *Die Religion des Alten Testaments* (Tübingen, 1932), containing illustrative passages with brief notes (one of the *Lesebuch* Series).

CRITICAL INTRODUCTION.   S. R. Driver, *Introduction to the Literature of the Old Testament*, holds its own for caution, compactness and completeness (9th Ed., Edinburgh, 1913).   Oesterley and T. H. Robinson, *An Introduction to the Books of the Old Testament* (1934) is more popular and suitable for introductory purposes.   Singularly comprehensive and valuable for its references to recent movements— for one of which he himself is responsible—is Eissfeldt's *Einleitung in das Alte Testament* (Tübingen, 1934): it includes Apocrypha, Pseudepigrapha, Text and Canon.

Other literature will be found in the notes that follow on the several chapters.

CHAPTER I. THE ENGLISH BIBLE. Among general literature, see Sir G. A. Smith, *The Preaching of the Old Testament to the Age* (1893); C. H. Dodd, *The Authority of the Bible* (1928); Dobschütz, *The Influence of the Bible on Civilisation* (New York, 1914); L. Diestel's *Gesch. d. Alt. Test. in d. christlichen Kirche* (Jena, 1869); Farrar, on the *History of Interpretation*, Bampton Lectures, 1885 (1886); S. A. Cook, *The Place of the Old Testament in Modern Research* (Cambridge, 1932).

For the English Versions, see primarily, *Encyc. Brit.*, "Bible, English," with the literature cited; J. H. Lupton, *Dict. Bible* (Hastings), Vol. V, pp. 236–71; F. Westcott, *A General View of the History of the English Bible* (3rd Ed., 1905), by W. A. Wright, whose *Bible Word-book* (1884) deals with English archaisms; W. F. Moulton, *The History of the English Bible* (5th Ed., 1911). Also, Ira M. Price, *The Ancestry of our English Bible* (New York, 1934).

On the literary aspects, see L. H. Wild, *Literary Guide to the Bible* (1922); C. A. Dinsmore, *The English Bible as Literature* (1931); P. C. Sands, *Literary Genius of the Old Testament* (Oxford, 1924); D. B. Macdonald, *Hebrew Literary Genius* (Princeton, 1933).

Page 14. Among other familiar but conventional phrases should be included "the skin of one's teeth," Job xix. 20; the Hebrew is unintelligible.

CHAPTER II. THE HEBREW TEXT AND CANON. A. S. Geden, *Outlines of Introduction to the Hebrew Bible* (Edinburgh, 1909): includes text, versions and a chapter on the Pentateuch. For the text, see T. H. Weir's useful *Short History of the Hebrew Text of the Old Testament* (1899), and C. D. Ginsburg's elaborate *Introduction to the Massoretico–Critical Edition of the Hebrew Bible* (1897). Among special studies are B. Pick, *Hebraica*, Vol. IX, 47 ff., on printed editions, Rabbinical and polyglot Bibles; Albrecht, *Zeit. f. d. Alt-test. Wissens.* (1920), pp. 160 ff., on the minute peculiarities of the Massoretic Text, and W. E. Barnes, *Journ. of Theol. Stud.*, I (1900), pp. 387–414 on the *tikkunē sōpherīm*. See also the concise survey by Burkitt, *Encyc. Bib.*, article "Text and Versions."

On the *Canon*, see monographs by Ryle (1892) and Wildeboer (trans. by B. W. Bacon, 1895); and the article by H. W. Robinson, *Expository Times*, Dec., 1935, pp. 119 ff.; also W. M. Christie, "The Jamnia Period in Jewish History," in *Journ. of Theol. Stud.*, XXVI, pp. 347–64.

The *Apocrypha and Pseudepigrapha*, edited by R. H. Charles, 2 vols. (Oxford, 1913), contain annotated translations with introduction; and among the various contributions of W. O. E. Oesterley to post-exilic history and literature must be noted his convenient *Introduction to the Books of the Apocrypha* (1935).

Page 20. For Kahle's work, see the literature cited by Eissfeldt, *Einleitung*, p. 700 (above, p. 234).

Page 21. For the "battle of the vowel-points," see Briggs (p. 233 above), pp. 216–26; B. Pick, *Hebraica*, Vol. VIII, pp. 150–173.

CHAPTER III. TRADITION AND CRITICISM. On the LXX in general, see Swete, *Introduction to the Old Testament in Greek* (revised by R. R. Ottley, Cambridge, 1914). S. R. Driver's commentary on the Hebrew Text of Samuel (Oxford, 1913), contains an introduction on early orthography, versions, etc. For the "Nash Papyrus" (p. 38), see *Proceedings of the Society of Biblical Archaeology*, XXV (1903), pp. 34–56; Burkitt, *Jew. Quart. Rev.*, XV, pp. 392 ff., XVI, p. 559 f.; N. Peters (Freiburg i. B., 1905); and R. H. Charles, *The Decalogue* (1923), pp. xiii ff.

For works on Biblical criticism, see above, p. 234. Of introductory books, D. C. Simpson, *Pentateuchal Criticism* (Oxford, 1924) is simpler, and that of A. T. Chapman, *Introduction to the Pentateuch* (Cambridge, 1911) is fuller and more technical. Wellhausen's *History of Israel*, Vol. I (1878) or *Prolegomena*—see p. 47—is still of outstanding interest, and Kuenen's *Historico-Critical Inquiry into the Origin and Composition of the Hexateuch* (1886) is still unequalled for its penetration. G. F. Moore's series of articles (Genesis, etc.) in the *Encyc. Biblica*—also his "Historical Literature" and G. B. Gray's "Law Literature"—are valuable summaries. The *Oxford Hexateuch*, 2 vols. (edited by Carpenter and Harford-Battersby, 1900), comprises a fine critical introduction (also published separately) and a translation specifying and justifying the analysis of sources. General accounts of the growth of criticism are given in the preceding. A. Duff, *History of Old Testament Criticism* (1910) is popular, starts early (Ch. II "how the Hebrews criticised their own literature"), includes a number of photographs of Biblical scholars. T. K. Cheyne's *Founders of Old Testament Criticism : Biographical, Descriptive and Critical Studies* (1893) is characteristic, and one-third of it is devoted to Driver's (then recent) *Literature of the Old Testament*.

Page 45 f. On the chronological discrepancies in Genesis, see esp. Driver's commentary on Genesis xii. 11 (with references)—the commentary is a valuable and popular introduction on the necessity and *rationale* of Biblical criticism.

Page 48. On the more recent developments in literary criticism, see Eissfeldt (p. 234 above). Bea, from the Roman Catholic standpoint, writes on the conflicting tendencies (*Biblica*, XVI, 1935, pp. 175–200). Attacks on the fundamental literary position have been answered by J. Battersby-Harford, *Since Wellhausen* (from *The Expositor*, July–Dec., 1925), and *Altars and Sanctuaries in the Old Testament* (1929, from *The Expository Times*, Vol. XL).

Pages 53 ff. On the critical analysis of the history, see the present writer's remarks in his edition of R. H. Kennett, *The Church of Israel, Introd.*, pp. xii ff., and his article "Pentateuch" in *Chambers' Encyc.*, and the relevant chapters in the *C.A.H.*

Page 59 f. On the twofold origin of the Patriarchal traditions and the Exodus–Conquest traditions—recently powerfully restated by K. Galling (*Erwählungs-traditionen Israels*; Giessen, 1928)—consult, in the first instance, the brilliant studies by Ed. Meyer (and B. Luther), *Die Israeliten und ihre Nachbarstämme* (Halle a. S., 1906), esp. pp. 127 ff., 415, 433, and Skinner's commentary on

Genesis (pp. xxiii n., 418, 422, 450, 507, 512). In the present writer's view the Exodus Traditions were imposed at a relatively late date upon the Patriarchal Traditions, which in their present form are not early; see the references at the end of the preceding note.

CHAPTER IV. LAND AND PEOPLE. Sir George Adam Smith's *Historical Geography of the Holy Land* (25th Ed., 1931) is inspiring and indispensable. Baedeker's *Palestine and Syria* (1912), though out-of-date in several particulars, is still invaluable for purposes of reference. F.-M. Abel's *Géographie de la Palestine*, Vol. I (Paris, 1933) is the work of a well-known expert. J. Garstang, *Joshua, Judges* (1931), and *The Heritage of Solomon* (1933), combine geography, archaeology, sociology and reconstructions of the history; the former is particularly well illustrated and contains important archaeological material. *The Call of Israel*, by W. J. Phythian-Adams (Oxford, 1934), makes useful contributions to our knowledge of the South of Palestine. On the political geography, the work of A. Alt is to be consulted: *Die Landaufnahme der Israeliten in Palästina* (Leipzig, 1925); *Die Staatbildung d. Israeliten* (1930), etc. Baikie's, *Lands and Peoples of the Bible* (2nd Ed., 1932) is an interesting little introduction.

For exploration and excavation, see F. J. Bliss, *The Development of Palestinian Exploration* (1906); R. A. S. Macalister, *A Century of Excavation in Palestine* (1925); and, on the more recent work since 1900, W. F. Albright, *The Archaeology of Palestine and the Bible* (New York, 1932).

For folk-lore and custom in particular, see S. I. Curtiss, *Primitive Semitic Religion of To-day* (1902); Sir J. G. Frazer, *Folk-lore in the Old Testament* (3 vols., 1918; Abridged Ed., 1 vol., 1923); Canaan, *Aberglaube und Volksmedizin im Lande d. Bibel* (Hamburg, 1914), and *Mohammedan Saints and Sanctuaries in Palestine* (1927). The *Quarterly Statements* of the Palestine Exploration Fund and the *Journal of the Palestine Oriental Society* contain interesting miscellaneous material.

For archaeology in particular, see P. Thomsen, *Palästina und seine kultur in fünf Jahrtausenden* (Leipzig, 1931) and F. M. T. Böhl, *Palestina in het Licht der jungste opgravingen en onderzoekingen* (Amsterdam, 1931). A.-G. Barrois writes a modest *Précis d'Archéologie Biblique* (Paris, 1935), and W. F. Badé, a practical *Manual of Excavation in the Near East* (Berkely, Cal., 1934). Vincent's book (p. 77 n.) gives the best introductory synthesis. J. Garrow Duncan, *Digging up Biblical History* (2 vols., 1931) gives much interesting material of a miscellaneous character. Special aspects are dealt with by S. R. Driver, *Modern Research as illustrating the Bible*: "Schweich Lectures for 1908" (1909), and S. A. Cook, *The Religion of Ancient Palestine in the Light of Archaeology*: "Schweich Lectures for 1925" (1930). Sir Charles Marston's *The Bible is True* (1934), has special references to the excavations of 1925–34.

Page 63. The reference to Sir G. A. Smith is to *The Early Poetry of Israel*: "Schweich Lectures for 1910" (1912), p. 29.

Page 64.   For Garstang's words, see *Heritage of Solomon*, p. 38.

Page 65.   Sir G. A. Smith's words are from *Historical Geography*, p. 59.

Page 67 and note.   See Garstang, *Heritage*, pp. 141 and 138f.

Page 72f.   The references are to Bliss, *op. cit.* (above), p. 159f.; G. A. Smith, *Hist. Geog.* (Preface); and E. Robinson's *Biblical Researches* (1841) Vol. I, p. 374f.

Page 78.   See J. Garrow Duncan, *The Exploration of Egypt and the Old Testament* (Edinburgh, 1908), p. 10f.

CHAPTER V.   ISRAEL AND THE NATIONS.   The literature is abundant and is rapidly increasing.   Of general accounts, the most important is that of H. Gressmann, *Altorientalische Texte und Bilder zum Alten Testament* (2 vols., Berlin and Leipzig, 1926–27). Good, popular and illustrated collections by Ball, *Light from the East* (1900), and G. A. Barton, *Archaeology and the Bible*.   A. Jirku, *Altorientalischer Kommentar zum Alten Testament* (Leipzig, 1923) is useful for students; more introductory and popular is S. L. Caiger, *Bible and Spade* (Oxford, 1935) and W. L. Wardle, *The History and Religion of Israel* (Clarendon Bible, Oxford, 1936).

For ARABIA,[1] see Nöldeke's article "Arabs" in the *Encyc. of Rel. and Ethics*; Landersdorfer, *Die Bibel und die südarabische Altertumsforschung* (Münster i. W., 1920); D. S. Margoliouth, *The Relations between Arabs and Israelites prior to the rise of Islam* (1924); J. A. Montgomery, *Arabia and the Bible* (Pennsylv., 1934); D. Nielsen, *Handbuch d. altarabischen Altertumskunde*, Vol. I (Copenhagen, 1927).

For BABYLONIA and ASSYRIA, see besides the works referred to elsewhere on this chapter, Luckenbill, *Ancient Records of Assyria and Babylonia* (Chicago, 1926).

For EGYPT, Breasted, *Ancient Records of Egypt*, 5 vols. (Chicago, 1906–07); A. Erman, *Literature of the Ancient Egyptians* (trans. by Blackman, 1927); T. E. Peet, *Egypt's contribution to the literature of the Ancient World*: "Schweich Lectures for 1929" (1931)—see also his *Egypt and the Old Testament* (Liverpool, 1922); A. F. Knight, *Nile and Jordan : the archaeological and historical inter-relations between Egypt and Canaan* (1921); A. S. Yahuda, *The Accuracy of the Bible* (1934)—with reference to Genesis and Exodus; and A. Mallon, *Les Hébreux en Egypte* (Rome, 1921).

There are interesting comparative studies in *The Psalmists*, edited by D. C. Simpson (Oxford, 1926): Babylonian (Gressmann), Egyptian (Blackman), etc. (S. R. Driver, T. H. and H. W. Robinson); in *Myth and Ritual*, edited by S. H. Hooke (1933), essays by Blackman (Egypt), Gadd (Babylonia), and others.   Also L. W. King, *Legends of Babylon and Egypt in relation to Hebrew Tradition* (1918), and W. L. Wardle, *Israel and Babylon* (1925).   Gunkel's fine commentary on the Psalms gives much illustrative matter.

[1] I.e. the old pre-Islamic culture ranging from (about) 800 B.C. downwards.

Page 81 n.   For the inscriptions, see G. A. Cooke's invaluable handbook, *North Semitic Inscriptions* (Oxford, 1903); Diringer, *Le Inscrizioni antiche Ebraiche Palestinesi* (Florence, 1934); and the great Paris, *Corpus Inscriptionum Semiticarum*.

Page 82.   On the decipherment of the scripts, see Macalister, *Camb. Anc. Hist.*, I, pp. 117 ff., 123 ff., and (for literature), p. 626.

Page 83 f.   A handy popular account of the Ras Shamra tablets is given by J. W. Jack (Edinburgh, 1935).

Page 87, ll. 4 ff.   For the tablet, see C. H. W. Johns, "The Influence of Bab. Mythology upon the Old Testament," in *Cambridge Biblical Essays*, edited by Swete (1909, pp. 22–52), esp. p. 43.
For the Sixth Dynasty Egyptian text, see Breasted, *Ancient Records*, I, p. 162.

Page 88.   For Rachel and the Teraphim, see S. Smith, *Journ. of Theol. Stud.*, XXXIII, p. 33 f.; Albright, *Arch. of Pal.*, p. 138 f.

Page 91.   For Amenemope, see below (p. 243).

Page 94.   The Amarna Period.   See the popular account by J. Baikie, *The Amarna Age* (1926); and the sketches by S. A. Cook, *Camb. Anc. Hist.*, II, pp. 336–51, and—more generally—Hammerton's *Universal History*, I, Ch. 21.

Page 98.   For the Elephantine papyri, see Cowley, *Aramaic Papyri of the Fifth Century* B.C. (Oxford, 1923), and the elaborate article by L. Hennequin in the Roman Catholic *Dict. de la Bible*, *Supplement*, II (Paris, 1934), pp. 962–1031.

CHAPTER VI. THE RELIGION OF THE OLD TESTAMENT.   This chapter is especially indebted to R. H. Kennett, *The Church of Israel* (Cambridge, 1933), pp. 139–87, "the Grammar of Old Testament Study," cf. pp. xxv, n. 3, xxviff.; see also his *Ancient Hebrew Social Life and Custom*. Further, Pedersen (above, p. 234); W. Robertson Smith, "the Poetry of the Old Testament," in *Lectures and Essays*, pp. 400–51 (1912); Sir G. A. Smith, *The Early Poetry of Israel in its Physical and Social Origins* (1912), and his essay on "the Hebrew Genius as exhibited in the Old Testament," in *Legacy of Israel* (Oxford, 1927), pp. 1–28; T. H. Robinson, *The Genius of Hebrew Grammar* (1928); H. W. Robinson, "Hebrew Psychology," in *People and the Book*, edited by Peake (Oxford, 1925), pp. 353–82; and "Prophetic Symbolism," in *Old Testament Essays*, edited by D. C. Simpson (1927), pp. 1–17; *The Religious Ideas of the Old Testament* (1923), cf. also below, p. 240.

Page 101 n.   See esp. S. Cave, *Redemption, Hindu and Christian* (1919), pp. 26 ff.; cf. also N. Macnicol, *Indian Theism* (1915), pp. 10 ff.

Page 105.   G. A. Smith, cited from *Legacy of Israel*, p. 10.

Page 106.   G. A. Smith, cited from *Early Poetry of Israel*, p. 10.

Page 112.   W. Robertson Smith, cited from *Religion of the Semites*, p. 400 (cf. p. 549 in the 3rd Ed.).

Page 113 n.   See G. Buchanan Gray, *Hebrew Proper Names*, p. 254 f.

R

CHAPTER VII. THE GOD, THE PEOPLE AND THE LAND. The whole chapter owes most to W. R. Smith's *Religion of the Semites* (see also 3rd Ed. Index *s.v.* "Groups"). The fundamental problem is the extent to which a god is regarded as an integral or organic part of a social group—and in that respect is "immanent"—or is essentially independent of it—and as such is "transcendent."

CHAPTER VIII. THE UNSEEN WORLD. See Oesterley, *Immortality and the Unseen World* (1921); C. F. Burney, *Israel's Hope of Immortality* (1909); and esp. R. H. Charles, *A Critical History of the Doctrine of a Future Life* (2nd Ed., 1913).

Page 127 f.   On the local sanctuaries, see A. von Gall, *Altisraelitische Kultstätten* (Giessen, 1898), and G. Westphal, *Jahwes Wohnstätten nach den Anschauungen der alten Hebräer* (Giessen, 1908).

Pages 128, 130.   For traces of sun-cult, see Morgenstern, *Hebrew Union College Annual*, VI (Cin., U.S.A., 1929), pp. 1–37; F. J. Hollis in *Myth and Ritual*, edited by Hooke (1933), pp. 87 ff.

Page 130.   On the deities, Name of Baal and Face (or Presence) of Baal, see Cook, *Rel. of Anc. Pal.*, p. 179 and n. 2.

Page 132.   On the "naturalness of the supernatural," see pp. 188 f., 206, and the writer's *Ethical Monotheism*, p. 20 f.

Page 133.   That the Hebrew Sheol was once believed to have a ruler is suggested by the title "the king of terrors" in Job xviii. 14.

Page 134.   For Davidson's words, see his *Theology of the Old Testament*, pp. 505 and 412, 415 f., 447. Cf. Stanley, *The Jewish Church* (Edition of 1875), I, lect. vii, p. 133: "The future life . . . was overlooked, set aside, overshadowed by the consciousness of the living actual presence of God Himself." It should be observed that among ancient and rudimentary peoples there were often "religious experiences" of no mean quality, and that the explicit feeling of the physical difference between life and death is often later than the apparent inability to realise that the physical change has removed the dead man from his environment.

Page 135.   See Burney, *op. cit.*, p. 104.

Pages 136, 138.   For the North Syrian inscription, see Cooke, *North Semitic Inscriptions*, no. 61, p. 162; Lagrange, *Etudes d. Rel. Sem.*, p. 493.

Page 137.   T. H. Sprott's words are from his interesting and suggestive book, *Modern Study of the Old Testament and Inspiration* (Cambridge, 1909), p. 157 f.

Page 139.   On the "spirit," see H. W. Robinson, *The Christian Experience of the Holy Spirit* (1928).

Page 141.   See *Ethical Monotheism*, pp. 15 ff.

CHAPTER IX. ETHICAL MONOTHEISM. The prevalence of monotheistic ideas and tendencies among even primitive peoples need not be questioned, see E. O. James, *New Commentary* (edited by Gore, etc.), pp. 672–76, and in *The Sociological Review*, XXVII (1935), pp. 328–43. But their significance is not to be exaggerated, see *Journ. of Theol. Stud.*, XXXIII (1931), pp. 1–17. See in general, the writer's *Ethical Monotheism in the Light of Comparative Religion* (West London Synagogue Assoc., 1932).

Page 145. On the interpretation and distribution of the various types of Hebrew proper names, see Gray's monograph, *Heb. Proper Names* (1896); M. Noth, *Die israelitischen Personennamen im Rahmen der gemeinsemitischen Namengebung* (Stuttgart, 1928). See also Nöldeke's article in *Encyc. Bib.*, col. 3271 ff., and the material in Baudissin's *Kyrios* (p. 234 above).

Page 145. For the Samaritan ostraka, see J. W. Jack, *Samaria in Ahab's Time* (Edinburgh, 1929), pp. 37 ff., also Gray in *Expos. Times*, Nov., 1915. For the period, cf. also Jack, "la Situation rel. d'Israël au Temps d'Achab," in the *Rev. de l'Hist. d. Religions*, CXII (1935), pp. 145–68.

Page 147 f. On the non-prophetic religion, see esp. G. F. Moore's series of articles in the *Encyc. Bib.* (High Place, Idol, Massebah, Nature-worship, Sacrifice, etc.); and cf. Harper, *Amos and Hosea* (Edinburgh, 1935), *Introd.*, pp. xxxi.–c., on the "pre-prophetic movement."

Page 150. For the evidence from Elephantine, see S. A. Cook, *Anc. Rel. of Pal.*, pp. 149 ff. An exact parallel to Anath-yahu is found in the stele of Mesha (the Moabite stone) where Chemosh is the chief god, but a certain Ishtar (or Ashtar)-chemosh is named (l. 17).

Page 154. For Skinner's words, see his *Prophecy and Religion*, p. 160 f.

Page 158. See Davidson, *Theol.*, p. 288, and pp. 284, 481. Cf. Box, in the *Clarendon Bible*, Vol. V. ("Judaism in the Greek Period"), p. 130.

Page 159. On angelology, see in particular, F. Stier, *Gott und sein Engel im Alten Testament* (Münster i. W., 1934).

Page 164. On Davidson's remarks, see further his *Old Test. Prophecy*, pp. 367, 370; *Theology*, pp. 262 f., 385. For Skinner's words, see *op. cit.*, pp. 319 and 311.

CHAPTER X. THE PROPHETS. W. R. Smith, *The Prophets of Israel to the close of the Eighth Century* B.C. (1882, 2nd Ed. with Introd. by Cheyne, 1902), is still a fine introduction; Hölscher, *Die Profeten* (Leipzig, 1914); Lods, *Les Prophètes d'Israël* (Paris, 1935); T. H. Robinson, *Prophecy and the Prophets in Ancient Israel* (1923); J. Powis Smith, *The Prophets and their Times* (Chicago, 1925); Duhm, *Israel's Propheten* (2nd Ed., Tübingen, 1922); and the writer's sketch in *C.A.H.*, V, pp. 458 ff. A. B. Davidson, *Old Testament Prophecy* (Edinburgh, 1903) contains much of value. Among commentaries, special mention may be made of Cheyne's *Isaiah*; G. A. Smith, *Isaiah* and *The Minor Prophets*; A. B. Davidson, *Ezekiel*, and Peake, *Jeremiah*. Among monographs are to be named G. A. Smith, *Jeremiah* (1923); A. C. Welch, *Jeremiah* (Oxford, 1928); and esp. J. Skinner, *Prophecy and Religion : Studies in the Life of Jeremiah* (Cambridge, 1922).

The comparative study of the prophets' ideas was immensely influenced by H. Gressmann, *Der Ursprung der israelitisch–jüdischen Eschatologie* (Göttingen, 1905); cf. Cripps, *Amos* (1929), Index *s.v.* "Eschatology." On the sociological aspects in particular, see W. C. Graham, *The Prophets and Israel's Culture* (Chicago, 1934); Louis Wallis, *God and the Social Process* (Chicago, 1935); and the original and suggestive work of O. Weber, *Das antike Judentum* (*Gesammelte Aufsätze z. Rel.-soziologie*; Tübingen, 1923; from the *Archiv. f. Sozialwissenschaft*, XCIV, 1918).

Page 167. On this aspect of the Book of Daniel, see esp. the incisive monograph by H. H. Rowley, *Darius the Mede and the Four World Empires in the Book of Daniel : A Historical Study of contemporary Theories* (Cardiff, 1935).

Page 173. For the story of Wen-Amon, see Breasted, *Camb. Anc. Hist.*, II, p. 192 f. (and the full text in his *Ancient Records*, Vol. IV, pp. 274 ff.); cf. also R. A. S. Macalister, *The Philistines* (1913), pp. 29 ff.

Page 176. Burkitt's paraphrase is cited from his interesting sketch of the Prophets of Israel in *The New Commentary*, p. 426.

Page 177. Besides Peake's interpretation, in his commentary on Jeremiah xlv., where he is following Cornill, see Skinner, p. 347 f.

Page 179. The literature on the Servant of Yahweh shows no signs of decreasing; esp. suggestive is H. W. Robinson, *The Cross of the Servant* (1926). For the present writer's views, see *C.A.H.*, III, pp. 499 ff.

Page 184. See Skinner, p. 223; cf. p. 219.

Page 185. Deuteronomy. Here I am indebted to Causse, "La Transformation de la Notion d'Alliance et la rationalisation de l'Ancienne Coutume dans la réforme Deutéronomique," in *Revue d'Historie et de Philosophie Réligieuses* (1933), pp. 1–9, 289–323.

Page 189. On the prophets' "sanity," see W. R. Smith, *Old Test. in Jew. Church*, p. 285 f.

CHAPTER XI. THE POST-EXILIC AGE. C. G. Montefiore, in the *Hibbert Lectures for 1892* (3rd Ed., 1897), Chs. V–IX, is still very helpful. Useful studies by L. E. Browne, *Early Judaism*, and *From Babylon to Bethlehem* (Cambridge 1920 and 1926); J. W. Hunkin, in *Palestine in General History*, lect. 2 (1929); T. K. Cheyne, *Jewish Religious Life after the Exile* (New York, 1898); Nairne, *The Faith of the Old Testament* (1914); Lods (p. 241 above); A. C. Welch, *Post-exilic Judaism* (Edinburgh, 1935). Handy classification of the post-exilic material in W. H. Bennett, *Religion of Post-exilic Prophets* (Edinburgh, 1907); Kittel, *Geschichte des Volkes Israels*, Vol. III (Stuttgart, 1927 and 1929) deals at great length with the period, and Ed. Meyer, *Ursprung und Anfänge des Christentums*, Vol. II (Stuttgart and Berlin, 1921), writes with special reference to the Persian and Hellenistic trends. For these cf. also A. v. Gall, Βασιλεία τοῦ Θεοῦ (Heidelberg, 1926).

For the criticism of the Biblical narratives, see in particular the writings of Torrey, starting with his *Ezra Studies* (Chicago, 1910). The work of Edwyn Bevan on the historical side includes, *The House of Selencus* (2 vols., 1902); *Jerusalem under the High Priests* (1904); chapters in the *Camb. Anc. Hist.*, Vol. VIII, Ch. 16, Vol. IX, Ch. 9; and "Hellenistic Judaism," in *The Legacy of Israel*, pp. 29–68. Not less invaluable on the religious side is the work of R. H. Charles, especially handy is his *Religious Development between Old and New Testaments* (Home Univ. Library), see also above, p. 235.

Suggestive also for the Hellenistic age are A. Causse, *Israël et la Vision de l'Humanité* (Paris, 1924); cf. also his *Les Dispersés d'Israël* (Paris, 1929), on the origin of the Diaspora; W. W. Tarn, *Hellenistic Civilisation*, Ch. VI (1927); C. H. Dodd, *The Bible of the Greeks* (1935).

For the Wisdom literature in particular, see Toy in the *Encyc. Bib.*, Cols. 5322–49 and his commentary on Proverbs (1899). For the recently discovered sayings of Amenemope and the question of Israel's indebtedness to Egyptian and other foreign sources, see the translation by F. Ll. Griffith, with notes by D. C. Simpson on the Hebrew parallels, in the *Journal of Egyptian Archaeology*, XII (1926), pp. 191–239; also Humbert, *Recherches sur les sources Egyptiennes de la littérature sapientale d'Israël* (Neuchatel, 1929); Oesterley, *The Wisdom of Egypt and the Old Testament* (1927) and his commentary on Proverbs (1929). For general discussion, see W. Baumgartner, *Israelitische und altorientalische Weisheit* (Tübingen, 1933), and in the *Theolog. Rundschau*, 1933, pp. 259ff.

Page 195. For the post-exilic priestly religion, see also the commentaries on Leviticus and Numbers.

Page 198. See Davidson, *Prophecy*, pp. 321, 430.

CHAPTER XII. THE OLD ISRAEL AND THE NEW. Page 213f. See Oesterley, *II Esdras, the Ezra Apocalypse* (1933), and C. G. Montefiore, *IV Ezra, A Study in the Development of Universalism* (1929).

Pages 215ff. Cf. also the present writer in *The Bible and Modern Rel. Thought*, IV, 8 (Dec., 1933), and *The Modern Churchman*, XXIV (1934), pp. 471–84.

Index of Biblical and other Passages

All references are made to the R.V. The apocryphal and pseudepigraphical references are placed at the end.

General Index

References to books of the Bible and the Apocrypha should be supplemented by those in the preceding Index.

256